UNIVERSITY OF CAMBRIDGE
ORIENTAL PUBLICATIONS

No. 14
JAPAN'S FIRST GENERAL ELECTION, 1890

JAPAN'S FIRST
GENERAL ELECTION
1890

R. H. P. MASON

Lecturer in Asian Civilization
Australian National University, Canberra

CAMBRIDGE
AT THE UNIVERSITY PRESS
1969

Published by the Syndics of the Cambridge University Press
Bentley House, 200 Euston Road, London N.W.1
American Branch: 32 East 57th Street, New York, N.Y.10022

Library of Congress Catalogue Card Number: 68–23915
Standard Book Number: 521 07147 x

T

Printed in Great Britain
at the University Printing House, Cambridge
(Brooke Crutchley, University Printer)

CONTENTS

CONTENTS

PREFACE

This book is substantially an account of the general election of 1890, and is based very largely on reports in the newspapers of that time. By this method, it did not prove too difficult to obtain a reasonably full and accurate picture of events as they occurred: in other words, to give fairly confident answers to the questions 'what happened at the election?' and 'why did it happen?', within the restricted framework of the election itself.

The basic newspaper material does not seem to have been used previously. As a matter of deliberate choice, therefore, the writer has let it speak for itself, and has generally refrained from blending his long-term interpretations with more concrete reportage on the election. This has been done in the hope that others will feel free to use the substance of this book for their own ends, even if their ideas on the subject conflict with the theories propounded here. It follows, moreover, that secondary sources have been at a discount. This is partly because time stultifies omniscience; but chiefly because it is considered that the main value of the work rests in its attempt to present fresh material freshly.

Wider problems of interpretation remain the most baffling. Why was a form of representative government adopted in Japan? What axioms of Japanese political behaviour can be deduced from a study of the 1890 election? The Introduction and Conclusions have been composed with a view to expressing some personal opinions on these important and controversial topics. However, two or three general observations may not be out of place here. First, a good many books seem to have been written with the breakdown of Japanese parliamentary institutions foremost in their authors' minds. Perhaps this one started with wondering why a system entailing parliament has been the effective method of government in Japan for most of the seventy-five years since its introduction. Secondly, it is the writer's belief that the bureaucratic settlement, as embodied in the

vii

institutions that became operative in 1889 and in the events of the first decade of parliamentary rule, while undeniably authoritarian and traditionalistic, did also represent an assimilation of Western ideas as well as forms. Thirdly, he also believes that Meiji society throughout the period was an open and dynamic society. Even after 1889, many areas of national life, including the day-to-day operations of the political system, were left open to dissent and innovation.

Some technical aspects: All place names have been checked for their readings in Yoshida Tōgo's *Dai Nihon Chimei Jisho*, an invaluable and fascinating work. Personal names proved more of a problem. In a few cases, it has been impossible to verify the readings given. In keeping with native custom, family names precede personal names. Translations, unless otherwise stated, have been made by the writer, who must of course take full responsibility for any errors in these and other aspects of the book.

Finally, some acknowledgements: Dr C. Sheldon has most generously and sympathetically given much of his time in helping to prepare the typescript for publication. Also, the writer has continued to receive encouragement and practical assistance from Professor W. Beasley, Mr E. Ceadel, Professor E. Crawcour and Mr Satō Seizaburō. Thanks are also due to Mrs S. Thomas for all the hard work she has so cheerfully undertaken with her typewriter.

R. H. P. M.

Canberra, 1967

History not Theory.
Evolution not Revolution.
Direction not Destruction.
Unity not Disruption.

Joseph Conrad, *Under Western Eyes*

At present, it is the responsibility of the government to follow a conciliatory policy...so that we
may control but not intensify the situation, and
relax our hold over government but not yield it.

Itō Hirobumi (cf. Beckmann, *The Making of
the Meiji Constitution*, p. 132)

Gentlemen, this year is truly an auspicious year.
It is the year in which we emerge from despotism
and slavery, and are born a people of constitutional liberty.

Itagaki Taisuke (election address given
in Mito on 18 June 1890)

INTRODUCTION

Japan's first general election took place as a result of the promulgation of the Meiji constitution[1] on 11 February 1889. This constitution allowed for a bi-cameral Imperial Diet. The Upper House (*Kizoku-in* or House of Peers) of the new Diet originally had 252 members. The majority of these belonged to a hereditary peerage set up a few years before, but this House also contained a considerable number of commoners.[2] The Lower House (*Shūgi-in* or House of Representatives) had a total of 300 seats, all of which were to be filled by direct election from among the people.

Under the terms of the constitution, formal sovereignty resided in the Emperor alone, but actual authority was divided between the Diet and a Cabinet of officials. The Diet possessed certain important rights which, apart from one very minor exception, were shared by both Houses in common. The most notable of these rights was the provision that bills had to have the assent of a majority of members in both Houses before they could become law. The annual budget, too, was subject to this veto. Moreover, the Government had to assemble the Diet at least once every year. The franchise for the House of Representatives was at first very restricted but, since it was regulated by a separate Law of Election promulgated together with the constitution, increasing the number of voters was to prove a comparatively easy matter.

On the other hand, the statesmen who had been in office since the beginning of the era in 1868 did their best to ensure that the innovations of 1889 would not deprive them of their control of the executive power. As has often been pointed out, the Government was authorized to carry on with the previous year's budget should a finance bill be rejected by the Diet. This was not so oppressive as it sounds in a period of rapidly rising national expenditure; and of even greater significance was the fact that the Meiji constitution was clearly written with the idea of 'transcendental' or non-party Cabinets in mind, even though the wording did not rule out the possibility of party Cabinets in the future. The ministers of State were theoretically appointed and dismissed by the sovereign; and for the first decade or so of constitutional rule, they were most reluctant to acknowledge that they were also responsible for their actions to the Diet, and so to the people. This dispute over ministerial responsibility between bureaucrats entrenched in the Cabinet and politicians elected to the House of Representatives was already well under way at the time of the first general election.

The Meiji constitution, as first operated, embodied what was essentially a family conception of the State. The Emperor was an august but somewhat remote Head of the Household. The 'elder brothers' in the Cabinet were empowered to carry on his government under what was hoped would be the friendly scrutiny of the 'younger brothers' in the Diet. This view of affairs was in many ways the one best suited to the political traditions of the nation, and actual domestic and international circumstances in the 1880s. However, in the nature of things, it was bound also to come under increasingly severe pressure from the large body of 'progressive' and Liberal-minded opinion represented in the Lower House.

In the context of overall political development, the constitution of 1889 is perhaps best seen as a conservative but sincere attempt to arrive at a *modus vivendi* between these two important groups: the bureaucrats in office and the Liberals in opposition. The latter had been pressing their demand for a constitution and a representative national assembly since 1874, and their campaign has come to be known as the *Jiyū Minken Undō* (Liberty and Popular Rights Movement). Thus, the political history of Japan for the sixteen or so years before the election of 1890 had been marked by much tension and conflict, with the advocates of popular rights continually urging the bureaucrats to move more quickly than they wished in the direction of administrative reform, and with the bureaucrats having to use all their skill to avoid the twin dangers of isolation and complete defeat.

Liberal demands were not met in full, but by a policy of piecemeal concessions. Often these concessions were made to appear more substantial than they really were, and the bureaucrats in their pronouncements from the throne always laid great stress on the underlying principle of gradual advance. Nevertheless there was not much doubt from 1875 at the latest that a constitution entailing representative institutions would be inaugurated eventually. From then on, the disputes were mainly over questions of the timing, theory and provisions of the proposed new system. Therefore though the period from 1874 to 1889 was one of tension and conflict, it was a special sort of tension and a special sort of conflict. The predominant pattern was not that of head-on collision between two wholly antagonistic and resolutely unyielding sets of forces. Rather, there was a long drawn out process of interaction between two opposed, certainly, but in some ways complementary and not permanently irreconcilable power groups.

An understanding of the exact nature of this interaction is essential for a proper appreciation of Meiji constitutional problems and history as a whole. At its highest level, it took place within the group of administrators that had come to power as a result of the restoration of *de facto* sovereignty to the throne in 1868. These men had as their grand aim the thorough reconstruction of the State along Western lines. Prominent among them were: Kido Kōin, Ōkubo Toshimichi, Yamagata Aritomo, Itō Hirobumi, Ōkuma Shigenobu, Inoue Kaoru, Kuroda Kiyotaka, Itagaki Taisuke, Matsukata Masayoshi and Gotō Shōjirō. The members of this little band of talented nation-builders were often seriously at odds with each other. Yet most of them were extremely influential in one capacity or another for a period of over forty years or more and on balance they had more to unite than divide them.

Divisions arose from persisting fief rivalries, personal ambitions, and differences of temperament as well as from open disagreements on matters strictly political. At the same time, there were other, unifying factors also at work. Most Meiji statesmen had known in their youth something of the frustrations and hardships attendant on the life of a non-shogunal samurai of middling or lower rank under Tokugawa feudalism. The system had made it inconceivable that men of their class should have power on the national level. The most they could aspire to was a rather insecure authority in their native fiefs. Consequently, while as former samurai they retained much of their sense of themselves as a governing élite, as former dissatisfied samurai they were ready to initiate a policy of wholesale reform once they got the chance. Despite a number of relatively minor upsets and failures, therefore, peaceful and successful change from above was the dominant theme of the Meiji era. It passed quickly from restoration to renovation, and ended up with having accomplished what amounted to a revolution.

There was another youthful experience which the Meiji leaders had in common: the bitterness of knowing that their country, under the Tokugawa Shogunate, had been helpless against Commodore Perry and his warships in 1853 and 1854. They desired to reconstruct the State not only for its internal good but also for its external safety. Patriotic indignation was married to a concern for personal advancement. Everything pointed to the need to strengthen the Empire against the West by making it as like the West as possible.

Identical class background, patriotism, and a strong interest in Western civilization—there were other elements, too, in their emotional and political situation to keep the Meiji leaders whether in or out of office in fundamental sympathy with one another. The national ideal of service to the throne, to which they ostensibly owed their initial success and which they themselves sedulously fostered, was even for them something more than an obligatory public attitude. With it went a sense of responsibility for the welfare of their fellow-subjects and compatriots.

Furthermore, empiricism was a notable trait of the political behaviour of this group as a whole. Both for the bureaucrats who were permanently in office and for the Liberal leaders who several times resigned from the Government only to re-enter it again, politics were pre-eminently the art of the possible. This meant that while they kept to the end their capacity for quarrelling among themselves, each successive dispute usually resulted in some sort of compromise rather than a lasting rupture. To repeat: the pattern of constitutional development from 1874 onwards is one of intense but localized conflict within an overall framework of interaction. Behind all this lay the collapse of the *Baku-han* system (*Baku*, an abbreviation of *Bakufu* or Shogunate; *han*, an autonomous fief or Daimiate), and the urgent need to put something in its place. The constitution of 1889 was, in a sense, the delayed but logical response to the Restoration of 1868. The latter had initially been nothing more than a successful *coup d'état*, the achievement of which had not been crowned by any comprehensive or durable political settlement. The entire period 1868–89 has the flavour of an interregnum.

The Liberty and Popular Rights Movement started in October 1873, when the Great Council of State (*Dajōkan*)[3] was divided on the question of whether or not to go to war with Korea, and the minority in favour of war resigned in protest against the majority decision for peace.[4] By 1873 the Council was in the hands of the real makers of the Restoration, a handful of the more talented Court nobles and the group of young but extremely able minor samurai already mentioned. These latter were all from the four great 'Restoration' fiefs in the south-western parts of the Empire: Satsuma in the extreme south of Kyushu; Chōshū in the most westerly part of Honshu; Tosa on the Pacific coast of Shikoku; and Hizen in the north-western region of Kyushu behind Nagasaki. This *Satchō-Tohi* coalition had been formed in the preliminary stages of the Restoration, and had lasted more or less intact until the great split of October 1873. After that date, we tend to find *To-Hi* 'renegades' in the van of opposition to their former *Sat-Chō* colleagues in the Government.

The councillors who had advocated hostilities with Korea were: Saigō Takamori (Satsuma), Etō Shimpei (Hizen), Soejima

5

Taneomi (Hizen), Itagaki Taisuke (Tosa), Gotō Shōjirō (Tosa), Furusawa Shigeru (Tosa). After their defeat on this issue, Saigō, an outstanding figure in the War of the Restoration, returned home to Kagoshima prepared to sympathize with reactionary attacks on the new régime. His course of action led eventually to the Satsuma rebellion of 1877, in the final battle of which he lost his life. Etō died as the defeated leader of a much smaller rising in Hizen in 1874. It was the Tosa (modern Kōchi prefecture) group of statesmen, headed by Itagaki, that turned to the far less traditional, and ultimately far more successful, method of peaceful political agitation as a means of prosecuting their case against the Government. Between them, Tosa and Itagaki gave birth to Japanese Liberalism.

Not only was the movement for popular rights originally confined to Tosa; it was also in those early days an expression of samurai class grievances. By 1873, many samurai in all districts were keenly dissatisfied with the Government. Xenophobic and haughty, impoverished and largely ignorant of the real state of the nation and its relations with the outside world—these men had been won over by the Restoration cry of 'Revere the Emperor; expel the barbarian!', and had looked forward to seeing the new rulers do just that. Instead, they found the Council determined to introduce Western ways, as the basis of its programme of national renovation. Furthermore, the replacement of fiefs by prefectures in 1871[5] had been followed by the steady whittling away of the hereditary stipends and special privileges of the samurai class as a whole. Not unnaturally, the latter grew discontented, though no special blame can be attached to the Government for what was taking place. It was on these feelings of wrathful disappointment among members of what was by far the most politically conscious class that Itagaki and his colleagues relied for their policy of Liberal propaganda against the Government.

In this way, Tosa-regional and samurai-class interests counted for much in the earliest Liberal organizations. The first of them was the *Aikoku-kōtō* (Patriotic Party), set up by Itagaki and a

6

small group of sympathizers in Tokyo in January 1874. The Patriotic Party was never anything more than a discussion club and is unimportant in itself; however on 17 January 1874, it sent a memorial[6] to the Council, asking for the establishment of an elected national assembly, which was the first public statement of the aims of the new Liberal movement.

Two months later, Itagaki was back in Kōchi city and busy founding the Tosa *Risshi-sha* (Society For Establishing One's Aim In Life). This, though it remained a purely local association, was in many ways the parent body of the Liberal movement. It had two distinct functions. One was to assist the economic rehabilitation of former samurai of the Tosa clan; the other was to strive for the attainment of the political ideas of the Patriotic Party.

The next step was the founding of the *Aikoku-sha* (Patriotic Society) at Osaka in February 1875. The founders of this new society were the leaders of the Tosa body. They hoped to free their political activities from some of their regional ties and economic sectionalism by setting up a new headquarters in the city which was the geographic as well as commercial centre of Japan. With this in mind, Itagaki and his adherents sent out invitations to other progressive but regional and samurai-connected clubs in different parts of the country, asking them to send delegates to a meeting to be held in Osaka. A number of them did, and it was from this meeting that the Patriotic Society was born, without disrupting existing groups.

Within three weeks of its founding, however, the Patriotic Society was dissolved. This sudden dissolution came about partly as a result of insolvency; but the main cause was Itagaki's decision to re-enter the Government. Concurrently with the parleys that had been going on among the leaders of the Society For Establishing One's Aim In Life and kindred organizations, a completely different set of talks had been in progress between Itagaki and Kido Kōin, on the one hand, and senior ministers still in the Government on the other hand. This second set of talks, known as the Osaka Conference, resulted in a general agreement between the parties concerned on the desirability of a definite but gradual transition to constitutional rule.[7] It was on the basis of this compromise that Itagaki rejoined the Council, and by doing so left the Patriotic Society, of which he was the chief architect and chosen leader, with little option but to disband.

This setback to the growth of the popular rights movement, severe though it was at the time, was not lasting. In October 1876, Itagaki again resigned from the Council, this time on the grounds that his *Sat-Chō* colleagues were not keeping good faith with regard to the decisions made at the Osaka Conference, and resumed his stance of Liberal opposition. Then, in the summer of 1878, the Patriotic Society was revived. From the time of its re-establishment, the society, with Osaka still as its headquarters, quickly grew into what its founders had originally meant it to be. That is to say, it became the controlling body of a national movement for popular rights, embracing all sections of the population and superimposing itself on the old provincial allegiances.

The next few years produced a spate of political clubs and discussion groups throughout the land, many of them affiliated to the Patriotic Society. The latter, for its part, embarked on a campaign of radical propaganda with the intention of forcing the Government to give way to its demand for a parliament, and held regular conventions in Osaka for delegates from its affiliated clubs. Closely linked with these developments was the tendency for the Liberal movement to draw more of its support from the urban middle and rural landlord classes, and be less just a mouthpiece for samurai discontents.

At the fourth of the Osaka conventions, which opened in March 1880, the name of the Patriotic Society was changed to The Union For The Establishment Of A Parliament (*Kokkai Kisei Dōmei Kai*). In November of the same year, the title of this—the most prominent still of all the popular rights associations—was altered again to The Great Japan Parliament Supporters Association (*Dai Nihon Kokkai Kisei Yūshi Kai*). At the same time, it was decided to found 'a party with fixed principles and based upon the idea of freedom'.[8] This resolution bore fruit on 29 October 1881, when the *Jiyū-tō* (Liberal Party) was formed in Tokyo, within three weeks of the promulgation of an Imperial rescript that promised an elected parliament in 1890.[9] As its first president the Liberal Party appropriately chose Itagaki Taisuke himself. Its vice-president was Nakajima Nobuyuki, later first Speaker of the House of Representatives. The Great Japan Parliament Supporters Association was amalgamated with the new organization.

These developments were the culmination of all that had gone before and marked the final stage of the transition from regional samurai clubs to a national political party with no restrictions on membership, clearly enunciated principles,[10] an organized structure and a great deal of support throughout the country.

If the popular rights movement had never moved out of the context of its regionalist and *ci-devant* origins, it would have certainly been capable of drawing attention to the ills that had engendered it, but it would have been without permanent or national significance. It was the signal achievement of Itagaki Taisuke, and to a lesser extent of Gotō Shōjirō, that they were able out of such relatively unpromising material and in a remarkably short time to inspire associations of a less restricted and more durable type. These associations subsisted on an essentially theoretical notion of liberty, which could be forsaken for collusion with the Government as readily as it was substantiated by violence against it, and on a natural proneness to make common but ephemeral cause on controversial topics of the day. Moreover, they retained all the stresses of individual temperament and regional affinities that had marked their antecedents. Yet, in spite of this, these later groupings were recognizable political parties. They represented, in a general and reasonably unified way, some national or class interests that were of importance to the Empire as it was becoming, and not merely a decayed vestige of what it had been.

Two other important political parties were established in Tokyo within a few months of the founding of the Liberal Party. The *Rikken Teisei-tō* (Constitutional Imperial Party), a Government sponsored body, was launched in March 1882; and Ōkuma Shigenobu, having recently resigned from the Council, started the *Rikken Kaishin-tō* (Constitutional Progressive Party) in April 1882.

Ōkuma's resignation[11] had taken place in October 1881, amidst conditions of great popular excitement and in conjunction with the promulgation of the rescript of 12 October 1881.[12] The departure of Ōkuma, perhaps the most influential figure in the Council after the death of Ōkubo Toshimichi in 1878, had come about ostensibly because of differences of opinion with his colleagues—notably Iwakura Tomomi, Itō Hirobumi and Kuroda Kiyotaka—over the pace of constitutional development and the sale of certain Government properties in Hokkaidō. The real situation may have been that Ōkuma felt himself in danger of political eclipse, as he was by 1881 one of the two representatives of the former fief of Hizen left in the senior councils of what was a predominantly *Sat-Chō* Government. Moreover, he and Itō were the two obvious contenders for the authority of Iwakura Tomomi, a Court noble who had played a major part in the Restoration *coup* and subsequent decisions, and was now in poor health. Therefore Ōkuma might have been feeling tempted to secure his own position by riding the new wave of a parliament when he submitted a memorial[13] in March 1881, advocating the summoning of an elected parliament within two years and the transfer of control of the administration to the leader of the party with the largest number of seats in the chamber.

Whatever the case, Ōkuma's views on the constitutional issue, were made known in the press, which also alleged that he had protested against the Council's willingness to let Kuroda have the Hokkaidō properties at a 'give-away' price towards the end of July 1881. Naturally, they earned him an immense amount of popularity with the growing body of petitioners for a par-

liament and with the general public. The attitude of the other
ministers soon ceased to be a matter just for editorial censure
and became the subject of protest meetings up and down the
land. In Tokyo and Osaka, the political temperature ran dangerously high. Ōkuma's colleagues, badly shaken, regarded him
as little better than a traitor; and eventually Itō took the lead
in forcing his resignation. At the same time, Itō prevailed upon
the Council to reverse its previous decision with regard to the
Hokkaidō sale, and to mollify public opinion still further by
announcing a firm date for the opening of a parliament. Ōkuma
had lost a war for himself, but had won an important battle for
his country. The whole affair had been one of the most spectacular manifestations of the sustained, but usually muted, fac-
tional and personal rivalries that went on within the higher
circles of the Meiji leadership.

The Progressive Party, then, when it was formed in the
March and April of the following year, was pre-eminently
Ōkuma's party; and the fallen giant was henceforth to devote
some of his abundant energies to retrieving his power by means
of party politics. His principal helpers in this new venture were
a group of well-educated and talented young bureaucrats, who
had resigned from office in sympathy with him. Among them
were Shimada Saburō, Ozaki Yukio, Inukai Tsuyoshi and Ono
Azusa. Ōkuma could also count on a great deal of support from
the Tokyo intelligentsia in general, chiefly because of his life-
long friendship with the renowned scholar and Westernizer,
Fukuzawa Yukichi. In the sphere of commerce and industry,
the new party had the even more influential favour of Iwasaki
Yatarō and his Mitsubishi Company.

The separate worlds of learning and big business were the
mainstays of the Progressive Party, in its initial stages at any
rate. Thanks to its good organization and conspicuously able
leadership, however, the party also attracted all those, in the
country districts as well as the towns, of substantial means and
moderate views who were unnerved by the extremism of the
Left wing of the Liberal Party. In this manner, it gradually

grew into the party of the educated and well-heeled middle classes everywhere, professional as well as business and academic.

As a party of fairly wide appeal and a cautious but sincerely held reformist outlook,[14] the Constitutional Progressive Party was destined to play a vital and, generally speaking, worthy role in the future scheme of Japanese politics. Its underlying spirit is best expressed in some words used by its founder in his inaugural address: 'While I am emphatic in my rejection of precipitous change, I feel that it is important to distinguish our party from those which mask their real conservativism by pretending to stand for gradual progress.'[15] Itagaki and his followers explained Liberalism to the people with a fervour that had a revolutionary and unitary side to it. The Progressives were much less doctrinaire and, because of their relatively late appearance, had nothing of the Liberals' tradition of protest. They based themselves firmly on the English model of sedate constitutionalism and were in fact openly pluralist, unanimously non-violent, and undeniably plutocratic in outlook.

These differences are partly accounted for by the fact that the great industrialists of the cities, who were the most powerful financial supporters of the Progressives, had little cause to grumble at the Government's policy of subsidies for heavy industry. The rural entrepreneurs and landowners, on the other hand, who paid the land-tax that provided the Government with the greater part of its revenues, were prompted by their pockets to make common cause with the Liberal intellectuals who declared: 'The people whose duty it is to pay taxes to the government possesses the right of sharing in their government's affairs and of approving and condemning.'[16] In addition to these cleavages of material interest, personal ambition and innate differences of 'Right wing' and 'Left wing' political temperament were responsible for the existence of both a Liberal Party and a Progressive Party. Although these two parties remained separate and were often hostile, both of them were 'popular' in the sense of standing up for the people against the Government.

It may seem oddly premature that opposition parties should have been formed eight years before the actual inauguration of the representative system. Perhaps even more remarkable was the relatively speedy emergence of political groupings as widely based as these from a matrix made up of familistic obligation as well as the already noted regionalism and class distinction.[17] Moreover, any waste of political enthusiasm as a result of the duplication was doubtless compensated for by the greater opportunities given men of talent and ambition.

Apart from this, the early formation of both a Liberal and a Progressive party was a reflexion of the overall Japanese political situation at the beginning of the 1880s. For, given that power is vested in a well-trained bureaucracy seemingly aloof from public opinion, the rise of an organization like the Liberal Party, laying great stress on inviolable rights in theory and sometimes rebellious in practice, is not surprising. It can only be termed felicitous that this confrontation of an entrenched officialdom with an opposition of demagogy should have been resolved, potentially at any rate, by the emergence of another, more moderate, parliamentary group. This second group acted as a central and beneficial catalyst, working to make the bureaucrats more receptive to democracy on the one hand, and the Liberals more mindful of the necessities of power and the niceties of parliamentary rule on the other.

Thus, there was already in 1882 a fore-glimpse of the dominant pattern of Japanese political strife for a generation to come —strife, that is, between a power-holding public service and an opposition divided into a headstrong radical element on the Left and a party of conservative reform in the Centre. In so far as parliamentary democracy has made advances in Japan, its progress has chiefly resided in the fusion of the bureaucracy with the forces of a proclaimed but restrained Liberalism. These forces were first represented by the Progressive Party.

The third national party, the Imperial Party, was never remotely comparable with the other two, either from the point of view of size of membership or in terms of crusading vigour. Its leaders were Fukuchi Genichirō, Mizuno Torajirō, Maruyama Sakura, Misaki Kemenosuke, Seki Naohiko and Watanabe Asaka. The first three were all owners of prominent newspapers, which usually supported the Government. The party did not make a great impression on the general public. Nevertheless it did have a number of affiliated societies in the provinces, and a sprinkling of sympathizers coming, in the main, from the lower echelons of the prefectural administrations, and the ranks of primary school-teachers, village priests, and businessmen with an interest in official contracts.[18]

The Imperialists' programme[19] is worth having a look at on two counts. The first of them is the unexpectedly subdued nature of its conservativism. Here, it is perhaps as well to remember that this party, too, had used the word 'constitutional' in its title. The manifesto was unequivocal in asserting that the Emperor alone had the power to issue the constitution and decide on its terms. Nevertheless, having made this typically statist pronouncement, it envisaged a bi-cameral assembly of which at least one House would be elected, and even went so far as to say that this parliament should be able to exercise the legislative power, admittedly under the necessity of having to secure the Sovereign's assent to any bills it might pass. Also, of the three major party programmes, only that of the Imperialists made specific reference to the need to safeguard freedoms of speech, association and publication.

All this may be taken as a true reflexion of main-stream conservative opinion, emanating from key figures like Itō Hirobumi, Inoue Kaoru, Kuroda Kiyotaka and Yamagata Aritomo. This main-stream current of opinion in the bureaucracy, which was to prevail for the next eighteen years, was conservative but not ultra-conservative. It accepted the need for a constitution and a national assembly, and was prepared to carry on the business of government within the limits imposed by them. As has been explained, these limits the ruling bureaucrats hoped to set themselves and as far as possible in their own favour. Yet for all that, they had in the Imperial Party manifesto and elsewhere signified their willingness to govern under the terms of a constitution and in accordance with the personal freedoms and parliamentary forms it would guarantee. Therefore, properly speaking, their attitude was conservative but not reactionary. It should be clearly differentiated from that of the Ultra-Conservatives, to whom any kind of constitutionalism was really anathema, and who wished to halt the process of Westernization over very wide areas of national life. The Ultra-Conservatives were not yet organized in a party at the beginning of the 1880s.

The second great point of interest in the Imperial Party declaration was a certain degree of similarity between it and the Progressive platform. Both parties wanted a restricted suffrage and a hard currency; and both manifestos also made explicit reference to the throne, in sharp contrast to the silence of the Liberals on this point. Moreover, in advocating the sovereign claims of the Emperor and a bi-cameral legislature, the views of the Imperial Party were somewhat closer to those of the Progressive Party which favoured a two-chamber system and the sovereignty of the Emperor-in-parliament, than to the ideas of the Liberal Party. All of the Liberals wished to see the people alone made sovereign, and a section of them was uni-cameralist in outlook. These resemblances portend the eventual coming together of the moderate bureaucrats and conservative parliamentarians, mentioned earlier.

Finally, the Imperial Party to some extent made up for its lack of popular support by its influence in the field of journalism. Even after the collapse of the party, its former leaders continued to make use of the columns of their newspapers for a generally able exposition of the Government's point of view.

The years 1881–2 saw an efflorescence of political parties in the warm sun of constitutional promise. Apart from the three major national parties already described, there were numerous local political associations. Many of these regional clubs were affiliated to one or other of the big parties; others were not. However, before long, a certain chill bleakness had set in on the political landscape.

Widespread agricultural distress, caused by a series of bad seasons from 1881 to 1885 and a deflationary policy enforced by the Government, led to general unrest and a number of small uprisings, planned or actually carried out. The extremist section of the Liberal Party was deeply implicated in these *emeutes*. The revolts themselves were quelled without any trouble, but they stirred the authorities into passing stringent laws to curb the influence of political parties. At the same time, there was also a parting of the ways within the Liberal Party itself after radical members rejected the moderation recommended by their party's leaders. Further quarrels broke out within the Liberal Party over the wisdom of Itagaki and Gotō Shōjirō's plan to tour Europe in the early months of 1883. They went; but it was alleged in the Progressive Party's newspapers and elsewhere that the Government had secretly given them funds for their jaunt. The Liberal press replied with counter-charges that an improper financial connexion bound the Progressive Party to the Mitsubishi Company.

In this atmosphere of violence, repression and recrimination, the decision to disband the parties was both wise and timely. The precedent was set by the Imperial Party which voluntarily went out of existence on 24 September 1883. This was supposedly done at the behest of Itō Hirobumi, who had returned from Germany in a mood of hostility towards political parties.[20] On 29 October 1884, the Liberal Party decided that a temporary dissolution was the best means of avoiding the odium of seeming to be responsible for the scattered outbreaks of rebellion and the hardships of Government vigilance. Though the Progressive Party never got to the point of formally disbanding itself, it contained a faction which strongly favoured this course. Moreover, it was seriously disabled as an effective political force by the resignations of its president (Ōkuma Shigenobu) and vice-president (Kōno Binken) in December 1884.

Thus, by the end of 1884, party activity, which had been so much in evidence two or three years before, was moribund. However, it took on a new lease of life before the end of the decade, when both Liberals and Progressives re-mustered their forces and other parties were formed. As these second generation parties were those that actually took part in the election of 1890, they will be discussed in a later chapter. Here it will suffice to note that the agricultural depression and the fear of agrarian revolution in the years 1881–5 had increased the power of the conservative and richer village capitalists in the rank and file of the Liberal Party, though the leadership of the party kept alive memories of its samurai and radical origins for a decade or so after 1885.

In the meantime, while their Liberal and Progressive opponents were taking shelter from the storms, the bureaucrats spent the years from 1881 to 1889 preparing for constitutional government under the aegis of Itō Hirobumi. The sociological relationship of this bureaucracy to the embryonic forms of parliamentary government is of considerable account in the constitutional history of the era.

The Meiji bureaucrats, though revolutionary in many ways, were also, as heirs to the Tokugawa Shogunate, the guardians of a tradition of effective bureaucratic control that went back to 1600. In Japan, a fully developed bureaucracy preceded the creation of representative institutions by several hundreds of years. Therefore, not unnaturally, the bureaucrats felt that they had a more vital as well as venerable *raison d'être* than the new-fangled parliamentary institutions and the politicians who sought power through them. After all, the very Diet itself was in a sense a bureaucratic innovation; so, too, were the administrative reforms leading up to the promulgation of the constitution. The bureaucrats represented the established order of things; Liberalism was a new, and possibly disruptive force. This was the exact opposite to the position in Britain, where the older institution, Parliament, has traditionally ranked higher in terms of power and general esteem than the Civil Service.

Again, it is important to realize that the Meiji bureaucracy was essentially a managerial class. This, too, stemmed directly from changes in the social function and attitudes of the samurai under the Tokugawa régime. During the two hundred and fifty years' peace of the Edo period, the fighting retainers of the late middle ages had become, as a class, a literate and salaried administrative élite. This means that the senior Meiji statesmen were not a landed, or otherwise economically independent, established upper class; and the term 'oligarchs' which is so often used to describe them is dangerously misleading because it has patrician overtones. These men were either administrators in office or comparative 'nobodies', and they had nothing else to fall back on in the event of failure in their public careers. Accordingly, they were more ready than other powerful ruling minorities, than the French or Russian aristocracies for example, to make concessions to their political opponents. This was one of the reasons for the empirical attitude already noted.

The bureaucrats were also pre-disposed by the Tokugawa past to think in terms of the Confucian ideal of the welfare of the nation as a whole. Of course, the notion that government should be basically for the people does not necessarily mean that it should also be by the people; and the Meiji bureaucrats often took the Cromwellian view that their duty was to do what was good for the people, and not what the people wanted. Yet, on balance, Meiji statism was Confucian benevolence brought up to date; and certain clear-sighted and influential persons such as Ōkubo and Kido believed, before the popular rights movement began and as a result of their travels in the West, that the State would function better as a constitutional monarchy under which the subjects would be allowed some say in deciding policy.

This appreciation of the situation was deepened by the dangers inherent in the post-revolutionary situation immediately after 1868, and also by a widespread sense of bewilderment at the disappearance of the familiar regulative machinery of the Baku-han system. Moreover, the prospect of indefinite arbitrary rule by the Council, unsystematic and difficult to manage at the best of times, was generally displeasing. In short, a predominantly agrarian society, just roused from two hundred years of seclusion and used to having its life determined in all particulars and at all levels by a mixture of written law, precedent and custom, was finding it hard to adjust to conditions of rapid and revolutionary change imposed by decree. This was as much the case for the rulers as it was for the ruled. Thus, Kido at one point says frankly that men would live to regret the Restoration, if the only alternative was chaos checked by tyranny. He regarded the constitutional systems of Europe as a model for Japan and quoted a saying to the effect that 'the Constitution is the mind of the State; the officials are its members'.[21] About the same time (1873), Ōkubo was writing that it was better to retain the system of absolute monarchy (i.e. Council vested with full powers of sovereignty) for the time being; but that 'in the future, we will not be able to keep the same kind of government'.[22]

Parallel with this desire for consolidation and legitimization, and often opposed to it, was the régime's aim of strengthening the Empire by modernizing it through a policy of bureaucratic centralism. In the long run, these two purposes were not so incompatible; in the short run, it was vastly more difficult to combine them. Yet the attempt had to be made. Before representative institutions could be expected to work at the national level, it was necessary first to do some nation building. On the other hand, it was impossible for the Government to start on its task of nation building, if all sections of public opinion were implacably hostile to it. It lacked the military and financial means to go ahead on its own for very long. From this underlying dilemma flow many of the shifts and changes, as well as much of the fascination, of early Meiji constitutional history. From it, too, came the bureaucrats' liking for 'gradualism'.

The political and social traditions of the Empire as formed under the Shogunate, as well as its post-Restoration difficulties, therefore, did much to persuade the bureaucrats to follow that path which, as Itō Hirobumi once said, 'slowly but steadily constitutionalized the monarchy'.[23] The process was perhaps accelerated, rather than initiated, by regional jealousies and personal enmities within the Government, and by the rise of the Liberty and Popular Rights Movement. These bureaucratic turnings towards constitutionalism can be observed quite clearly in two important aspects of early Meiji political history. One was the attitude of the Council to the throne. The other is the history of experiments and reforms in the constitutional field before 1889; these latter were introduced by the bureaucrats partly of their own initiative, partly in response to the challenge of the Liberals' agitation and Ōkuma's defection.

With only rare exceptions, autocracy had not been practical politics in Japan for the previous thousand years; and the Meiji statesmen, though they elevated the throne, did so as bureaucrats and not as courtiers.[24] They were never lacking in the outward deference they felt was due to the ruler and frequently hid themselves behind his formal omnipotence in times of trouble; but, at the same time, they knew and acted as if their real work lay with the State and people as a whole. Thus, the constitution, when it was promulgated in 1889, was ostensibly a gift from the Emperor to his subjects. In reality, it was a kind of statutory compact between the governing bureaucrats and the remodelled nation they had called into being. They had moved from the steps of the throne to the rostrum of a parliament. In doing so, they had led their compatriots from the gloomy caverns of feudal disintegration and aristocratic reaction to the light of bureaucratic modernism.

As for the record of constitutional experiment and reform before 1889, two of its most important items were touched on when outlining the growth of political parties. The Osaka Conference of February 1875 led to the rescript of 14 April 1875; and the events culminating in Ōkuma's fall from power were inseparably linked with the rescript of 12 October 1881. In the first of these rescripts, the Government made known for the first time, in clear and definite terms, its intention to introduce a constitutional system 'by degrees'. In the second, it committed itself to summoning a parliament in 1890. These were milestones along the route that had begun with the Charter Oath, sworn by the Emperor in April 1868, and the promulgation of Japan's first written constitution, the *Seitaisho*, in June 1868.[25]

The Charter Oath[26] was an epoch-making document, in which the new Government pledged itself to have matters decided by public opinion as expressed in assemblies 'widely convoked'; to abolish the Tokugawa class distinctions of samurai, farmer, artisan and merchant; and to seek knowledge throughout the world. All these promises were eventually made, good; some sooner than others. The *Seitaisho* was a crude and contradictory scheme of government, which gave consultative powers to a feudal, bi-cameral assembly. The members of the Lower House of this assembly (*Kōgisho* or *Shūgi-in*) were nominated by their respective fiefs.

These feudal parliaments proved worse than useless, and were soon abolished. The Government had found it impossible to get help with its plans for modernization, involving the destruction of the fiefs and the special status of the samurai class, from representatives of a milieu of insular and ignorant reaction. The Charter Oath did not go into abeyance, however. It kept its significance as a kind of declaration of progressive intent to which both sides made trenchant and frequent appeals in the ensuing years of constitutional conflict.

Mention has been made also of the recommendations on constitutional policy submitted by Ōkubo and Kido in 1873. Between them, these two statesmen initiated the basic Government policy of a gradual introduction of constitutional forms, starting with local government institutions. In 1874, a year before the Osaka Conference, the Emperor announced that he would summon a Conference of Prefectural Governors (*Chihō-kan-kaigi*), in partial fulfilment of the promise made in the Charter Oath.[27] This was strictly in keeping with one of Kido's suggestions, and the latter regarded the Conference as a sort of prototype parliament. The Conference of Prefectural Governors met for the first time in 1875, and again in 1878. Its debates were animated and its trappings dignified, but its occasional nature and the quickening pace of political developments robbed it of any chance it might have had of growing into a proper national assembly.

A more important innovation was the setting up of elected consultative assemblies in the prefectures (*fu* and *ken*) in 1878. This was followed by a similar measure for the towns and villages in 1880. These assemblies, though restricted in their powers, doubtless improved day-to-day administration of the provinces and had a vital role as a preliminary stage in the administration's long-term plans. They were also an embodiment of those feelings of localism which were such a widespread and powerful influence at the time of the election of 1890. Another unintended but invaluable function was that of training future opposition candidates for the Diet. As first set up, the assemblies were found to be not entirely satisfactory in practice, and the whole system of local government was overhauled by Yamagata in 1888.[28]

In 1879, the Emperor asked each of the principal ministers for his written opinion on the constitutional problem. The answers were virtually unanimous in their desire to keep moving forward, slowly but surely, in the direction of an elected parliament. In other words, the Government was prepared to come to terms with the Liberals; but in its own way, and in its own time. Yamagata wrote: 'We need not be wise men to know that it will have to be done sooner or later.'[29] In the same vein, Itō declared: 'At present, it is the responsibility of the government to follow a conciliatory policy...so that we may control but not intensify the situation, and relax our hold over government but not yield it.'[30] It was on this still somewhat fluid stage of planning that the Ōkuma 'bombshell' of March 1881 acted as a crystallizing agent, making concrete a decision that had already been taken in principle.

Before October 1881, the bureaucrats had managed to hold on to the initiative only by making small concessions; after October 1881, they enjoyed the initiative because they had made a major concession. That the influence of these men on the making of the constitution was the predominant one is shown by the finished product. As has been noted, it embodied ideas about the nature of sovereignty and ministerial responsibility that were of direct profit to the official class. Less obvious, but just as important and well documented, is the fact that this same group of main-stream bureaucrats was not really forced at the last minute into the decision to grant a constitution and establish a parliament, but arrived at it as a result of its own reading of the situation in which it had found itself from 1868 onwards.

Nevertheless the significance of the contribution of the Liberty and Popular Rights Movement to constitutional progress should not be under-estimated. It had served to create a public opinion about politics where none had previously existed. By advocating natural rights with their concomitant doctrine of popular sovereignty, by making open opposition to the legally constituted authorities a matter of legitimate convention, and by giving birth to political parties, it laid several of the foundations on which a fully representative system could be built in Japan. All this was in addition to its more immediate achievements of advancing the date, and doubtless broadening the scope, of the constitution. In this fashion, the Meiji constitution, in its timing as in its provisions, was more than anything else the product of the interaction of a Government of progressive but prudent intent with an opposition of radical but in some ways opportunist and often irresponsible persuasion.

By no means all the driving force for this movement towards a constitution came from the domestic conditions of uncertainty following on the disappearance of the old order. Western pressures and example will account for much. The problem of unequal treaties was in the forefront of national politics at the time of the first general election. In 1890, Japan was still in a position of having to grant preferential tariffs and rights of extra-territorial jurisdiction to no fewer than seventeen States. Needless to say, these privileges were not reciprocal. Though other factors entered into it, the Restoration movement was in origin and impulse pre-eminently a nationalist outburst against the humiliation of these agreements; and the modernization programme of the new régime was from first to last directed towards making good those weaknesses in administration, armaments, and technical skills that had incurred it. It is against this international background of a fervent desire to catch up— or, in Fukuzawa Yukichi's words, 'to escape from Asia, and enter Europe'[31]—that the emergence of parliamentary institutions must also be seen.

For the Liberalism of the great Powers of Europe and America was, in the long run, probably even more influential than their Imperialism. The Meiji Government was certainly anxious to promulgate a constitution in order to satisfy the treaty Powers that Japan, should extra-territorial rights be abolished, would be able to provide foreign residents with the same safeguards with regard to law and justice as they enjoyed at home. Moreover, an idea that a Liberal State was *ipso facto* a strong State quickly took root in Japan, and greatly influenced the thinking of both the bureaucrats and the leaders of the popular rights movement. Ōkubo, Kido, Itō and Yamagata all claimed at different times that it was necessary to have the people satisfied and able to co-operate actively with the administration, in order to reach the goal of modernization and full national sovereignty. On the other hand, the Liberals were always ready to use Japan's weakness *vis-à-vis* other countries as a stick with which to beat the Government, and agitated for representative institutions on grounds that included appeals to the common good as well as to the dogma of inalienable personal rights. Itagaki, himself, was apt to argue the case for Liberty in these potentially nationalist and neo-Confucian terms.

Yet, in addition to considerations of this kind, the Government and the educated part of the nation seem by and large to have been fired with enthusiasm by what they saw or learnt of the Occident. There was a feeling that Japan was about to be led to a loftier state of civilization. Among the younger leaders of Meiji society, at any rate, the fact that parliaments and constitutions were of importance to the more advanced exponents of that civilization was sufficient to ensure that they would one

24

day be found in a more prosperous and resplendent Japan.
'Progress is the most beautiful thing in the world'—so ran one
of the assertions in an early anti-Government manifesto.[32] Perhaps the idea of progress is the Occident's greatest gift to other
cultures. In the second half of the nineteenth century, liberty
was the genius of progress and the industrial revolution its
physical embodiment.

Inevitably, the industrial revolution was imported in its capitalist guise, along with a good deal of *laissez-faire* economic
theory. The full effect of these developments was not felt, however, until after 1890. Before then, the Government actively
encouraged new industries with its policies of temporary State-
ownership, subsidies, and the like.[33] The part played in all this
by the banking and mercantile communities, centred on Osaka
and Edo, which had grown up during the Tokugawa period, is
obscure. A few of the old concerns, like Mitsui and Kōnoike,
survived the shock of the Restoration but many did not. It
seems that the merchant class of the great cities, though it had
become financially powerful under the Shogunate, had been
content to remain a politically subordinate and fully integrated
part of the feudal order. At no time did it contemplate revolution. The Tokyo and Osaka traders tended to preserve this
rather submissive attitude, and with it a noticeable lack of
interest in politics, for a generation or so after the Restoration.

The businessmen and capitalist landlords of the countryside
were of a more independent turn of mind. Their enterprises
were far smaller than those of their urban counterparts, but
they and their families were often all-powerful in the economic
structure of the villages. This important element had a finger
in the Restoration, supported the popular rights movement,
and in some respects dominated the first general election. In
terms of the traditional background, the influence of this group
was partly the result of capital accumulating in the hands of
private individuals, partly the result of Tokugawa regionalism
and local village or group autonomy.[34]

Behind many of the contradictory facets of Meiji political

25

history lurked the Tokugawa past. As has been seen, the authority of the bureaucracy and the position of the former samurai as an élite were attributable to this. So, too, were the guiding principles of harmony between governors and governed, and the rule of law. The Meiji Japanese were also fortunate in inheriting a convention of conciliar rule, which stood them in good stead amid the schisms and dissensions of the first half of their era. Likewise, Tokugawa rationalism, together with a long-standing and increasingly utilitarian acquaintance with complex problems of economics and politics, made it relatively easy for Japan to take a creative interest in Western institutions.

The importance of regionalism and local autonomy cannot be over-stressed. Itō's description of nineteenth-century Japan as 'a vast village community'[35] does not seem to have been at all inaccurate. This was one of the strongest forces to which the centralizing programme of the new Government had to be adapted. To that extent, it was a power behind the Liberal movement both in its formative years and after 1881. On the other hand, the nascent political parties were divided over and over again along regional or parochial lines. The same was true of the Confucian family system. Its existence more or less precluded the emergence of perpetual one-man or arbitrary rule. At the same time, it unfailingly laid stress on duties rather than on rights; and its compulsive parent–child ethic was the source of factionalism in the parties and elsewhere. In short, despite the superficial comprehensiveness of the Emperor-orientated constitution of 1889, the Tokugawa legacy was such as to make the Meiji era nothing more than the starting point of that long process of friction and assimilation, whereby the institutions of Western individualism and the traditions of a family and bureaucratic State are being slowly accommodated—the one to the other.

CHAPTER I

ORGANIZATION AND ADMINISTRATION

The general election of 1 July 1890 was carried out under the provisions of the Law of Election of the Members of the House of Representatives.[1] As mentioned earlier, this law was formally enacted by the Emperor at the same time as he sanctioned the constitution, that is on 11 February 1889. Kaneko Kentarō had been the official mainly responsible for the drafting of the law. In the preamble to the law, it was stated that it had been adopted with the advice of the Privy Council (*Sūmitsu-in*), and on 2 March it was submitted to the Senate (*Genrō-in*) for inspection. The Senate merely put on record its acceptance of the law, without raising any objection and without entering into any discussion.[2] Presumably the Privy Council was less perfunctory in its handling of the Law of Election, but in a brief account of the drafting and ratification of the law[3] Kaneko did not mention that it met with any special difficulties there. The Law itself had many points in common with the rules for the election of members of the local assemblies, contained in the Municipal Code and the Town and Village Code of 1888; and, though not without defects, it was in general a sophisticated and well-constructed piece of legislation.

For the purposes of the election, the entire country, with the exception of Hokkaidō, Okinawa and the Ogasawara Islands,[4] was divided into 257 electoral districts. Forty-three of these returned two Members, the remainder one Member each. Thus, there was a total of 300 seats to be contested of which only twenty-five or so were completely urban. The various constituencies were grouped together in their respective prefectures, and given an identification number on the basis of these groupings. For example, the six constituencies in Kyoto *fu* were labelled Kyoto *fu* First Constituency, Second Constituency, and so on.

The 300 seats were distributed on a basis of one Member for every 120,000 persons.[5] This ratio was nothing more than a guiding principle. In fact, when they came to draw the electoral boundaries, the authorities found it convenient to make them conform as closely as possible to the already existing lines of demarcation that separated one sub-prefecture (*gun*) from another in the country areas, or one ward (*ku*) from another in the cities. Accordingly, though the theoretical norm of 120,000 inhabitants per Member was never altogether abandoned, the actual allocation of seats was done in a very flexible manner in the interests of adapting it to the local government framework.

Geography as well as administrative convenience seems to have dictated that a few relatively large islands such as Tsushima (population 32,000) or Oki (population 34,000) should have a Representative of their own, irrespective of the number of people dwelling on them. Except in the case of those prefectures which embraced these islands, the number of Representatives per head of population was not allowed to exceed the norm when calculated for a prefecture as a whole. As a result, the majority of constituencies did have more than 120,000 inhabitants per Member though there were variations not only between prefectures but also between the different constituencies within a single prefecture. The table opposite shows the average number of inhabitants per Member in each of the forty-five prefectures.[6] According to it, Fukui had the highest average (149,000) and Nagasaki the lowest (107,000). Tokyo had an average of almost 130,000 citizens per Member.

The national average of 131,274 inhabitants per Member was much higher than the equivalent figure for other parliamentary countries in Europe where Germany had the highest number of inhabitants per seat in the Diet. The German figure was 69,181. In the United States, on the other hand, there were 173,900 citizens for every Representative. In his memoirs, Kaneko draws attention to the fact that it took far more people to elect a Representative in Japan than in most other countries,

I. ORGANIZATION AND ADMINISTRATION

Fu or Ken	No. of inhabitants	No. of Members	Average population per Member
Tokyo	1,558,454	12	129,871
Kyoto	875,084	7	125,012
Osaka	1,281,150	10	128,115
Kanagawa	947,766	7	135,395
Hyōgo	1,521,817	12	126,818
Nagasaki	752,402	7	107,486
Niigata	1,665,378	13	128,106
Saitama	1,054,483	8	131,810
Gumma	718,215	5	143,643
Chiba	1,172,138	9	130,238
Ibaraki	998,976	8	124,872
Tochigi	684,341	5	136,868
Nara	496,431	4	124,108
Mie	909,702	7	129,957
Aichi	1,444,011	11	131,274
Shizuoka	1,058,226	8	132,278
Yamanashi	445,182	3	148,394
Shiga	667,563	5	133,513
Gifu	909,226	7	129,889
Nagano	1,111,946	8	138,993
Miyagi	736,628	5	147,326
Fukushima	913,459	7	130,494
Iwate	656,047	5	131,209
Aomori	530,292	4	132,573
Yamagata	741,896	6	123,649
Akita	682,928	5	136,586
Fukui	596,704	4	149,176
Ishikawa	745,110	6	124,185
Toyama	738,445	5	147,689
Tottori	394,333	3	131,444
Shimane	692,101	6	115,350
Okayama	1,062,155	8	132,769
Hiroshima	1,289,109	10	128,911
Yamaguchi	914,083	7	130,583
Wakayama	623,842	5	124,768
Tokushima	676,154	5	135,231
Kagawa	660,484	5	132,097
Ehime	906,414	7	129,488
Kōchi	569,874	4	142,469
Fukuoka	1,209,295	9	134,366
Ōita	781,554	6	130,259
Saga	553,423	4	138,356
Kumamoto	1,042,281	8	130,285
Miyazaki	407,827	3	135,942
Kagoshima	985,271	7	140,753
Totals	39,382,200	300	131,274

and half explains the policy on the grounds that if Japan had copied the West more closely in this matter, her House of Representatives would have contained approximately 520 members; and 'this would have been inconvenient for our country when it was having its first experience [of a parliamentary system]'.[7] What he probably really meant is that the Government was frightened of having too large a rebellious House to deal with.

This same mood of caution was even more strongly expressed in the restrictions placed on the franchise. In 1890, this was very narrow indeed. Women could not vote, and for men the qualifications were of three kinds: age, residence, and property. To be entitled to the vote, a man had to be more than twenty-five years of age. To be included on the electoral roll he had to have been living in a prefecture as a permanent resident for at least one year, and, in addition, to have paid at least ¥15 per annum in direct national taxes in the area concerned for a period of not less than one year previous to the drawing up of the roll. In the case of income-tax, the minimum time limit was three years.

The effect of these severe franchise qualifications was to reduce the number of voters to a mere 450,365 out of a population of close on forty millions—in other words, to 1·14 per cent of the total number of inhabitants of those regions of the Empire covered by the election. Only Shiga prefecture had over 2 per cent of its inhabitants on the electoral rolls, and in Tokyo the proportion of voters to residents was as low as 0·38 per cent. Kagoshima did hardly better with 0·41 per cent. The number of electors in relation to the number of adult (i.e. over twenty-five) men was one in twenty-five; and taking the population as a whole, there were eighty-seven persons for every one elector.[8]

The most disabling of these restrictions was undoubtedly that relating to direct national taxes. Though every other parliamentary country, with the exceptions of France, Germany and Switzerland, still had a property qualification to limit its franchise in 1890, and there was no demand in Japan at that time for unrestricted manhood suffrage, the choice of ¥15 as the minimum requirement made the Japanese electorate inordinately small in proportion to the total population. When discussing the reasons for the choice, Kaneko confined himself to the remark that 'Prince Itō was always a believer in gradual advance'.[9]

Taxation in 1890 was levied either on land or on personal incomes, and the land-tax accounted for by far the greater part of the national revenues. So much so, that at the time in question there were approximately 500,000 people paying ¥15 or more a year in land-tax, but only 14,000 paying the same amount in income-tax.[10] This last point is important for understanding the overweening influence of the rural areas in the elections. It is less easy to understand why the income-tax payers should have been further discriminated against by imposing on them a minimum period of payment of three years as opposed to one year. Possibly it was because the authorities felt that since the land-tax was the financial life of the State, the farmers had to be given the impression that they were being treated slightly more favourably than the city dwellers.

The small size of the electorate meant that the total number of voters in any particular constituency was often counted in hundreds rather than thousands. Moreover, because the constituencies did not all have the same number of inhabitants, the number of voters differed very sharply from one constituency to another. For the Empire as a whole, the average number of voters per constituency worked out at 1,714; but electoral districts with fewer than 500 voters were by no means uncommon, especially in the cities. In Tokyo, for instance, the constituency with the largest number of electors was Nihonbashi ward but even it could only muster 604. The Ninth Constituency (Koishikawa, Ushigome and Yotsuya wards) had just 182 names on its electoral roll, and four other metropolitan constituencies had fewer than 300. The reasons why Tokyo had such a small share of the electorate were that the majority of its citizens did not own immovable property within the city and not many of them paid ¥15 or more a year in income-tax.

I. ORGANIZATION AND ADMINISTRATION

In rural districts, as the franchise was tied ultimately to the value of land, a given acreage in well-favoured regions would carry with it the right to vote whilst the same or an even greater area of land in less fertile parts would not. Three single-member constituencies—Fukushima *ken* Fifth Constituency, Shiga *ken* Second Constituency and Mie *ken* Third Constituency—had more than 4,000 voters. As opposed to this, three other constituencies—Shimane *ken* Sixth Constituency (Oki islands), Nagasaki *ken* Sixth Constituency (Tsushima island) and Kagoshima *ken* Seventh Constituency (Ōshima islands)—had fewer than 60 voters each.[11]

The qualifications for candidates were similar to, but not identical with, those required of voters. To be eligible for election, a candidate had to be: a male Japanese subject, over thirty years old, and to have been paying for at least one year previous to the compilation of the electoral rolls ¥15 or more a year in direct national taxes in the prefecture where he wished to be elected. Once again, in the case of income-tax, the minimum time limit was extended to three years.

There was no residence qualification for candidates. In other ways, too, the regulations for candidates were slightly less rigid than might have been expected or, indeed, deemed advisable. Candidates for election did not have to pay any deposit to be forfeited if they failed to secure more than a stipulated share of the votes; and the law did not place them under any restraints with regard to election expenses as opposed to bribes. Moreover, candidates were free to stand for election regardless of whether or not they had been formally authorized by a political party or had been favoured with any kind of organized local support. Thus, the Law of Election was somewhat deficient in safeguards against irresponsible or reckless candidatures.

Certain persons were disqualified on professional grounds from standing for election. These were members of the Imperial Household Department, judicial officers, auditors employed by the Government, revenue officials, members of the police force, and also Shintō priests, Buddhist clergy and teachers of religion.

I. ORGANIZATION AND ADMINISTRATION

Local government officials were not allowed to contest seats in areas under their own jurisdiction.

The ban on the Buddhist clergy may have been interpreted as a reversion to the hostile attitude to their religion shown by the Meiji Government in its early years, and was not without repercussions. There were cases of priests renouncing their vocation to take part in the election.[12] According to a newspaper article written in July 1890, so many petitions for the restoration of the clergy's right to be elected had been submitted to the Senate since the promulgation of the Law of Election that, for the convenience of the petitioners, a special inter-denominational writing room had been set up at the Kōmyō temple in the Shiba ward of Tokyo.[13] One of these petitions, recorded a few days later as having been handed in to the Privy Council, originated in two villages in Yamaguchi prefecture and carried 168 signatures.[14]

Apart from petitions, the Buddhist priests were capable of defending their interests by more questionable methods. In the spring of 1889, an organization known as the *Sonnō Hōbutsu Daidōdan* (Confederation for Honouring the Emperor and Revering the Buddha) was formed, including in its ranks both priests and lay believers, and spread to every province. In some places, the more fervent members of this organization used violence in an attempt to prevent Christians or non-believers from being elected to the town and village assemblies. Though this violence did not always achieve its objective, it was sufficiently successful to suggest suddenly to a number of candidates in the general election of the following year the wisdom of enrolling themselves in the *Sonnō Hōbutsu Daidōdan*, or buying Buddhist family altars if they did not already have them, or helping the Buddhist priests to write speeches. The tone of the latter was presumably political rather than pastoral.

To disturbances of this sort, in favour of priests being allowed to stand as candidates, some of the leaders of the sects were prepared to turn a blind eye. Those who were not, suggested at a conference of representatives from a number of sects, held in

Tokyo during April 1890, that the clergy should make every effort to bring about by peaceful means the election of those candidates who were known to be believers in Buddhism.[15]

In addition to forbidding candidatures by persons belonging to the categories listed above, the Law of Election also withheld from certain other classes of people both the right to be elected and the right to vote. These were lunatics, idiots, undischarged bankrupts, members of the armed services not on the retired or temporarily retired lists, heads of noble families, and persons who had been deprived of their public rights or whose public rights had been suspended. Those who had undergone imprisonment for one year or more were also in danger of losing their electoral rights, as the Law stated that three years had to pass after the completion or pardon of their sentences before they could be entitled to vote or be elected. The same rule was enforced with respect to persons who had been punished for gambling. Finally, anybody against whom a criminal charge had been laid, and who was in detention or on bail, could not elect or be elected until the completion of legal proceedings.

It was by virtue of this last ruling that Kobayashi Yūshichirō, editor of the *Tōhoku Nippō* (a Niigata prefecture newspaper), nearly forfeited his right to stand as a candidate. He had been sentenced for libel, and was in the process of appealing to the Supreme Court at the time of the election campaign. His lawyer made a special request for an alteration to the time-table of the Supreme Court so that his client's case could be concluded before the election. The Court acknowledged the justice of this request and held an extraordinary sitting on 17 June. At this sitting, the public prosecutor agreed with the defending counsel that the plaintiff had been the victim of a miscarriage of justice and asked for the appeal to be upheld.[16]

Other people were not so lucky. In May, the Toyama prefectural office asked the Home Office for a ruling on the legal technicality of whether an offender sentenced to concurrent terms of imprisonment for several offences, but later pardoned for the major crime and so released from gaol, was eligible for

34

electoral rights. The Toyama authorities had based their query on the case of certain Liberal militants who had been sentenced in September 1887 to five years for subversion overseas and to one month for having harboured criminals, sentences to run concurrently. These prisoners had been released in February 1889 under the terms of a special amnesty to celebrate the inauguration of the constitution. In the instructions he sent in reply, the Home Minister (Saigō Tsugumichi) said that the amnesty had been for political offences only; and that in the case in question, those sentenced to confinement for one month on 24 September 1887 for the common criminal offence of having harboured criminals would be given back their electoral rights on 23 October 1890, i.e. three years after the expiry of their sentences.[17]

The chief sufferer from this ruling was Ōi Kentarō, a prominent radical leader of the Liberal Party. Condemned in 1886 to nine years' imprisonment for having attempted to stir up a Left-wing revolt in Korea in the previous year, with the idea of starting the 'liberation' of east Asia there, he had been prematurely released from gaol in February 1889. On 23 June 1890, the Osaka Court of Petty Offences ruled that Ōi was not eligible to stand as a candidate in the election, because other sentences given at the same time for minor felonies had not been absolved by the amnesty. The Court also held that he was not entitled to vote as he had recently changed his permanent domicile.[18]

The governor of a prefecture was responsible for the overall supervision of elections held within the territory under his jurisdiction. These governors had been appointed by, and were answerable to, the Minister for the Home Office. Yamagata Aritomo had been in charge of the Home Office from December 1885 to May 1890 when he was replaced by Saigō Tsugumichi, and he had been Prime Minister since December 1889. Therefore he was all but doubly responsible for the enforcement of the Law of Election; however, apart from cases like the Toyama query mentioned above, the Home Office did not often intervene directly in the management of the election.

The prefectural governors, too, tended to keep themselves in the background. They had to issue a certain number of proclamations, ensure that there was an adequate supply of ballot forms, check the electoral rolls and results of the voting, and generally keep a watchful eye on the way things were developing. But, essentially, a governor's function was to make sure that his subordinates were carrying out the real work of the administration of the election in a manner that was both proper and efficient. The burden of this real work undoubtedly devolved on those local government officials appointed by the governors to act as returning officers.

The returning officer for a constituency was already operating in it as either a sub-prefect (*gunchō*), a city mayor (*schichō*) or a ward head (*kuchō*). At a lower level of administration, the polling stations were put under the authority of the heads of the villages (*son*), towns (*chō*), or urban districts (*ku*) in which they were situated. Thus, in every case, the most onerous tasks of electoral administration—that is, the responsibility of being a returning officer, and the supervision of the polling stations—fell to the senior local government official in the area concerned. Sub-prefects and ward heads had been appointed to their posts; city mayors, like town and village heads, had been elected to theirs.

The Government, when drawing up the Law of Election, had tended to take for granted the honesty of these petty functionaries. Events were to prove this assumption largely correct so far as the returning officers were concerned; on the other hand, many others who were not returning officers used their position to influence the outcome of the election. Accordingly, in retrospect, it was felt by commentators on the election that it would have been better if the Government had issued supervisory regulations to prevent improper conduct by the minor officials in charge of, or attached to, the administrative offices in every urban ward, town or village.[19] An extreme example of such misbehaviour occurred in the Fifth Constituency, Saitama prefecture, where the heads of the towns and villages campaigned actively on behalf of certain candidates and even held a meeting to assess their suitability. Reporting this, the pro-Government *Tokyo Nichi Nichi Shimbun* castigated it as an unhealthy survival of the bad old custom of 'revere officials, despise the people'.[20] These local officials sometimes justified their partiality on the grounds that they were acting in their private, and not public, capacities; but the border between legitimate exercise of their rights as citizens and outright abuse of their office by way of fraud or coercion must have been frequently crossed.

The costs of the election in each constituency were to be met out of local taxes. There is no means of ascertaining what these costs actually were, but they are not likely to have been very great. The returning officers, the supervisors of the polling stations, and the clerks who worked at the polling stations or in the offices of the returning officers were all full-time local government officials. As such, they would have received no special emoluments for their electoral work. Similarly, the polling stations themselves were situated in public buildings, and so the authorities would not have had to pay rent for them. Consequently, it is difficult to see for what money would have been required, apart from such things as: the cost of printing special entry permits and ballot forms, of preparing the electoral rolls, and of supplying the requisite memorandum books and writing materials; the price of the ballot boxes, and the paying for the transport of them from outlying polling stations to the office of the returning officer after the voting was finished; and perhaps, the costs of any legal action arising from the election. A law suit, if it was chargeable to a constituency, could have involved it in fairly heavy expense; but expenditure on the other items cannot have amounted to very much.

The returning officer for a rural constituency instructed town and village heads to make a list of all persons qualified to be electors living in the areas under their control. On this electoral list were inscribed the name, official rank, profession, class (noble, *shizoku* or ex-samurai, commoner) and date of birth of each elector, together with the total amount of direct national taxes paid by him and the place or places in which these taxes were paid. Two copies of the list had to be prepared by 1 April of the year in which an election was held; and the town or village head was expected to forward one copy to the returning officer by the 20th of that month. The returning officer, after receiving these local preliminary lists, made up an amalgamated roll for the entire constituency. A duplicate of this amalgamated roll was then sent on to the governor of the prefecture. In the case of the cities, when a whole city or one ward thereof formed a constituency, the returning officer (*shichō* or *kuchō*) prepared the electoral roll without the help of preliminary lists. If several wards were joined together in one constituency, the heads (*kuchō*) had to draw up the preliminary lists for their own wards and forward them to whichever one of their number was acting as returning officer.[21]

For fifteen days from 5 May, the returning officer displayed the completed electoral roll at the office of the sub-prefecture, city or ward responsible for the management of the election. That is to say, at his own 'home' office. Any member of the public who felt that his own name had been wrongly omitted from the roll, or that somebody else's name had been mistakenly included in it, was supposed to make representations in writing within the period of inspection. On receiving such representations, the returning officer had to make inquiries and announce a ruling on the matter within twenty days.

This ruling could be contested at law, either by the person who had made the original representations or by the person about whom they had been made, provided the plaintiff filed a suit in a Court of First Instance within seven days of its publication. The courts were instructed to hear suits relating to the electoral rolls without delay. Appeals against the judgements of the Courts of First Instance could not be brought in the ordinary Courts of Appeal, but the Supreme Court could be asked to consider them. On 15 June, the electoral rolls were to be regarded as settled and complete. Only a judicial decision could change them after that date.

The rules for the preparation and amendment of the electoral rolls were one of the fairest and most carefully thought out features of the Law of Election. Doubtless for this reason, newspaper reports of litigation in connexion with the rolls were not very common. The following summary of one of these reports is given as a seemingly isolated example of what could happen, even though it concludes with the observation that 'such suits will be frequent occurrences from now'.[22]

The report in question concerned Kobayashi Kanichirō, a member of the *shizoku* class in Miyazaki prefecture. In May, he notified the returning officer for his constituency that his name had been mistakenly omitted from the roll of voters. The returning officer refused to enfranchise him; on the grounds that because of a special reassessment of the value of his land, it had been liable for a tax of only ¥13 between 1 January and 22 February 1890 and so he had not been in continuous possession of land assessed at a rate of ¥15 or more during the previous year. In fact, Kobayashi had paid more than ¥15 in direct taxes since March 1889; moreover, his current tax assessment was above the qualifying amount. On these grounds, he filed a suit against the returning officer in the Miyazaki Court of the First Instance, but lost his case. In the judgement of the Court, even though it was not disputed that he had never actually stopped paying a land-tax of ¥15 or more, he was not entitled to vote since he had not been in uninterrupted possession of land liable for this amount. Dissatisfied with this decision, Kobayashi travelled to Tokyo to seek legal advice; and at the time of the report, his counsel was preparing an appeal to the Supreme Court.

The connexion between the financial year, which ended on 31 March, and the electoral franchise accounts for the choice of April as the month for preparing electoral rolls, and, allowing time for the necessary administrative work and possible judicial proceedings, the fixing of the first day of July as the date of the election. The Law of Election determined this not only for the first general election, but also for every subsequent regular (i.e. quadrennial) choosing of a new House of Representatives.

Thus, at the outset at least, the dates of general elections in Japan were made to conform to the convenience of the financial machinery of the central Government, rather than being left to the less orderly dictates of political exigency or party stratagem.

On 1 July, the polling stations were to be opened at 7 a.m. and were to remain open until 6 p.m., though they could be closed earlier than this if all the voters in the area had voted.[23] As a general rule, polling stations were situated in the town, village or ward offices of a constituency, but additional stations could be opened elsewhere at the discretion of the local headmen. For instance, in Tokyo *fu*, where there were approximately ninety-one polling stations distributed among twelve constituencies,[24] the nine electoral districts comprising inner Tokyo had only one polling station apiece and in each of these nine cases, it was a ward office (*kuyakusho*). In the outlying, semi-rural regions of the metropolitan area, however, primary schools, temples and charitable institutions were all used for balloting, as well as the more usual village offices (*mura-yakuba*).

Speaking of the country as a whole, in the urban and more populous rural districts, the electors did not have to go very far in order to vote; but the same was not true of less densely inhabited regions because the number of electors was too small to justify the setting up of a polling station in every village. In Fukuoka prefecture, the authorities decided to provide one polling station for approximately every fifty-five voters. Even so, some of them had to journey more than twenty or thirty miles.[25]

As stated earlier, the person in charge of a polling station was the local ward, town or village head. This official was responsible for seeing that the voting was carried out in the prescribed manner, and he had to keep an election minute book in which details of the voting and any unlooked for contingency or error were to be recorded. To assist him, he had the clerks who were his subordinates in the everyday work of local administration. Furthermore, the Law of Election expressly stated that the headman had to nominate not less than two and not more than five election witnesses from among the electors of the district under his authority. He was to tell the persons whom he wished to appoint at least three days before the poll that their presence would be needed in the polling station from the time it opened on 1 July. The persons chosen, for their part, could not refuse the headman's request unless they had good reason.

In making this provision for independent witnesses, the Government was clearly trying to forestall any distortions of the electors' will by the officials in charge of the polling stations. However, as the nomination of these supposedly independent witnesses was left entirely in the hands of these same officials, there remained not a few loopholes for collusion and unfair practices. A headman who was determined to see his own man win had only to select witnesses who shared his views and lack of scruple, and the intention of this particular section of the law was undermined.[26]

The ballot papers were of uniform style in each prefecture, and were sent out by the prefectural office to the headmen responsible for the various polling stations through the local government offices in charge of constituencies.[27] Not only ballot papers were distributed in this way, but also ballot boxes,[28] entrance tickets, arrival numbers, special paper for recording the number of votes gained by each candidate and sundry rules and regulations.[29] These preparations were virtually completed in the Tokyo area by 26 June, when the various ward offices began handing out entrance tickets to the electors of the metropolis.[30] The other two *fu* (Kyoto and Osaka) and forty-two *ken* adhered to the same general procedure, though the time-table varied slightly from place to place.

These preliminary arrangements worked virtually without a hitch throughout the Empire, evidence of a general state of pacification extraordinary for a country which had been the scene of bitter civil strife not twelve years before, and of efficient local administration at any rate down to the sub-prefectural or ward office level. When the polls opened on 1 July, there was not a single elector who had not been in a position to check whether his name was on the electoral roll and who had not received the necessary entrance ticket beforehand; and there was not a single polling station that lacked ballot papers, ballot boxes, and the other equipment requisite for the election. Accidents did happen, but they were of a very minor nature. One such befell Takada Kiyonobu, the headman of Izumi village in Ehime prefecture. About 23 June, he went from Izumi to the sub-prefectural (Kita Uwa *gun*) office in Uwajima to collect the voting papers for his village. Having done that and before returning home, he stopped in Uwajima to do some shopping. In one shop he put the leather bag containing the ballot forms on the counter only to have it disappear in a moment or two. A search of the premises having failed to reveal it, he was obliged to report to the police and the Kita Uwa office that the voting papers had been stolen.[31]

The ballot papers were not printed with the candidates' names. The elector himself had to write down the full name of the person, or persons in the case of two-member constituencies, for whom he wished to vote. Then, the elector had to write down his own name and place of residence, and affix his personal seal by way of signature. Ballots inscribed in the native *kana* syllabary, or having names that were clearly recognizable though spelt with the wrong Chinese characters, were to be regarded as valid. Since it is more difficult to write personal names correctly in Chinese ideograms than in a phonetic script, this attitude on the part of the framers of the Law of Election of accepting anything unequivocally intelligible was fair and sensible.

The problem of the legibility of ballots was complicated by the existence of illiterates among the voters in numbers amounting to several hundreds or perhaps even a few thousand for the country as a whole.[32] With this in mind, the authors of the Law of Election inserted an article[33] allowing illiterate voters to ask one of the polling station clerks to write their votes for them. After the clerk had written down the vote at the elector's dictation, he was to read it out; then the elector himself had to cast the vote in the normal way if he was satisfied that the clerk had heard him correctly. Moreover, the legislators had intended to have this done as privately as possible, in conformity with the principle of secret ballots. On the other hand, nothing could prevent the local headman or his clerk, with the connivance of any onlookers there might have been, from writing what they wished on a proxy ballot; and, in fact, many petty deceptions seem to have been carried out. Suematsu Kenchō declared in his talk on the election: 'There are fears that nothing can remove that, when it came to the actual voting, if an illiterate asked for a proxy, Gombei was written as Hachibei or Gosuke as Rokusuke, as a result of collusion between the headman and the clerks. I was often a witness to this most baneful, for the electors, practice.'[34]

The ballot boxes were made of wood. They had two lids, each of which was fitted with a different lock. One of the two keys was held by the headman in charge of the polling station; the other was kept by the election witnesses. The inner lid was slotted, and the boxes remained locked, with the outer lid off, while the voting was in progress. Before the voting began, the officials and the witnesses publicly opened the boxes to show that they were empty to the electors already gathered at the voting places.

The system of election in single-member constituencies was similar to that used in Britain; that is, the candidate with the greatest number of votes, regardless of whether this majority was absolute, was declared the winner, and each voter had only one vote. In the two-member constituencies, each voter could write down the names of two candidates, and the two with the highest number of votes were returned for the constituency. In the event of a tie between two candidates, the elder was to be deemed elected; and should the dates of their birthdays happen to be the same, the election was to be decided by drawing lots.

Only the most salient features of the actual procedure for voting were laid down in the Law of Election itself; detailed

43

instructions were left to the Imperial Ordinance No. 3 of 9 January 1890.[35] The contents of this ordinance were later clarified and publicized in an item headed Instructions to Voters, which appeared in several leading newspapers towards the end of June. Voting was not compulsory; but an elector wishing to vote had to go in person to the polling station, taking with him his registered seal and the entrance ticket he had already received from the authorities and stamped with his seal. When he surrendered his entrance ticket, his name was checked against the electoral roll and he was given a ballot paper. This he took to a voting booth and, having cast his vote in the way outlined above, he folded the paper, stuck down the gummed edges and dropped it in the box. After that, and after collecting his 'umbrella, cane, or other hand luggage', he had to leave the polling station promptly and peaceably.[36]

The authorized procedure for voting, then, made the actual business of casting a vote reasonably straightforward and as fair and as private as possible, although the arrangements for the special category of illiterate voters certainly left something to be desired. Perhaps this, more than any other single thing, testified to the essential integrity of the Government's attitude towards the election. Moreover, the electorate can have hardly been left in ignorance of what was required of it. The articles of the Law of Election relating to the management of the polling stations, together with the prescribed punishments for breaches of the law or other criminal activities in connexion with the election, were displayed at every polling station. More positively, the Law of Election had been promulgated for over a year, and the Imperial Ordinance No. 3 for nearly six months, before the day of the election. Nation-wide local elections, too, had been held in the preceding twelve months.

For the rest, the newspapers, as has been indicated, did their share in informing the public. In addition to the 'Instructions to Voters', there were other articles like the detailed commentary on relevant sections of the Law of Election and the administrative regulations for voting which the *Sanyō Shimbun* of

Okayama prefecture issued as its editorials for the period 12–15 June. The editor prefaced it with a declaration that it was just as important to have a knowledge of the rules for the election, so as not to make procedural mistakes when voting, as it was to make inquiries about the candidates. In Kanagawa prefecture, the electors of Tachibana sub-prefecture met together for a special voting rehearsal on 15 June. They wanted to ensure a good turn out on the actual day of the election, and so avoid any possibility of disgracing their prefecture or offending their local deity, Hachiman.[37]

Promptly at six o'clock on the evening of 1 July, those in charge of the polling stations were to declare the poll closed, and shut the ballot boxes by putting on the outer lids. Thereafter nobody at all could vote; no matter what extenuating circumstances there might have been for those who had failed to do so or were too late in coming to the polling station. During the night of 1 July, the ballot boxes remained at the polling stations where they were kept under strict guard. The guards in some places were local government clerks. They were told to try to sit up all night without falling asleep, and to make sure that they held on to the boxes if in fact they did happen to doze.[38] In the majority of the constituencies, groups of electors also kept watch; and almost everywhere the police, too, were called on to mount guard. Despite precautions of this nature, there were suspicions in at least one prefecture that boxes had been illicitly opened and their contents tampered with, under the cover of darkness.[39]

On 2 July, the various polling stations forwarded their ballot boxes, together with the minutes of the voting, to the local government office responsible for the constituency. On this journey, the boxes were accompanied by a police escort and at least one of the official witnesses to the voting. In the case of remote islands where it would not have been possible to send in the ballot boxes on 2 July under the usual arrangements, the prefectural governor was empowered to hold the election earlier, between 15 and 30 June, and have the boxes sent to the mainland by 1 July.

After the returning officer had received all the ballot boxes for his constituency, he had to hold a counting and declaration of the poll meeting. This was known as the Election Meeting. In a few places, notably inner Tokyo and the urban constituencies of Kyoto *fu* and Osaka *fu*, the counting of the votes was completed on 2 July; but over the greater part of the country, the boxes were not opened until 3 July and sometimes the counting went on until 5 or 6 July.[40]

Having formally convened the Election Meeting and before going on to open the ballot boxes, the returning officer was required to co-opt an Election Committee of at least seven persons from among the witnesses assembled from the various polling stations. Then he opened the boxes and counted the votes in the presence of this committee; at the same time, he had to count the total number of voters. Any discrepancy between the two figures was entered in the official minutes of the Election Meeting.

The next step was for the returning officer to inspect the ballots with the assistance of the Election Committee and decide which of them were valid. Invalid ballots were those which:

(i) Were written by persons whose names did not appear on the electoral roll. This did not apply, however, to voters who had brought with them to the polling station a court order to the effect that their name should have been on the roll.

(ii) Were not made out on the official voting paper.

(iii) Were not inscribed with the voter's name.

(iv) Were inscribed with the name of a person not qualified for election; but in the case of a two-member constituency, such a ballot was to be valid for any person named therein who did have the proper qualifications.

(v) Were illegible or ambiguous with regard to the name of the voter or the person for whom he voted.

(vi) Contained extraneous matter, writing, or drawings. When this additional material was meant to be of help in identification, however, the ballot was to be considered valid.

If the validity of a ballot was in doubt, the returning officer was competent to decide the matter after conferring with the members of the Election Committee. Consequently the application of the rules for determining the validity of ballots varied somewhat from place to place.[41]

On completion of the work of adding and sorting the ballots, the returning officer announced the result of the election to those assembled at the meeting place. When details of the entire proceedings had been entered in the minute book and signed by him and the members of his Election Committee, the Election Meeting was declared closed.

Electors could attend the Election Meeting for their constituency, but were under strict orders to behave themselves. They had to preserve complete silence at the command of the returning officer, and they were not supposed to show either by word or by gesture any sign of approval or disapproval when the results were read out. The problem of controlling visitors to the Election Meetings seems to have loomed rather large in the minds of the authorities, and it was discussed at a special conference of returning officers for the Tokyo *fu* constituencies. This conference was held on 30 June; and a newspaper intimated that such words as 'patrols', 'firemen', 'police', 'clubs' and 'pumps' were overheard while it was in progress.[42] Even if this report was true, the event proved its forebodings unduly pessimistic as the Election Meetings in Tokyo and elsewhere passed off without incident.[43]

The final duty of the returning officer for a constituency was to report the result of the election to the governor of the prefecture. The governor then sent official notifications of election to the successful candidates, asking them to say whether or not they accepted. The persons elected had to let the governor know their decision within ten days if they were residing in the prefecture concerned, within twenty days if they were not. Failure to reply by then or a declaration of unwillingness to serve as a Representative meant that the governor had to order a new election in the constituency unless there had been a tie vote.

If a candidate had managed to get himself elected in two constituencies, he was to tell the authorities which he wished to represent. Though there was nothing in the Law of Election

47

to prevent a candidate standing in two separate constituencies and a number of them did so, there were in fact only two cases of double election. In Ehime prefecture, Suzuki Jūen was returned for both the First and Fourth Constituencies; and in Ōita prefecture, Motoda Hajime was equally fortunate in the First and Fifth Constituencies. In both instances, the constituency for which they refused election had to go to the polls again.[44]

Once it was settled that he was lawfully and willingly elected, the new Representative received a certificate of election from the prefectural governor. The governor also had to send in a report to the Minister for Home Affairs, detailing the names, qualifications, and personal histories of the candidates returned for his area. Thus, in its concluding stages, the election procedure came back into the hands of the Home Office bureaucrats. These were the people who had organized and initiated it, and then withdrawn while the subordinate provincial officials, the candidates, and the electors ran the course they had mapped out. From this rather elevated point of view, the first general election was a masterpiece of impartial and nation-wide administrative organization.

The Law of Election provided that ballots should be kept for sixty days if they were valid, and for one year if they were not, and then burnt. Connected with this was another article[45] which made it possible to challenge the legality of a result by bringing a suit in a Court of Appeal. These suits had to be filed within thirty days of the official publication of the names of those elected, and plaintiffs were required to deposit a sum of ¥300 with the judicial authorities. This sum was to be used in part payment of costs of the suit; and if the plaintiff lost his case, he was obliged to pay the whole amount of legal costs. A person whose seat in the House of Representatives was thus placed in jeopardy retained it pending the decision of the court. In fact, none of the elected Members were unseated as a result of legal actions initiated by their defeated opponents. No doubt the ¥300 deposit protected some of them.

To recapitulate for a moment the principal features of the

I. ORGANIZATION AND ADMINISTRATION

electoral system of 1890, these were: irregular and mainly single-seat constituencies; an electorate that was no more than 1·14 per cent of the total population; a heavy preponderance of rural voters; a high property or income qualification for candidates as well as electors; a procedure for the supervision of the voting itself that relied too heavily on the probity of town and village headmen or other minor local government officials; election by simple majority, with every elector having only one vote except in the case of two-member constituencies; signed but otherwise secret ballots; notable efficiency and a sense of fair play on the part of the senior officials responsible for the drafting and enforcement of the Law of Election, notwithstanding any limitations or defects inherent in the foregoing. Constituency sizes, and the size and composition of the electorate were all crucial. However as their importance will become more apparent with the development of the story of the election, here it is only necessary to point out they provoked controversy before and after the polling[46] and touch on some of the administrative issues they and the other provisions raised.

As in all cases where proportional representation is rejected in favour of single-member constituencies and election by relative majorities, it sometimes happened that in a particular prefecture a minority of votes secured a majority of seats. For instance, in Kagawa prefecture, the Progressive Party managed to return only one Representative with its total of 1,241 votes, whereas the Liberals got three seats for 1,160 votes. In Ehime the figures were: Progressives, 3,542 votes and two Representatives; Liberals, 3,260 votes and five Representatives.[47] Though these anomalies in the separate prefectures tended to balance out over the country as a whole and the prevailing sentiment of opposition to the Government was quite adequately reflected in the House of Representatives, in the next few years there were a number of suggestions for a change to multi-member constituencies consisting of whole prefectures, and a voting system based on proportional representation.[48] As always, it was a case of having to weigh the claims of accuracy against the

49

advantages of expediency. With regard to the problems of securing both fair and effective representation, as a technical matter, the Japanese do not appear to have fared worse than anybody else. This was because from the outset they could keep an open mind on the subject. The whole business of a national election being without precedent, there were no traditionalist impediments or interested opposition to what was in effect a policy of trial and error.

Critics of the system of small, sub-prefectural election districts also argued that it favoured candidates with strong local connexions who were resident in the area. Such candidates did not necessarily have in them the making of a good Representative, but they nevertheless came off best when pitted against an outsider, however talented.[49] Similarly, it was alleged that many capable men were prevented from standing as candidates, because of the ¥15 a year minimum tax qualification. This line of argument had special relevance to Japan, where, as a result of the peculiar antecedents of the *shizoku* class, wealth was by no means a sure indication of superiority in learning or ability.[50]

While neither of these last two objections was without foundation, the first House of Representatives contained not a few men of sterling worth and quick wits, and in this respect did not compare unfavourably with later Houses elected with fewer restrictions and from bigger constituencies. Also, almost one-third of its Members belonged to the *shizoku* class. Another point in favour of small constituencies and having nothing to do with the ¥15 tax qualification for candidates, was made by Kaneko himself: small constituencies were more in keeping with the extremely narrow 'village politics' of the time.[51]

This same village factor lay behind the attack in one section of the press[52] on the requirement that ballots should be marked with the voter's name as well as the candidate's. The attackers assumed that information about an elector's choice would be eventually divulged by the official witnesses co-opted by the returning officer when he counted the votes. Not only would the prospect of such leakages materially influence the voter's decision but also, it was claimed, knowledge about who had voted for whom would cause estrangements in the all-important social life of a village. Consequently the system of signed ballots would give rise to coercion or disinclination to vote at all. If such abuses had been at all widespread, however, both the rate and the pattern of the voting would have been different from what they were. Clearly, the reason for having the ballots signed was that it would help ensure that only those entitled to vote did in fact do so. Complete anonymity will tend to be a consequence of full suffrage. On the other hand, it is to be expected that an electorate restricted to the most wealthy tax-payers would not have been unduly susceptible to unfair persuasion or apathy. Indeed, far from being reticent about their intentions many electors up and down the land allowed their names to be used in electioneering advertisements which announced in advance that Messrs X, Y and Z had decided to vote for Mr so-and-so.

All this simply indicates the truth that the Law of Election, like any other law, had to operate as part of an authoritarian political structure in a social environment as peccable as it was patriotic, parochial as well as purposeful. There were, then, certain political and social limits to what the Law by itself could achieve, and these are often really to blame for its less fortunate aspects and consequences. To take another example, the failure to provide adequate supervision for the headmen in charge of the polling stations should not be judged without taking into account the enormous social influence they wielded in addition to their political powers. It would have been difficult in the society of 1890 to devise regulations strong enough to keep them completely in check. In fact, it seems that the drafters of the Law had wished to have policemen on duty inside as well as outside the polling stations while the voting was going on, but in many places this scheme was abandoned in view of accusations that it could be construed as Government interference.[53]

Generally speaking though, the police and the courts played a vital and salutary role in the management of the election. Faced with the welter of corruption, petty trickery, and minor violence that attended the campaign, one wonders what sort of stained monster the infant Japanese parliament would have been, but for the careful midwifery it received from the law and its guardians. It must be stressed that, in complete contrast to what went on at the time of the second general election two years later, the Government refrained from abusing its executive or judicial powers to secure the electoral defeat of its opponents. The law was neutral, and so was its enforcement by the police and the higher political or judicial authorities. A single case of something that may be an infringement of this principle occurred during a meeting of the Kyōbashi Ward Political Discussion Group, held in Tokyo on 28 June, at which some of the candidates for the House of Representatives made speeches. The speakers gave full expression to their views but one of them, Nakajima Matagorō, was cautioned by a policeman for straying off the subject. As the matter at issue was trivial, Nakajima left it at that.[54]

However, before describing the various activities undertaken by the police in connexion with the election, the legal statutes which gave them the power to act the way they did should be summarized. The Law of Election itself contained a section entitled Punitive Rules, which had for its scope the following offences: fraudulent entries in the electoral roll; bribery of any kind, indirect or direct, and no matter whether goods, money, or employment were actually given or only promised; acts of violence against electors; mass intimidation of electors; riots at polling stations or Election Meetings. The penalties for such crimes varied in accordance with the degree to which the perpetrators achieved their objectives, but in any case they were hardly lenient. For the more serious offences, such as corruption that had achieved its effect, violence and creating a public disturbance, the Law authorized imprisonment for a term of between two weeks and six years and a fine of two to three hundred yen. Persons accepting bribes were to be given the same punishments as those who offered them.

Feeling, as the election campaign got under way, that this

section of the Law of Election was not achieving its purpose, the Government promulgated on 29 May the Supplementary Penal Regulations for the House of Representatives Election Law.[55] These Supplementary Regulations made some additions to the list of actions constituting breaches of the Election Law proper. Through them, the definition of bribery was widened to cover the serving of food or drink to electors on their way to or in the vicinity of either the polling stations or the places where the Election Meetings were held; and also to cover offers of transport to or from the polling stations or Election Meeting places, offers of lodgings and offers of expense money.

Likewise, individual, as opposed to mass, intimidation of the electors became a punishable offence for the first time as did the abduction of electors on election day, or the hindering of their movements with the idea of preventing them getting to the polls. Another new offence was the spreading of rumours about who was or was not eligible for election, and false stories to the effect that a particular candidate would not accept his seat in the House of Representatives if elected. Article IV of the Supplementary Regulations made election demonstrations subject to police control. It read:

Persons who, in the sub-prefectures and cities where there are polling stations or Election Meetings, assemble in large numbers or go about in bands, or light bonfires or pine torches, or make a noise with bells, drums, or conch shells, or horns, or make use of flags or other emblems, in order to stimulate election fever, and do not obey police orders to desist, shall be sentenced to not less than fifteen days' and not more than three months' imprisonment with light labour, and shall be fined not less than five yen and not more than fifty yen.

These Supplementary Regulations were not opposed in the press. The *Tokyo Nichi Nichi Shimbun* remarked that it was far from being surprised by the rigour of the legislation.[56] More significantly, the 'opposition' papers—the *Yūbin-Hōchi Shimbun*[57] and the *Kokumin Shimbun*[58]—both admitted the need for such laws in a society where public morality was of a shamefully low standard. The *Kokumin Shimbun* asserted that the offences enumerated in the Regulations were a photographic record of what was happening in all districts at the time, and that this was true even in the case of Article IV which read like a page from a medieval chronicle.

The Punitive Rules in the Law of Election, as well as the Supplementary Penal Regulations, were directed primarily at the triple abuses of corruption, violence and public disorder. A fairly sharp distinction should be made between the actual polling and election results on the one hand, and the events of the campaigning that preceded them on the other. The abuses were not sufficiently serious to have vitiated the outcome of the election as a whole and so render the holding of it pointless. Nevertheless they did occur on many occasions in many different places, and a few instances of what will be a recurrent theme in subsequent chapters will give some idea of the conditions with which the police and courts had to deal.

No part of the country was absolutely free from corruption, but it was perhaps more rife in Saitama prefecture than anywhere else. One case that came to light towards the middle of June involved a number of the inhabitants of two villages, Kambe and Tagaya, in the sub-prefecture of Kita Saitama. These people had been sending out sums of ten sen, together with the visiting card of a local celebrity who was standing for election. The Shintō priest of another village in the area, Sukage, had also been sending out money on behalf of the same man. A confession by one of the electors, who apparently had accepted the bribe only to find his conscience getting the better of him, disclosed what was going on. The priest, when summoned by the village office at which the elector had made his confessions, sent word that he was not at home, but later told the police that he had received a sum of money to be used as bribes from an agent for the candidate. The agent then had to report to the courthouse at Kumagaya to undergo preliminary interrogation, and at least eighteen other persons were summoned for questioning in connexion with the case.[59] Later, it was alleged that an opposing candidate had bribed the original informer to make a spurious confession.[60]

54

Violence, like bribery, was endemic, but most of it was on a small scale. Kumamoto, Kōchi, Ishikawa, Toyama and Niigata prefectures were frequently mentioned as having been particularly notorious trouble spots;[61] and one may perhaps add Yokohama city to this list.

In the Fifth Constituency, Kumamoto prefecture, the turbulence of the two rival political parties, Nationalists and Progressives, obliged the police to fall back on their emergency powers and order them to disband in Yatsushiro sub-prefecture. This order was put out on 24 June and behind it lay a whole series of minor incidents, culminating in a set fight between adherents of the two factions armed with swords and clubs. The battle, which took place probably on 22 or 23 June, had been started by the Nationalists; but the Progressives do not seem to have been much in awe of the swordsmen hired by their opponents, and rallied well enough to start gaining ground. The newspaper report neglected to say how many combatants were involved, but this was evidently quite a major affray over a fairly wide area, as the correspondent did state that skirmishing had been particularly fierce near the twin villages of Kagumi and Miyanohara. Apparently no one was killed, even in these two settlements where the 'warfare' was at its hottest. Elsewhere, on the evening of 23 June, a member of the Nationalist faction had met with a supporter of the Progressives, and the two had started to fight. By the time the police arrived, the Nationalist had already pushed his adversary over, and had bitten him on his cheek, side and right arm.[62]

Cases of the police or other executive officials ordering the dissolution of political organizations were extremely rare; and in the above-mentioned instance, the ban applied to only part of the constituency concerned. Earlier in the election campaign, the Home Minister himself had intervened to authorize the total proscription of an association known as the Sanyō Society of Righteousness (*Sanyō Gikai*). This society was active in Himeji, a medium-sized town in Hyōgo prefecture. Its members had Liberal connexions and were also linked with the Himeji Young Men's Club.

55

Their record of disorderly conduct dated from November 1889, when some of them, in order to give vent to their hostility to the Government's plans for treaty revision, attended a speech meeting on that subject, heckled the speakers and assaulted somebody in the audience. Shortly afterwards other members challenged to a duel the writer of a series of articles that appeared in a Kōbe paper. There then came a brief interlude for internal re-organization. In January 1890 the society, having invited Count Itagaki to address it, held a meeting of its supporters from all over Hyōgo prefecture. At this rally it decided to work with Itagaki rather than with the leaders of rival Liberal factions. In February, the society was responsible for assaulting Tanaka Tokitarō, the editor of a Himeji journal, while he was opening a meeting. As a result of this outrage, the police asked for a membership list. In the same month, the society appointed a candidate for election to the House of Representatives in the Seventh Constituency of Hyōgo prefecture.

The decision to compete in the parliamentary elections seems to have bereft the Sanyō Society of Righteousness of whatever shreds of respectability remained to it. On 9 March, members rioted with drawn swords at a meeting of supporters of the Progressive Party held in the village of Kokubunji, Shikitō sub-prefecture; and on 25 March, they caused a disturbance during a Progressive Party speech meeting at another place, Masuisan, in the same sub-prefecture. Throughout April and May, they were responsible for a series of similar outbreaks in the constituency, as well as finding time to challenge the Progressives to a debating contest. The Home Office order dissolving the society was issued on 6 June. Undaunted, its ex-members announced their intention of setting up a Hyōgo Prefecture Patriots Club.[63]

This preliminary sketch of the circumstances in which the police all too frequently found themselves may be appropriately concluded with a translation of an item which appeared in the *Tokyo Nichi Nichi Shimbun* for 20 June. It was headed 'Violence at A Speech Meeting':

56

I. ORGANIZATION AND ADMINISTRATION

At a Progressive Party speech meeting held on the 16th of this month by a certain Mr Katō of Usui village, Nakakanbara sub-prefecture, Niigata prefecture, the audience was thrown into a state of great confusion during the speech of the second speaker, Mr Shigeno Tamaki. (A member of the staff of the *Mainichi Shimbun*.) A gang of hooligans stood up together and, overturning the dais, assaulted the speaker. In a state of affairs which even the police lacked the means to control, Mr Shigeno had his head injured and his face was dripping with blood. Could anything be more outrageous?

The examples given—one from Kyushu, the second from the Kansai area, and the third from the Tōhoku region—show that violence was not limited to any one particular district. To repeat, most of the incidents in themselves did not amount to very much; the battle between the Progressives and Nationalists in the Fifth Constituency, Kumamoto prefecture, was on a bigger scale than the great majority of cases where participants in the election campaign took the law into their own hands. Nevertheless, the police in all areas were understandably apprehensive lest small outbreaks should multiply as the campaign ran its course, and eventually reach their climax in a deluge of major riots and attacks on or just after the day of the election. Therefore they took great care to guard the polling stations and their environs while the voting was in progress. Similarly, they made efforts to ensure that the ballot boxes would be safe after the polls had closed, and that there would be no disorders at the declaration of the poll meetings.

After making inquiries of the returning officers, the Police Commissioner in Tokyo decided to allocate one sergeant and five constables to every polling station.[64] In Kagawa prefecture, election fever ran high enough to warrant the posting of 'several hundred' policemen to each constituency during the last week of the campaign.[65] If this report is accurate, since there were five constituencies in the prefecture and its total force of regular policemen would have hardly exceeded four or five hundred,[66] one must assume that many of the constables involved were borrowed from other prefectures or else had been specially recruited to supervise the election.

57

Two hundred such special force policemen were in fact distributed among the 219 polling stations in Kanagawa prefecture. These men were to work in conjunction with another hundred who had been assigned to the constituencies earlier. On 29 June, the Chief-Inspector of the Prefectural Police Department, accompanied by the Chief Inspector of the Public Peace Preservation Department, set out on a tour of the outlying districts in order to check the arrangements made for the safety of both polling stations and ballot boxes.[67] For Yokohama city itself the police control was especially strict. The solitary polling station was protected by a force consisting of four police-sergeants, ten uniformed police-constables, and ten constables in Japanese dress. In addition, stationary guards were on duty at thirty strategic points in the city. This show of strength completely demoralized the Yokohama gangsters who had been actively concerned in the election right down to the evening of 30 June.[68]

These and similar precautions in other parts of the country achieved the desired effect. As will be shown later, the assaults and rowdyism that preceded the voting had been perpetrated by a type of person who was not likely to stand his ground when confronted by a superior force. Organized political violence on a wide scale was hardly ever attempted; and when it was, it met with the fate meted out to the Sanyō Society of Righteousness. Still, there is no saying what might have happened on the day of the election if the police had not adopted a very firm attitude. As it was, despite the unruliness of the campaign, and despite a number of half-hearted endeavours on the part of known trouble-makers to stir up incidents in front of the polling stations on election day, the voting itself was everywhere peaceful. A Tokyo journalist, reporting the election scene in the capital, could write: 'In front of the gate of every polling station, white-uniformed policemen were placed on guard; and beside them, the sparrows pecked for their food and the dogs slept.'[69]

From the provincial centres, too, the telegrams, without a single exception, all brought the same message: 'Voting completed; no incidents.'[70]

CHAPTER II

PARTIES, PRINCIPLES
AND ISSUES

Contestants for election in 1890 may be divided, for the purpose of discovering their predominant political colouring, into three major groups: the Liberal-Progressive factions, the Conservative factions and the Independents. The majority of candidates belonged to the last group, which was non-party. The principal parties were all descended from the three earlier national political associations of Liberals, Progressives and Imperialists. Indeed, the *Kaishin-tō*, it will be remembered, had never formally dissolved itself, even after the resignation of its leader, Ōkuma Shigenobu, in 1884; and it was the same organization and the same platform that bore the label 'Progressive' in the first general election.

(1) THE 'DAIDŌ DANKETSU'

The case of the Liberals was very different. After the dissolution of their party in October 1884, there was virtually no legitimate political activity among the ranks of the Government's opponents until 1886 when Gotō Shōjirō started a campaign against the administration's alleged mishandling of the treaty revision problem. All this time there had been a steady growth in the extent and depth of popular feeling against the existing treaties; and this feeling could be quite easily converted into a formidable expression of hostility towards the authorities.

Inoue Kaoru's scheme for revision had finally broken down in the summer of 1887; partly because of the uncompromising policies of the treaty Powers, partly because of affronted Japanese opinion. Sensing this opportunity, and making clever use of the failure of the Itō Cabinet's rather fatuous policy of excessive fraternization with the Occidental diplomatic communities, Gotō worked hard to combine all the different

59

disaffected elements—conservative, moderate and radical—in one large body of agitators. The name of this organization was the *Daidō Danketsu* (Unionist League); its slogan was Unity in Diversity (*Daidō Shōi*, i.e. 'alike in great matters, of differing views in small'); its avowed aim was the rectification of the diplomatic situation; its real purpose, the unseating of the *Sat-Chō* clique.[1]

This revival of party activity gained force with explosive speed. Speech meetings were held throughout the country; and in the capital, petitions flowed into the Senate, or else were presented at the private residences of the ministers of State. These petitions were the same in form and substance; and since they were limited to three demands—that is, reduction of the land-tax, freedom of speech and assembly, and an improvement in the country's diplomacy—they were collectively known as the Petition on Three Serious Matters. In September 1887, the Home Minister, Yamagata Aritomo, announced that all petitions would be rejected, and that anyone submitting a petition would be severely punished. The following month, Gotō and his closest confederates founded the *Teigai Club* ('87 Club), a political but non-party organization designed to hold together the adherents of the *Daidō Danketsu* movement.[2]

Meanwhile groups of these adherents were continually moving into Tokyo from the provinces, and the political temperature of the metropolis was rising to heights last reached at the time of the Hokkaidō Development Board scandal in 1881. At the beginning of December, Gotō presented a lengthy memorial to the Lord Chamberlain, asking that it should be passed on to the Emperor.[3] Immediately afterwards, he (Gotō) left for a successful and inflammatory speech-making tour of the north-eastern prefectures, where resentment at the victory of the south-western forces at the time of the Restoration still rankled in the hearts of many. The Emperor, it seems, was not allowed to see Gotō's memorial; and on 26 December, the Government struck a hard blow at his movement by promulgating the emergency Peace Preservation Ordinance.[4]

The effect of this ordinance was to shift the opposition from the capital to the countryside. Article IV of the new law empowered the authorities to order the removal of anybody they considered likely to promote civil strife or disorder to a place more than three *ri* (about seven miles) from the Imperial palace. Applying the power conferred by this article with prompt and relentless vigour, the police by the evening of 28 December had brought about a mass exodus of upwards of 570 prominent party politicians from the inner regions of Tokyo.

However, the opposition, though foiled in its first objective of putting immediate and unbearable pressure on the Government, proved itself quite capable of carrying on the struggle from the provinces. Itagaki Taisuke had emerged from his political retirement in the previous autumn, and was actively engaged in realizing the aims of the *Daidō Danketsu*. Gotō, himself, revisited the north-eastern regions in the summer of 1888. Prior to this, Ōkuma had re-entered the Government as its Minister for Foreign Affairs. This development, which had taken place in February 1888, had a number of important repercussions including a relaxation of the hostility so recently displayed by the Cabinet to the Unionists.

The incessant scheming and campaigning began to bear visible fruit in October 1888, when the *Daidō Danketsu* took formal shape for the first time at a series of conventions of local politicians held in Chiba, Osaka and Kumamoto. The new association, as such, remained non-political; but it acknowledged Gotō as its leader, and accepted a common programme of action. It also decided to issue a 'party' journal to be called *Seiron (Political Discussion)*.

The *Daidō Danketsu* soon crashed. The Government, conscious of having gained something of a Pyrrhic victory in December 1887, had invited Ōkuma to assume the responsibility for treaty revision as a gesture of conciliation towards its opponents. Though Ōkuma had long since severed his formal connexion with the Progressive Party, the unofficial links between him and his sympathizers had not been impaired. Therefore, after their ex-leader had entered the Government, many

Progressives became first of all lukewarm in their zeal for the *Daidō Danketsu* and later, when Ōkuma's proposals for treaty revision were made the subject of heated controversy, openly antagonistic to the attitude of their political allies. Thus, the situation arose that the Progressives and their press came out in favour of Ōkuma and the Government on the subject of treaty revision; while the Liberals and the Conservative extremists continued to maintain a stance of unflinching opposition. The promulgation of the constitution in February 1889, together with the special amnesty for political offenders that marked the occasion, also served to ease the strain of the previous year, and naturally won some measure of public esteem for the Government.

The death-blow for the *Daidō Danketsu*, however, was dealt it by its own leader. In March 1889, Gotō Shōjirō unexpectedly entered the Cabinet as Minister of Communications. The motive behind the invitation to Gotō is clear—as always, the Meiji statesmen were not unwilling to win over their most dangerous enemies if the chance to do so offered itself. They preferred reconciliation to isolation. As for Gotō, his career was one of amiable adventurism in both business and politics. Though not without talents and insights which were of value to the Liberal movement, he made his way by remaining friendly with more powerful figures than himself in all quarters at all times. It is possible that he had deliberately used the *Daidō Danketsu* as a means of advancing his own fortunes, private as well as public. Certainly, he took a delight in emphasizing the superior spending power of the Ministry of Communications, when replying to a group of erstwhile followers who had taunted him with the lowliness of his new post in terms of Cabinet rank.[5]

The Government, at the time when it had begun negotiations with Gotō, had extended an invitation to Itagaki, too, with the idea of persuading both of them to rejoin it.[6] If this stratagem had worked, it would have been a major tactical victory for the *Sat-Chō* bureaucrats. Itagaki refused for himself, however, while advising Gotō to accept. He told Gotō that as the constitution had now been promulgated, it would be better for the Liberal cause if he were to take part in the affairs of State as a member of the Government and as a kind of forward scout for the more slowly moving battalions of full party Cabinets. From other evidence it looks as if Itagaki's protestations in this matter were genuine; and this theory of infiltration was Gotō's own principal defence of his actions.[7]

The remaining leaders of the *Daidō Danketsu*, stricken by their chief's defection, were soon divided into two factions.[8] The more radical, under Ōi Kentaro, Arai Shōgo, Ishizaka Masataka and others, wished to retain the technically non-political character of the organization; opposed to them was a group led by Kōno Hironaka, Inoue Kakugorō, Ōe Taku, Inukai Takeshi and others who wished to turn it into a properly constituted political party. At the beginning of May 1889, Itagaki tried hard to heal the division between these two sections of his supporters, making a special journey from Kōchi to Tokyo. His efforts proved unavailing, however, and on 10 May, the 'political party faction', now calling itself the *Daidō Club*, held a meeting in Tokyo at which a formal statement of policy was discussed and approved. The other section of the *Daidō Danketsu*, the 'non-political party faction', adopted the name Unionist Harmony Society (*Daidō Kyōwa Kai*), and entered into a spirited but sadly wasteful strife with its sister body in Osaka and elsewhere.

(2) THE LIBERAL FACTIONS—THE 'JIYŪ-TŌ', THE 'DAIDŌ CLUB' AND THE 'AIKOKU-KŌTŌ'

In this way, the once formidable *Daidō Danketsu* came to an inglorious and rancorous end. It passed beyond recall in October 1889, when the severe wounding of Ōkuma Shigenobu in a bomb outrage brought about the indefinite postponement of treaty revision so destroying the only basis for an alliance between the Liberals and extreme Conservatives. Itagaki, now that Ōkuma was in hospital and Gotō in the Government, alone of the three outstanding leaders of the old popular rights movement, was able openly to take to the hustings. Thinking of the election, he went on trying to get some semblance of order and unity out of the broken ranks of Liberalism. His plan was to re-found the Liberal Party, making it wide enough to attract both the *Daidō Club* and the *Daidō Kyōwa Kai* each of which would be dissolved. When he suggested this to the various leaders, he encountered many obstacles in the form of regional jealousies and personal rivalries. Undeterred, he then sent out invitations to all the notables of the popular rights movement, asking them to attend a meeting in Osaka on 17 December. He proposed in his letters that the meeting should discuss the formation of a new party.

The *Daidō Club* leaders travelled *en masse* to Osaka in response to these invitations; so, too, did their opposite numbers in the *Daidō Kyōwa Kai*. But the latter, taking offence at Itagaki's professed intention of reconciling the two factions as revealed in a preliminary interview they had with him, refused outright to attend the actual convention. As a result, only the *Daidō Club* element was present when Itagaki opened his meeting on 19 December. To them, he explained what he had had in mind when he arranged the conference, and read out a draft prospectus for a new party. This he wanted to call not after the old *Jiyū-tō*, but after the still earlier *Aikoku-kōtō* (Patriotic Party). The meeting heard him out; but it came to an end without anything definite being decided. As soon as these proceedings had finished, the *Daidō Club* opened a separate meeting of its own to discuss the proposed change of name. In the end, it rejected the suggestion that it should start calling itself the *Aikoku-kōtō*.

Itagaki's initiative did lead to something. However this was not one large and re-invigorated Liberal Party decked out with a 'Patriotic Party' label. Rather, it was the formation of three, instead of two, splinter parties. After having brusquely rejected Itagaki's overtures, the *Daidō Kyōwa Kai* stole his policy and set about reviving the *Jiyū-tō*. A provisional inauguration ceremony for the new party was held then and there in Osaka

2. THE LIBERAL FACTIONS

preceding a full-dress affair in Tokyo, on 21 January 1890, at which the metamorphosis of the *Daidō Kyōwa Kai* into the *Jiyū-tō* was properly effected. The revived *Jiyū-tō* did not have a single national leadership, but was divided into two wings. These corresponded to the two great geographical divisions of Japan. There was a *Kantō Jiyū-tō* based on Tokyo, the president of which was Ōi Kentaro; and there was a *Kansai Jiyū-tō* based on Osaka, under the control of Kobayashi Kusuo. There followed a convention in Tokyo of all the leading members of the new Liberal Party from 21 to 23 February, which produced a statement of the party's principles and aims, in effect, an election manifesto.[9]

While the *Daidō Kyōwa Kai* was busy turning itself into the *Jiyū-tō*, its rivals in the *Daidō Club* were also closing their ranks and preparing for the election. The *Daidō Club* manifesto received unanimous assent at a party convention which took place in the capital on 4 May. Kōno Hironaka acted as chairman. As with the *Jiyū-tō*, the *Daidō Club* policy statement was not just an election manifesto; its leaders took the opportunity to make public for the second time the unchanging axioms of their political beliefs, as well as to put forward a series of vote-catching promises.[10] Again like the *Jiyū-tō*, the *Daidō Club* used the *Kōtō Nakamura Rō* for its election convention.

The day after this, 5 May, Itagaki, who had not abandoned his scheme for reviving the *Aikoku-kōtō* after the fiasco of the Osaka conference in the previous December, and who had in the meantime made a speech tour in the south-western provinces, called a meeting of his closest adherents. More than 500 of them came to the meeting. The *Kōsei-kan*, in the Kobiki-chō district of Tokyo, had been hired for this gathering which was the occasion of the official re-birth of the *Aikoku-kōtō* and also of the publication of that party's general prospectus and election programme.[11]

It was these three splinter parties, then—the *Jiyū-tō*, the *Daidō Club*, and the *Aikoku-kōtō*—which, together with the *Kaishin-tō*, represented the 'popular rights' end of the Japanese political spectrum in the general election of 1890. The history of the rapid rise and fractious fall of the *Daidō Danketsu* illustrates very well the general political temper of the times, and, in particular, the endemic weaknesses of the Liberal movement. The opponents of the Meiji bureaucracy could present a united front on a single issue of overriding importance and far-reaching appeal; but for long many of those most closely associated with the political party movement found it next to impossible to coalesce into a broadly based organization, owing allegiance to a single leader. Moreover, although the popular rights agitation was never permanently damaged by official repression some of its champions were not immune to offers of Government posts. The disputes and secessions of the Liberal and Progressive party politicians meant that they faced their enemies in the Government with badly divided forces when it came to the election and suffered accordingly. On the other side of the political gulf, within the ranks of the bureaucracy, the desire for a 'transcendental Cabinet' can have been only strengthened by the discords in the 'popular' camp.

These strictures can be fairly made on one—the organizational—aspect of party politics because the Liberal cause in 1890 still carried with it the marks of its origins. While it would be possible to attempt to rationalize the conduct of characters like Gotō by arguing that the party movement from first to last was nothing more than a means of getting back into power, this theory fails to explain why he and Itagaki resigned from the Government in the first place. Nor does it give proper weight to the increasingly important social infra-structure of the movement whereby it was giving political voice, and before long chances of political leadership, to groups hitherto without these rights and opportunities. Consequently, although an element of opportunism is undeniable, it would be better to think of the Liberty and Popular Rights Movement as having come into existence as an instrument of struggle—struggle to wrest concessions from the authorities, and struggle to teach the people basic democratic theory. It had not only drawn into its upper echelons its share of trimmers, but also had raised to that level many men of great talent and imaginative zeal, such as Kōno Hironaka, Sugita Teiichi and Yuasa Jirō.

Self-seeking or not, all these leaders were persons of strong character and individualistic bent; many of them had 'done time' in prison. Moreover, in the conditions in which it had taken root, the popular rights movement had been forced to put a premium on abstract principles—Liberty...Independence...Progress—and to rely heavily on its political theorists. This was the only way its sponsors could justify their bid for power but this stress, imposed by circumstances of opposition on the Liberals, enhanced their penchant for polemics amongst themselves as well as in their relationship with the Government. Finally, there was the always simmering feud within the movement between the militant minority in favour of direct action against the Government and the more cautious majority which believed in enforcing its political claims by peaceful means. The dissolution of the first *Jiyū-tō* had afforded ample proof of this basic cleavage, but had hardly put an end to it.

Thus, the years 1873–89 were a period of power-seeking without responsibility, a period of politics given over to theory and propaganda during which the internal ethos of the Liberal movement also lent itself to individual initiative and ambition. This in turn gave rise to bitter personal rivalries, and a serious difference of opinion over the use of force substantiated by armed uprisings on the part of frustrated extremists. In some ways, these tendencies were fortified by the general course of events in the 1880s, with their agricultural depression, Governmental arbitrariness, and the mounting tension over the treaty problem. Again, over the whole national scene hung the miasma of a vanished feudalism; some of its less auspicious traits—regionalism and factionalism—have already been described.

In view of all this, the breakdown of the *Daidō Danketsu* followed by the appearance of three rival heirs to the mantle of the original Liberal Party is quite intelligible, though this does not mean that it and similar disruptions in the future were anything but disastrous for the Liberal cause as a whole. On the other hand, what the advocates of Liberty lost by their failures in the sphere of organization, they to some extent recovered by the good sense that they showed in compiling their respective election declarations. This was a task for which they were well qualified, and they made the most of both their previous experience in political debate and the opportunities presented to them by the Government.

Compared with the short, abstract declaration of principle issued by the Liberal Party in 1881, these manifestos were more moderate, more specific and longer. The differences reflected the general post-1884 resurgence of traditional feeling; they also reflected the imminence of the first parliamentary election. After all, the Liberals would have had a plausible case in 1881, had they argued that as the Diet was not to be summoned for a further nine years, it was hardly the time to frame a detailed electoral programme; even though this sort of consideration had not deterred either the Progressives or the Imperialists from being more precise about their intentions.

However, after making full allowances for alterations in the country's mood and in the tactical requirements of the situation, the greater conservativism of 1890 arose, at any rate in part, from a falling off of radical fervour in the Liberal ranks. Allusion has already been made to the principal reason why the Liberal movement underwent this change of heart, that is, the growing influence of the wealthy rural capitalist element within the party. Attitudes towards the throne are a touchstone of this trend towards moderation. The document issued in 1881 had been rather remarkable in that it contained no mention whatsoever of the Imperial House; now, in 1890, the *Daidō Club* was implicitly, the *Jiyū-tō* explicitly, and the *Aikoku-kōtō* effusively monarchist. Therefore in this respect (as in others) the Liberal position had moved appreciably closer to that of the Progressives over the intervening years.

The greater pragmatism of the 1890 manifestos is even more readily apparent. The *Daidō Club* went furthest in this direction.

68

It introduced its programme to the public in a very cut and dried manner under short headings, such as 'The Strengthening of Independent Sovereignty', or 'The Introduction of Party Cabinets'. The *Jiyū-tō* was about as pedestrian, though it did preface its proposals with the general statement that it was a party based on a belief in Liberty. The *Aikoku-kōtō* stood alone in making a deliberate effort to recapture the spirit and terminology of the earlier and more heroic age of the popular rights movement. Even so, sandwiched between the somewhat high-flown perorations on Liberty and Natural Rights that begin and end the *Aikoku-kōtō* manifesto, there are some temporizing reservations as well as a compact legislative programme.

Another important and obvious feature of the election manifestos is the similarity of their recommendations. They all came out in favour of: (i) equal treaties with the foreign Powers; (ii) responsibility of the Cabinet to the Diet; (iii) reduction of the land-tax and a policy of financial retrenchment; (iv) extension of the authority of the organs of self-government; (v) abolition of the Peace Preservation Ordinance and the amendment of other regulations which they held infringed the freedoms of speech and assembly; (vi) a reduction in the number of officials; and (vii) the withdrawal of special Government subsidies for commerce and industry.

In all these matters, there was virtually complete agreement among the three Liberal parties not only about ends but also about means. The solitary slight exception to this seems to have been that whereas the *Jiyū-tō* and *Aikoku-kōtō* both asserted the need for specifically party Cabinets, the rather more conservative *Daidō Club* was content with a resolution that ministers of State should be obliged to acknowledge their responsibility to the Diet as well as to the Emperor. In their policies on armaments, too, the Liberal politicians more or less thought alike. The *Aikoku-kōtō* would undertake no more military preparations than were strictly necessary for national defence and decisively rejected policies of aggression. Though the *Daidō Club*, on the other hand, planned to enlarge the army and navy in keeping with the gradual increase in the economic strength of the country, both it and the *Jiyū-tō* promised to revise the conscription system in order to shorten the periods of active or reserve service it entailed.

The recommendations listed above show that the Liberal opposition could launch a shrewd and damaging attack on the Government in matters relating to its personnel as well as its policies. In some respects this attack was unfair, but that simply made it all the more effective. The unequal treaties were in many ways the Achilles heel of those in power; and to raise an unthinking cry for the revision of them was a sure means of winning popular support and at the same time bedevilling the Government's diplomatic efforts. Yet though the Liberal manifestos all contained a clause saying that equal treaties would be signed, none of them went on to elaborate exactly how foreigners could be brought to view the question with the same urgency as the Japanese did. The promise to reduce the land-tax would produce an equally favourable response from the predominantly rural electorate. Again, though, there was more than a tinge of irresponsibility in this proposal. Granted that the manifestos implied or explicitly declared that economies would be made by streamlining the administration and dismissing supernumerary officials, the amount of money thus saved would have hardly compensated for any large-scale reduction in the land-tax. This was still the Government's main source of revenue. Moreover, by 1890 it was apparent that treaty revision would be hastened, to say the least, by acquiring a powerful army and navy, and that would require money.

The same general judgement may be passed on two of the other planks in the Liberal platform—consolidation of local self-government, and a thinning out of the numbers of Civil Servants at all levels of administration. These pledges were good politics, but both of them were to some extent poor statesmanship.

The process of centralization had gone a very long way in the first two decades of the Meiji period; and this development could be made to seem all the more onerous when contrasted with the fief autonomy of Tokugawa times. Therefore, even so late as 1890 the Government's opponents were able to rely, to some extent, on a backwash of regional sentiment, no doubt strengthened by the day-to-day excesses of bureaucratic centralism. Furthermore, regional loyalties were still a major dynamic of the Liberty and Popular Rights Movement. Nevertheless there was something a little unreal in 1890 about some of the more particularist statements to be found in the Liberal manifestos; such as that emphasizing the separate rights of the provinces, or another to the effect that local custom should be made the basis of the Municipal and the Town and Village Codes. Anything but a uniform and fairly closely supervised system of local self-government would have been hampering and wasteful to a country in the throes of modernization.

Likewise, the demand for a reduced Civil Service might have proved a little more difficult to realize in practice than it had been to make on paper. Certainly, the bureaucracy was overstaffed, and the Government itself issued orders for the dismissal of redundant officers in the weeks preceding the election. But it is probable that the Liberals tended to exaggerate for their own ends the quantity of 'drones' living at the tax-payers' expense; and since the officials, civil and military, were in many ways the standard-bearers of Japan's progress their number could not have been cut back too ruthlessly. The Liberals were on good tactical ground, though, in making plain their animosity to the bureaucrats. There is no reason to doubt Suematsu Kenchō's word on this matter:

[Judging] by the experiences of the recent general election, it would appear to be very hard for an official to become a Member [of the House of Representatives]. Apparently, officials were generally detested so far as the election of Members was concerned. In so saying, I would appear to be praising myself; because I was elected while holding an official post. However, consider my election to have been quite exceptional![12]

In Suematsu's opinion, many electors feared that if they elected officials to the House of Representatives, the Government

71

would pass whatever legislation it pleased without paying attention to public opinion. Not unnaturally, such a prospect was
the reverse of pleasing to them, as Suematsu also made clear
when he talked of the voting public's disenchantment with a
state of affairs as a result of which:

The present Government, even though there have been some comings
and goings amongst the ministers, has been in the hands of the same
group of people ever since the Restoration.[13]

A little earlier than this, but still on the same point of the
electors' desire for change, Suematsu had said that there was
a vague but widespread hope that the political scene would be
radically altered as a result of the institution of the Diet, and
that the latter 'would be of great use to the people in every way'.
Other evidence proves that he was correct in his assessment of
the general temper of the electorate in this matter of Government versus people.

It was these circumstances that gave the call for party or
Diet-controlled Cabinets such a prominent place in all three
manifestos, and made it the opening shot of a bitter struggle
that went on for the greater part of the ensuing decade. Indeed,
both in terms of the situation as it existed in 1890 and in terms
of future constitutional development, this demand was the key-
stone of the Liberal (and Progressive) programme. Once the
principle of party government was conceded, the rest (reduction
of the land-tax, strengthening of local self-government, etc.)
could be expected to follow in so far as it was practicable.
Moreover, a party Cabinet, if it still desired, would have no
difficulty in abolishing the more obnoxious relics of the past
such as the Peace Preservation Ordinance, which the Government had soon ceased to invoke but could do so at any time;
and in removing minor irritations like red-tapism, not to mention the latent tyranny of the Newspaper, Public Meetings, and
Publications Regulations. The country's lack of experience in
representative government as well as internecine Liberal
squabbles enabled the bureaucrats to argue with a fair degree
of plausibility that transcendental Cabinets were better for the

time being. Yet nothing is perfect, and as has been pointed out earlier, making the Cabinet responsible to the Diet was the next step in obtaining a fully effective parliamentary democracy for Japan.

Compared with the promise to introduce party Cabinets, the attack on Government subsidies or other forms of protection for private industry was of a lesser order of political magnitude. In 1890, these subsidies were still inconsiderable and they were to be multiplied many times during the next two decades. From the Liberals' point of view, however, hostility towards any special financial help for the modern manufacturing and trading combines of the cities accorded as well with their underlying dogma of *laissez-faire* as it did with a commitment to cut the land-tax and with their general concern for the sectional interests of the rural areas where most of the voters lived. Even though a policy of 'no subsidies' was unrealistic so long as Japan had not regained tariff autonomy and remained in the infancy of industrialization, problems of national economy, like setbacks in diplomacy, could still be laid at the door of the Liberals' enemies in the administration.

As has been noted, the manifestos put out by both the *Daidō Club* and the *Jiyū-tō*, but strangely enough not that of the *Aikoku-kōtō* in spite of its greater emphasis on the theory of Liberalism, contained suggestions for electoral reform. These suggestions consisted in the main of a pledge to make the constituencies larger, implying that in future they would each return several Representatives, and a promise to widen the franchise by lowering the age and tax qualifications for electors. Perhaps the reason why the *Aikoku-kōtō* did not include electoral reform in its planned legislation for the first Diet was that this programme was deliberately restricted to what the party considered to be the most urgent of urgent matters. Be that as it may, there can be little doubt that the *Daidō Club* and *Jiyū-tō* politicians were serious and in many ways justified in putting forward these proposals. The existing electoral system cried out for a more liberal suffrage in particular.

73

The general impression left by the three Liberal manifestos as a whole, even after taking into account their inconsistencies and electioneering opportunism, is one of solid worth and purposeful zeal. Their overall efficacy, both as a means of winning votes and as a pointer to future developments, was proved by the results of the election in which the three Liberal factions between them won almost half the seats in the House of Representatives, and by what happened after it was all over. Treaty revision was eventually accomplished by direct and secret negotiations between the Meiji Government and the Powers concerned, without either the concurrence or the interference of the Imperial Diet. The Liberals could have hardly quarrelled with the outcome of these 'private' talks; since they abolished extra-territorial jurisdiction forthwith, and ensured that Japan would regain her tariff autonomy at the end of a fixed number of years.

In other matters—notably, the introduction of party Cabinets, the widening of the franchise, the curtailment of expenditure, and the abolition of the Peace Preservation Ordinance—interested Members of the House of Representatives fought on until they won most or part of what they and their spiritual forbears of 1890 had wanted. Only on the issue of decentralization do they seem to have scored a complete blank; but there, they were to a not inconsiderable extent forestalled by Yamagata's broad-minded and thorough approach to the problems of local self-government. The new Municipal and Town and Village Codes were only just going into operation at the time of the election. Apart from this, as has been explained already, the more regionalist overtones of the Liberal pronouncements on local government were not appropriate to the age.

If, in the last analysis, Liberal ideas on regional autonomy constituted an inapposite vestige of Japan's feudal past, yet another and more important aspect of their election manifestos was becoming obsolescent in terms of Western European political development. This was the conviction, running all through the declarations, that Liberty would of itself completely cure

74

the evils of society. Already in 1890, outside Japan, *laissez-faire* carried to this extent had a taste of mid-century *naïveté* and selfishness for disciples of Shaftesbury and readers of Zola, not to mention the Fabians. The corollary of this was the Japanese Liberals' general lack of interest in matters of social, as opposed to political, reform.

The *Jiyū-tō* declared that it would amend the education system and encourage the spread of learning; the *Aikoku-kōtō* looked forward to improving the prison system, but whether it was actuated in this by philanthropic motives or by thoughts of saving the tax-payers' money is not clear. Apart from these minor, if not quite meaningless, affirmations, the Liberal manifestos were bereft of any black and white proposals for the betterment of social conditions. Their prevailing philosophy was that of upper-class individualism; and their overriding objective was to bring about a decrease in the powers and expenditures of the Government.[14]

The ideological sections of the *Aikoku-kōtō* manifesto raised two or three interesting points. First, they contained a definite attempt to clarify the position of the followers of Itagaki *vis-à-vis* the Imperial House. Briefly, the argument was that Liberalism by making the monarchy constitutional would enhance it, whereas absolutism could only endanger it by antagonizing public opinion; and further, that rendering the Empire strong and independent by correct application of Liberal principles would make manifest the innate glory of its Sovereign. The Emperor, in other words, was to be the topmost and most resplendent flower on the Liberal tree. Not being permitted to govern himself, he was thereby to be made an all the more secure, and still semi-divine, symbol of the greatness and prosperity of his subjects under Liberal rule. For Japan, republicanism was out of the question; and this was probably as good a way as any of trying to solve the knotty problem of reconciling the formal omnipotence of the dynasty with the actualities of constitutional government. In advancing these ideas, the *Aikoku-kōtō* undoubtedly drew much moral support from the example of England.

Elsewhere in what have been called the 'ideological sections' of its manifesto, the *Aikoku-kōtō* urged the need for a large united party in the 'popular' camp, so that radical politicians would be able to meet for the forces of the Government on something like equal terms in the Diet. This again was an important issue. Not only would a large number of small parties in the House of Representatives have made it easy for the Government to control the Diet rather than the other way round, but it was of special relevance to the election of 1890, when the Liberals themselves were split into three factions and there were many Independent candidates. These last were a threat to party candidates if only because the concept of a political party, avowedly organized to advance personal ambitions or sectional interests, ran counter to the Confucian and feudal ideal of disinterested public service. As a result of this, there was always an inclination in many minds to vote for Independents simply on the grounds that they were Independents. This sort of antagonism was a constant worry to the advocates of popular rights; and none of them was more conscious of its injurious effects than Itagaki himself. The use of such terms as 'Patriot' and 'Public' (*Aikoku-kōtō*, Public Party of Patriots; *Aikoku-sha*, Patriotic Society) in naming his Liberal organizations was one of the means he devised for trying to rid them of the stigma of being thought a cabal.

Finally, at the very end of the *Aikoku-kōtō* manifesto, there appeared a passage about the possibility of Japan exerting her influence all over the world as the Oriental fortress and protagonist of freedom and independence. This glittering hope was held out in contrast to a supposedly existing limbo of alienation: 'Ah, our land of the dragon-fly is an orphan isle! If we are ardent in our devotion to true liberty, shall we not make our country's glory shine through the five continents?' Short and vaguely couched, it is hard to know exactly what to make of these sentences; but they would seem to confirm other evidence that expansionism and a sense of national mission were sentiments affecting all quarters of the political world in Meiji Japan. In this

76

case, though, the implication was that the way to world-wide influence lay through moral leadership rather than military hegemony.

Itagaki, in the speeches he made during the election campaign, played upon these three themes of constitutional monarchy, stable parties and world influence; as well as dealing with the other main issues such as the necessity for financial retrenchment and the disadvantages of too much centralization. When talking on 18 June to a gathering at Mito, he used the metaphor of a strong colt to describe the vigour that a constitutional and parliamentary State would derive from its institutions. Part of his purpose here was to show that the people could expect an improvement in the country's diplomatic position, and by implication an extension of its international prestige, if they adopted the principles of Liberalism. At the same time, in saying that the Emperor would be made to accept the honour of riding this strong colt, he was attempting to explain the Liberal conception of the relations that, properly speaking, should have subsisted between the Sovereign and his subjects. In the section of the speech immediately preceding this, he had alleged that 'absolutist' methods of honouring the Emperor would amount to 'elevating him by burying the common people under the ground and leaving His Majesty above it'.[15] He was uncompromising in his declarations that Liberalism, as it would increase the welfare and happiness of the mass of the Imperial subjects, was the best way of showing loyal respect to the throne. Conversely, the statist thinking of the Meiji bureaucrats he considered to be disloyal to the throne; and, what was more, illogical in itself: 'If it were said, "you people shall be poor, but your State shall be rich and powerful"—who would submit to such an argument?' Itagaki asked, after stating that 'The Liberalism which our party advocates is individualism. That is to say, it is the view that if one sets out to enlarge national rights, one must widen popular rights. If it is desirable to make the State wealthy and strong, one must make individuals wealthy and strong.'

It will be seen that the attack was made not so much on the long-term Meiji objectives of strengthening the State and

77

enlarging national rights, as on the means whereby the Government was seeking to attain them. Furthermore, even though there was an unequivocal assertion of the individualist basis of Liberal philosophy, Itagaki's words on this occasion would seem to indicate that he still had to appreciate the fact that at the root of Western individualism lay the purpose of realizing the full potentialities of man as a personal soul rather than as a national subject. This is a point to be made more in sorrow than anger; and it should not be taken as a completely damaging reflexion on either Itagaki's outlook or the achievements of the popular rights movement. Just over twenty years had elapsed since the overthrow of feudalism and the diplomatic position of Japan was still critical in a world where Britannia's imitators in domestic freedom had come to be her chief competitors for rule beyond the waves. In these circumstances, it was of very great credit to Itagaki and the cause for which he had fought that he should have been able to give such a trenchant exposition of one side of the Liberal case and to insist that individual rights must take precedence over State rights, at any rate in so far as the goal envisaged by the latter was unattainable without giving proper scope to the former.

This speech showed that Itagaki had remained consistent since the birth of the Liberal movement in Tosa to his belief in the need to build a strong Empire on the energies of an emancipated people, living under a representative system. On the other great questions of parties and the part they should be expected to play in a national assembly, however, there was an unavoidable rejection of the early emphasis on abstract principles. Having won recognition of popular rights, a further task was to justify the existence of a political party as a necessary mediatory link between the people and the power he had encouraged it to seek. As a result, the theory of direct representation, implying that Representatives would be no more than delegates of the voters and bound to obey them in every particular, was demolished with the observation that as the majority of electors were fools, this would inevitably lead to a government of fools. 'The object of a representative system', he declared, 'is to make use of the wise.' The proper task of a Representative was, in his opinion, to represent indirectly the views of his constituents. This trend away from militantly doctrinaire theories about the mandate of the people was indicative of the power of the upper-class and politically moderate forces behind Itagaki's main-stream Liberalism, and displayed a growing appreciation of the nature of parliamentary government as known in England. In less theoretical terms, it was yet another step towards the Progressive position, foreshadowing the long period of control of the House of Representatives by two parties that shared the same general conservative point of view.

But, if Representatives were not to be the talking puppets of their masters in the constituencies, how was the bond of representation to be retained at all, and how were the voters going to be able to discriminate between honest men and rogues? Itagaki's answer was given in one word—'principle'. Men of principle would, if elected to parliament, remain true to their beliefs as a general criterion of public morality while exercising their right to use their own judgement in mundane politics. Further, by persuading candidates to disclose their principles before the day of the election, the voters would be able to sort the sheep from the goats. Finally, principles were the thing around which political parties were formed; therefore it was of the utmost importance that electors should vote for candidates belonging to a party, and not for Independents. Thus, from two points of view—from the point of view of checking the tyranny of government, and from the point of view of obtaining a House of Representatives that would effectively represent the general interests of the electors—'political parties are the foundation of a representative system of government'.

Itagaki argued in favour of a system of strong parties founded on principle, and revealed the impact of his own personality, in these words:

Principles are the compass of the political world. Political parties are founded on them; and Representatives move in accordance with them.

79

The confidence which the electors have in their Representatives is nothing other than a confidence in their principles. Therefore, in electing Representatives, we must first of all discover their principles and ascertain their talents. To ascertain men's talents and to discover their principles is the way to become a people that gives its support to political parties, and to make clear the condition of the political world. Moreover, Representatives must on the one hand stand by their parties and advance their cause, and on the other hand reflect upon the parties and criticize them of their own accord. That is how it is. If the people sees fit to put its trust in principles and to discover men's talents by means of forming a large and vigorous party, it will ensure the creation of a perfect representative system from the first, without there being any opportunity for ruffians and flatterers to practise their arts.

Enough has been said to indicate how large these issues of State Rights versus Individual Rights, of theoretical Dynastic Absolutism versus practical Constitutional Monarchy, and of Independents versus Party Candidates loomed in his mind and presumably in the minds of his hearers too. The passages quoted will also have conveyed something of his point of view on these topics, and of the high plane of impartial morality and clarity of thought on which he could conduct a political debate. Some have called Itagaki the 'Rousseau', but—at any rate in relation to the positions he took up in 1890—he would rather seem to merit the epithet 'Gladstone' of Japan.

The Mito speech was delivered on 18 June. The previous day, Itagaki had covered much the same ground in an address given elsewhere in Ibaraki prefecture at Ōta-machi. This speech began with a short eulogy of constitutional government in which he congratulated his audience on the fact that, with the opening of the Diet, they were going to be born as 'genuine human beings'.[16] Then after describing in a suitably guarded way his view of how the constitution had been granted, in form as an act of grace on the part of the Emperor but in reality as a result of the unremitting efforts of the agitators for popular rights, the veteran campaigner made a series of rapier thrusts at what he held up as examples of the tyrannical and wasteful methods of the pre-constitution bureaucracy. The specific evils named were

2. THE LIBERAL FACTIONS

conscription (blood-tax) and general taxation. While dwelling on the theme of burdensome taxation and misuse of public funds by the Government, Itagaki was able to give some under-cover rubs to two other sores of the body politic—centralization and the failure to revise the treaties. This is what he said, in part:

Despite the fact that we, together with you, are burdened with taxes, two-horse carriages are driven round [in the capital], fat horses neigh at the gates, the notes of organs resound mightily in the *Rokumei-kan*, and the currency leaves the countryside to become the plaything of Government contractors in Tokyo. Our manufactures and industries are short of capital and are on the verge of extinction...looking at it from our point of view, we are entitled to ask whether the Government does not spend money wastefully. The value of land falls; more and more bank-notes are issued. Our misfortunes pile up; and starvation hangs over us morning and evening. However, we cannot give voice to our complaints. Truly, ours is a miserable and piteous condition. Gentlemen, I hope you will give this your fullest consideration. Could anything be more miserable and piteous?[17]

Reference to the *Rokumei-kan* was particularly astute. This was the name of a Western-style pleasure pavilion which had been specially constructed by the Government in Tokyo for entertaining the diplomatic representatives of the Treaty Powers. There, Inoue Kaoru, Itō Hirobumi and other high Japanese officials had passed the time in the years 1886–7 by playing cards or dancing with members of the foreign communities, in order to encourage them to persuade their home governments that Japan was sufficiently Westernized to have equal treaties. Not only did the manoeuvre fail to convince the governments of the Powers concerned of the merits of the Japanese case (history is more or less silent on the subject of what the foreign envoys, their staffs, and their respective families themselves thought of the entertainments), but it had made the Japanese Government unpopular with a large section of public opinion that did not like to see the nation's leaders behaving in too Western a fashion. Consequently, the *Rokumei-kan* episode could be easily presented by Itagaki and his friends as a very extravagant, ludicrous and dangerously Western fiasco.[18]

The manufactures and industries mentioned in the above

extract can be taken to mean rural enterprises like the distilling of sake or the making of soy sauce. It was certainly not the case that the Government was withholding much needed capital from the heavy industries in the cities. Even the rural industries were in much better shape, economically speaking, in 1890 than they had been six or seven years before at the worst of the agricultural depression. Similarly, the complaint that 'we cannot give voice to our complaints' was not so much a valid expression of an existing grievance as a piece of retrospective rhetoric, that is, a recriminatory allusion to the Government's use of such measures as the Peace Preservation Ordinance or the Public Meetings Regulations in its contests with the Liberals and their extremist supporters over the past ten years. Obviously it cannot be taken literally; otherwise, Itagaki and other opposition politicians would not have been allowed to make anti-Government speeches.

The Ōta-machi speech did not contain any of the analysis of fundamental problems concerning the status of the Emperor or the nature of the State with which Itagaki was going to grapple on the next day at Mito. However, in the second part of the Ōta-machi address, he did enlarge on the dangers of electing Independents. Party men, he said, were honourable, and not prone to theft or telling lies. In this, they stood in flattering contrast to their non-party opponents, in particular to those of them who were retired officials or members of the local assemblies, whom he accused of being both corrupt and stupid. He expressed the hope that at least 150 members of his own party would be returned to the House of Representatives; and his words were infused with the idea that parliamentary rule could be expected to function well only if the parties were represented in sufficient numbers.

Itagaki's criticisms and exhortations on these two occasions reached a wider audience than that for which they had been originally intended, as they were re-printed in the newspapers. Moreover, he was by no means exceptional in his efforts to win over the electors by arguing his case, and it is interesting to

2. THE LIBERAL FACTIONS

compare his remarks with two other examples of campaign oratory, also publicized in the press. The first is an address prepared by Okamoto Takeo for the voters of a constituency in Mie prefecture;[19] the second is a speech given by Matsuo Seijirō, a candidate for the Third Constituency in Tokyo.[20]

Okamoto was something of a lone bird whose aspirations for himself and his country brought him at length to a career in journalism in which he could make full use of his share of that unimpugnable good sense commonly associated with angels and writers of newspaper editorials. Before 1875, he had served the Government as a minor official; he had been a member of the Imperial Party for a short while when it was first formed in 1882; and in 1890, he was a leader-writer for the generally pro-Government *Tokyo Nichi Nichi Shimbun*. On the other hand, Okamoto had fought out of a sense of loyalty for the Shogunate in 1868, and had edited *Akebono Shimbun* (Daybreak Newspaper), a Liberal journal, for several years. Moreover, although he refused to join any other political party and apparently objected as much to the radicals' factionalism and self-interest as he did to the 'inevitable one-sidedness' of their opponents, his political opinions on the whole resembled those of the Liberals and Progressives. The development in Japan of a system of large, united and responsible parties, similar to that found in Britain or the United States, was of particular importance to him.

In these circumstances, Okamoto, a freelance and representative in many ways of what was most admirable in mid-Meiji attitudes, naturally decided to run as an Independent, when asked to be a candidate by a group of people living in the Second Constituency, Mie prefecture. Towards the end of May, he made a preliminary four-day tour of the area, in order to introduce himself and have his nomination confirmed.[21] On his return to Tokyo, he busied himself with composing a major campaign speech. Judging by the document, of which a draft version was published by his own *Tokyo Nichi Nichi Shimbun*, Okamoto's opinions were unequivocally intelligent, although they failed to get him elected and were characteristically

83

Utopian. It was in keeping, too, with what can be discerned of his career and temperament[22] that he should have concentrated on explaining the opportunities and dangers of the representative system as a whole. He spent little or no time in attacking either the Government or the popular rights parties.

The thinking of the bureaucracy was echoed in his argument that parliament's role was to assist the Cabinet, not to replace it, and to 'rectify the administration'. He did not advocate party Cabinets. Nevertheless, because the House of Representatives would be the junior partner in the administration, it was of the utmost importance to have it as strong and as upright as possible. This could come about only if the right sort of people were elected; and so everything depended on careful choice by the voters.

The rest of what Okamoto had to say was chiefly devoted to advising people on how to regard their responsibilities as voters. The model he wished them to bear in mind was England, where, he said, elections were usually fought keenly but fairly by two candidates representing the Liberal and Conservative Parties who had been chosen by the local members of the parties. He realized that it would have been virtually impossible for Japan to reach in a day the English level of internal stability and political maturity. Nevertheless this realization did not prevent him from urging that the Japanese should make every effort to ensure that their first House of Representatives would be an effective and honest one.

An ineffective or dishonest House, Okamoto argued, would prove worse in some ways than no House at all and would cause endless troubles in the future. Therefore, as this initial step under a constitutional system was all important, and as it was the electors who had to take it, and as the situation in the majority of constituencies was far from satisfactory, he felt himself justified in asking his audiences to take their responsibilities as voters very seriously indeed. To help them in their task of selecting worthy Representatives, he offered them four suggestions. These were: that they should choose competent men;

that they should not allow themselves to be swayed by bribery or intimidation in making their choice; that they should not surrender their right to vote; and that they should not give their votes to a large number of candidates and thereby make success the reward of a minority vote.

The first two of these points need no further comment for the moment. The idea behind the other two pieces of advice was that if for some reason the House did not fairly represent the majority opinion in the country, it would be without a *raison d'être* in logic and incapacitated in practice. Generally speaking, Okamoto thought that so long as the electors remembered and conformed to these four rules of conduct, constitutional government would have a fair chance of prospering from the start in Japan. One thing, he noted, the experiment of 1890 did have in its favour was that the constitution had been promulgated in times of peace and plenty. Japanese democracy, starting under the tranquil mandate of the highest in the land, would not carry with it the poison of having originated in strife or usurpation. This asset to some extent made up for the disadvantages of a tradition of 'dictatorship', and of being 'befogged on a limitless ocean' when it came to discriminating between the multitude of candidates.

A prominent feature of the election of 1890 was that usually at least four, and often as many as ten or twelve, candidates stood for each seat. Most of them had not been nominated by one of the recognized parties; neither had their candidature been solicited by local notables, in the way that Okamoto's had been. Unasked and completely of their own initiative they had presented themselves for election. In other words, they were— in the phrase of the time—'self-nominated' Independent candidates. The low calibre and questionable strategems of the great majority of these self-nominated Independents, together with the baneful influence they exercised on the election, were denounced, fully and fairly, in the following passage of Okamoto's speech:

If one goes around the provinces and sees what is happening in them at the present time, either there are people suddenly coming forward as candidates who had no status in political society hitherto, or else there are occasionally people who, belonging to old provincial families, have the singular good fortune [of being able to] rely on their friends among the electors and do not [have to] take into account their own strength even...And then, looking at the behaviour of these self-nominated candidates, when one sees that their behaviour is in most cases not straightforward and impartial, such as seeking a large measure of support by getting up on a rostrum and giving vent to their own views on politics, and that for the most part they are planning to get hold of votes in stealth and secrecy, it will be realized that they are having recourse to those measures which, in the normal course of events, should be most avoided in electing Members.[23]

The blame for this sorry state of affairs Okamoto laid in part on the leaders of the popular parties; because they had not maintained them at a high enough level of organization, and, in particular, because they had not ensured that there would be a reasonable and proper distribution of reputable candidates among the prefectures. Consequently there were cases of three or four candidates sharing the same political views but contesting the same seat, while in a neighbouring constituency there was nobody with Liberal convictions and a name for integrity in the list of competitors. He also blamed the local men of affairs in many areas for having failed to form nomination committees to pick men who would, if elected, be of service to their constituents and of credit to their country.

In order to rid the political world of the evils of self-nominated Independents and their electioneering methods, he called for the speedy formation of nomination committees of this kind in areas where they did not already exist. He wanted members of the prefectural or village assemblies or other men of local fame to serve on these committees. In addition to nominating responsible candidates, they were also to act as an electors' watch committee, examining the credentials of any others who offered themselves for election and 'driving away' all those contestants guilty of unfair practices. Only by measures such as these could a clean election be held, and a responsible and powerful House of Representatives returned.

The willingness of Okamoto, an Independent, to air these

views shows that Itagaki's censure of non-party candidates as a class could not have been applicable in each and every instance. On the other hand, both Okamoto and Itagaki had no time for the usual run of Independent candidatures. Perhaps, as Okamoto suggested, a broad distinction should be made between the numerous self-nominated Independents and the far fewer Independents who had been requested to stand by a responsible group in the constituency.

To continue comparing the opinions expressed by Okamoto with those revealed in the speeches of Itagaki, the former seems to have been rather less contemptuous of the electors. He at no time so much as hinted that he considered most of them to be fools. On the contrary, he was continually stressing the great powers for good or evil that the constitutional system had given to the electorate. Again, while Okamoto made it clear that the supreme value of an energetic, well-informed and incorruptible House of Representatives would lie in its ability to check stupid or tyrannical tendencies on the part of the bureaucracy, he did not bother to cite specific examples of Government arbitrariness or to delimit the prerogatives of the throne as Itagaki had done. His overriding concern had been to point out the dangers in having so many self-nominated candidates of little worth and no scruple, and to emphasize the importance of electing talented and honest men.

This last was an increasingly frequent theme in the candidates' speeches and newspaper editorials as the election campaign neared its end. Rather high-minded explanations of the people's rights tended to give way to outspoken diatribes on electoral corruption. Such was Matsuo Seijirō's speech. By occupation, a Tokyo lawyer and a member of the prefectural assembly, in politics Matsuo was a Liberal who had for a while dallied with the Progressives. His speech was one of several given by the local candidates at a discussion meeting in Kyōbashi ward on 26 June.

Following the same general line of argument as that used by Itagaki, Okamoto and many others, Matsuo began by drawing

87

the attention of his audience to the important role which the new Diet would play in the affairs of a constitutional country and, having made that point, went on to stress the need for clean elections. Once again, the high standard of parliamentary life in England was presented as the objective at which Japan should aim; and, like Itagaki, Matsuo was of the opinion that all candidates should be forced to make a public declaration of their principles. The main part of the speech, however, was entirely given over to bitter denunciations of the dishonest or unfair methods used by many candidates in their campaigns. The method he criticized most harshly was the shameless (and illegal) bribing of the electors—that is, the making of agreements in a society where drinking customarily precedes eating, 'after the glasses and before the plates'.

Thus, debate was not concerned with only large and abstruse topics like the position of the monarchy and the right of the parties to form the government of the Empire. The more circumscribed but nonetheless significant question of how the election should be conducted, or more properly speaking of how the election should not be conducted, was an increasingly serious issue at the time.

(3) ATTEMPTS TO AMALGAMATE THE THREE LIBERAL PARTIES AND TO ORGANIZE A COALITION BETWEEN THE LIBERALS AND THE PROGRESSIVES — THE KYUSHU CONFEDERATION OF PROGRESSIVE PARTIES AND THE 'KŌIN CLUB'

As has already been noted, when the Liberal Party, the Progressive Party and the Imperial Party were formed in the early 1880s, numerous regional associations of a political character were either already existing or came into existence. Most of these had been affiliated to one or other of the big national parties, though some of them had been independent bodies. Exactly the same sort of thing took place after revival of party activity in the years 1887 and 1888; and these local groups figure prominently in the records of the first general election.

For example, in Yokohama city, the seat was fought for by the *Kōdō Club* on the one side, and the *Kōyū-sha* in co-operation with the *Dōkō-kai* on the other.[24] The *Kōdō Club* (Justice Club) was the local landlords' stronghold and connected with the Liberals, while the *Kōyū-sha* and *Dōkō-kai* (both these names mean something like 'Friendly Society') represented mercantile interests in the city and were linked with the Progressives.

For present purposes, however, the most notable of these regional clubs were those to be found in Kyushu. There, every prefecture seems to have had at least one 'progressive' association; and as Conservatives were particularly strong in places like Kumamoto and Kagoshima, their opponents no doubt felt all the more keenly the weaknesses of their own divisions. In April 1889, representatives of the various progressive factions had met in Kagoshima and agreed to form themselves into a Kyushu Confederation of Progressive Parties. The groups that came together in this confederation retained their separate identities, but they do seem to have had a measure of success in framing an organization that would link them all together and so prevent them from cutting each other's throats.

On the other hand, although the Kyushu Confederation of Progressives contained elements that elsewhere would have enrolled under the banners of either the Liberals or the Progressives (i.e. the *Kaishin-tō*), none of its constituent parts achieved more than the most tenuous relations with the 'up-country' parties.[25] Thus, the Kyushu Confederation of Progressives was a precedent for uniting the Liberals with the *Kaishin-tō*, something which only the *Daidō Danketsu* movement had attempted before; and it was an example of the strength of separatism in the southern island's politics, something which had revealed itself most openly on the occasion of the Satsuma rebellion in 1877.

A year after its inaugural meeting, the leaders of the Kyushu Confederation of Progressives met again in Kagoshima on 17 April 1890, and resolved to do what they could to bring about a reconciliation between the Liberal factions and the *Kaishin-tō* on the national level. In effect, they were anxious to do for the country as a whole what they had done in one region of it. Not unnaturally, these developments in Kyushu had been closely watched by observers elsewhere and attracted much comment. Therefore when, in conformity to the resolution adopted at Kagoshima, four delegates of the Kyushu Confederation arrived in Tokyo at the end of May to open talks on the subject of a National Confederation of Progressive Parties, the newspapers of the metropolis were for a few days full of articles on the matter.

Meanwhile, for some time before this, attentive readers of the press of the capital had been able to follow the tortuous details of a completely separate series of negotiations. These had had for their more limited, but possibly even more essential, aim the bringing together of the three Liberal parties. In other words, in May and early June 1890, there was a definite movement afoot to unite the *Jiyū-tō*, the *Daidō Club* and the *Aikoku-kōtō*. Since their respective election manifestos had had so much in common, since there was a great deal to be gained from refraining from fighting each other at the polls, and since the potential rewards of making a united and determined stand against the Government in the House of Representatives were plain to see; a basis for rapprochement clearly existed. Indeed, the only real obstacle was the mutual jealousy and distrust displayed by the Liberal factions' leaders. The fact that union proved so difficult to achieve in practice was a fitting comment in itself on the virulence of those feelings, despite which three of the most senior people in the Liberal movement—Nakajima Nobuyuki, Takenouchi Tsuna and Katō Heishirō—busied themselves with arranging an understanding among the three parties.

Nakajima, Takenouchi and Katō first of all relied on holding private conversations with each of the three parties in turn, so that none of them should be directly aware of the others' attitudes. These discussions showed that there was a genuine interest in amalgamation on all sides. Nevertheless, there was disagreement over problems such as the date for making a firm decision on a common programme of action, and whether the proposed organization was to be a political or a non-political association.

If yet another election manifesto, this time in the names of all Liberal parties, had been issued within four weeks of the election, *Jiyū-tō*, *Daidō Club* and *Aikoku-kōtō* adherents who up till then had been fighting each other in the provinces might well have felt disheartened. On the other hand, the weakest of these three parties would benefit from incorporation in the other two, as this would ensure the election of its leaders at any rate, and would give them some followers to lead in the House of Representatives.

In the same fashion, the question of having a political or a non-political association depended for its answer on the immediate interests of each of the parties involved. A non-political body would have served to link the Liberal factions together in a very loose way, but would have been powerless to intervene in the election campaign on its own behalf. If it had done, it would have contravened the Public Meetings Regulations which made it obligatory for all organizations with any sort of interest in politics to register themselves with the police as political associations. A political association would have been able to campaign; but too great a display of vigour by an association representing all the Liberal parties in their new-found unity would have demoralized the existing party organizations in the country.

Behind haggles of this nature, lay the fact that both the *Jiyū-tō* and the *Daidō Club* were in relatively good shape to fight the election, and so were not very enthusiastic about putting themselves out of existence before knowing the results of the polls. The *Aikoku-kōtō*, on the contrary, as the latest arrival in the Liberal family, was still having its teething troubles. Therefore it was far more eager than the other two to have a quick merger.

At length, on 14 May, the three mediators changed their tactics, and brought delegates from the three parties face to face for the first time at a meeting held in the *Yanagi-ya* (Willow Inn), near Gofuku-bashi. As a result of this conference, the following agreement was reached:

1. The existing three party organizations shall be abolished, and a new, comprehensive political party shall be formed.

2. The party to be established as a result of this merger shall be called the *Kōin Club* [1890 Club]. It shall be an association of equals and shall have no leader.

3. The *Kōin Club* declares its support for the principles of Liberalism.

4. The *Kōin Club* shall appoint nine officers to manage its affairs. They shall be elected in equal numbers from each of the three former parties.

5. The *Kōin Club* shall be convened again not later than next August to determine its policies, and to carry out the official inauguration of the party. The need to preserve the spirit of the principles that have animated each of the existing parties is hereby affirmed.[26]

The general effect of the above was to usher in the union, not federation, of the three Liberal parties in principle, but to delay the practical consequences of this decision until August, that is until after the election. It was rather like a three-party marriage by proxy, with at least two of the prospective partners wanting to have a final night out before settling down to consummate the affair.

In this sort of strained situation, it was hardly surprising that they should have very soon begun to bicker among themselves. By the end of May, a major quarrel had broken out between the *Daidō Club* and the *Aikoku-kōtō* over the question of whether the *Kōin Club* was to be treated as the opening phase of full amalgamation or simply as the first step towards a federation of the three parties. The *Daidō Club* leaders in Tokyo had written to their supporters in the provinces to tell them officially of the formation of the *Kōin Club*, and to make a point of announcing that their party would continue to contest the election as a separate entity on the strength of the manifesto it had already issued. In addition, this letter went so far as to say that there would possibly still be a need for the *Daidō Club* even after the full inauguration of the *Kōin Club* in August.

3. KYUSHU CONFEDERATION AND 'KŌIN CLUB'

News of the attitude adopted by the *Daidō Club* leaders when corresponding with their followers in the country provoked an angry riposte on the part of the *Aikoku-kōtō*. Two of the leaders of the latter party, Kobayashi Kusuo and Kurihara Ryōichi, sent a written protest to Nakajima Nobuyuki and his colleagues.[27] In this protest, the *Aikoku-kōtō* complained that the *Daidō Club* letter to its supporters had contradicted the spirit of the agreement entered into at the *Yanagi-ya* by placing too much emphasis on independent competition at the elections. The *Aikoku-kōtō* spokesmen insisted that the *Kōin Club* had been founded to replace the existing parties, not just to associate them in a loose federation.

This dispute quickly developed from a fairly private exchange of letters into a newspaper war; and it seemed for a while as if the whole hard-won achievement of the *Kōin Club* was nearing collapse. In the words of one Osaka man of affairs, whose opinion had been canvassed by the *Tokyo Nichi Nichi Shimbun* and who was personally in favour of federation rather than amalgamation: 'Cats are cats, and dogs are dogs—and, when all is said and done, you cannot keep them in the same cage.'[28] Nevertheless, despite these unhappy beginnings, the *Kōin Club* did survive to play a brief but important part in the reunion of the Liberals after the election. Thus, it was in due course to fulfil the hopes of its original sponsors.

Even before the election, the *Kōin Club* was asserting its right to an independent existence in a number of ways. On 17 June, its founders, taking their stand on the phrase 'new, comprehensive political party' in the first article of the club's constitution, formally notified the police in Kyōbashi ward of their desire to be registered as a political association. Registration with the police, as has been explained, was the *sine qua non* for participation in the election campaign. The police, after the secretary had sent them a reminder, officially authorized the *Kōin Club* on 21 June. This allowed the secretary to start distributing its first and second reports to country members.[29]

The *Kōin Club's* membership in its application for registration

93

was given as forty-one.[30] On 25 June, however, the *Tokyo Nichi Nichi Shimbun* told its readers that 'applications to join the club have shown no signs of falling off of late'. Therefore the figure of forty-one must have meant only those who had been formally enrolled by 17 June and it would appear that recruiting of one sort or another had been going on for some time in anticipation of the official authorization. In Chiba prefecture, there had been more than three thousand applications for membership by 25 June;[31] and in other regions, things were sufficiently far advanced for the *Kōin Club* to be able to put forward its own candidates in the election. This was particularly true of Aichi prefecture, where the *Aichi Kōin Club* was very well organized and took the lead in representing the Liberal interest in every constituency.[32]

It is clear that the *Kōin Club* lost little time in trying to get itself accepted as a new and growing political group, with a mind and an organization of its own. In addition, it was able to shout its name from the hustings in some districts at any rate. Furthermore, within three weeks of its formation on 14 May, the club had won a rather sudden distinction in a field other than electioneering. This was because the delegates of the Kyushu Confederation of Progressive Parties approached the *Kōin Club* directly, without bothering to have separate consultations with the *Jiyū-tō*, *Daidō Club* and *Aikoku-kōtō*, when they appeared in the capital around the beginning of June with their scheme for a pre-election understanding between the Liberals as a united group and the *Kaishin-tō*.

The Kyushu delegates planned to hold talks with the leaders of both sides and soon got down to business.[33] The opening moves in this latest round of inter-party diplomacy had already been played by 4 June, on which date fourteen senior members of the *Kōin Club* entertained the visitors from Kyushu (whose numbers had risen from four to six) to a banquet.[34] This banquet took place in the *Jubi-ya* (Tea-House of Long Life and Beauty), in the Tsukiji district of Tokyo, and lasted from midday. While it was in progress, the *Kōin Club* hosts told their

94

guests that they personally all approved of federation with the *Kaishin-tō*, but would need to have this preliminary decision confirmed by the general body of members at the first full convention of the *Kōin Club* in August.

During the afternoon of the next day, the standing committee of the *Kaishin-tō* met privately, and unanimously adopted the following resolution:

Item. We shall meet the members of the committee from Kyushu to-day, the 5th, at 6.0 p.m. in the *Sanen-tei*, in Shiba park; and shall make the following reply, which has been agreed on by all the members of the standing committee of the *Kaishin-tō*. (However in the last ten days of July, we shall hold an extraordinary general meeting, and will ask the party members from the entire country to endorse this.)

Item. Since we have already approved of federation, we cannot leave this work to the gentlemen from Kyushu and just be lookers-on. In order that this intention should be fully seen in practice, we must first of all call on the members of the *Kōin Club* and make various arrangements with them.[35]

In conformity to the above resolution, three representatives of the standing committee of the *Kaishin-tō*—Katō Masanosuke, Shimada Saburō and Ozaki Yukio—went immediately after the end of the meeting to call on the various Liberal leaders. These, in turn, expressed their satisfaction with the way things were developing.

In this way, with or without the aid of wine and geisha, the attempts made by the Kyushu politicians to bring about a coalition of Liberals and Progressives at the national level had met with a success that was as quick as it was unexpected. As with the union of the Liberal factions, however, while the decision in principle to form some sort of institutional alliance had been taken by the parties concerned at the beginning of June, the practical working out of this decision was postponed by mutual consent until after the election.

The, in this respect, neutral *Tokyo Nichi Nichi Shimbun* was quick to point out the lack of logic in this attitude, which it likened to two enemies agreeing to have one more fight to the death before they became friends.[36] The same paper reminded its readers that it was highly unlikely that an enduring compact could be made between the Liberals and the Progressives so long as the treaty revision problem remained unsolved, as only a few months had passed since the two groups were at loggerheads on this issue. This raised the question of whether a party politician as Minister for Foreign Affairs could be trusted to look after the Empire's interests as competently as the bureaucrats had done. There were hints, too, in this editorial that: 'The essential element uniting the parties must have been congeniality of temperament rather than identity of principle.' However, this was a rather unfair insinuation, as the political platforms of the Liberals and the Progressives obviously had much in common. Though the leader-writer in this particular issue of the *Tokyo Nichi Nichi Shimbun* was insistent in his professions of sympathy for the trend towards federation in the popular parties, he concluded somewhat waspishly: 'We simply think that a free wedding is very wonderful, but fear that we shall soon have news of a divorce.' The same day, a member of the *Aikoku-kōtō* was reported to have expressed himself in very much the same vein.[37]

Not all the newspapers and publicists took this gloomy view of the prospects of the half-negotiated federation of the Liberal and Progressive parties. Admittedly, the leading *Kaishin-tō* newspaper, the *Yūbin-Hōchi Shimbun*, advised the party leaders in Tokyo to give very careful consideration to the Kyushu proposals, but it was quite ready to concede the necessity for a link of some sort between the major anti-Government parties.[38] The *Sanyō Shimbun* in Okayama prefecture was far more welcoming than this, and congratulated both the *Kōin Club* and the *Kaishin-tō* on having taken the first step towards federation, which it thought would be of benefit not only to the popular parties but also the Empire as a whole.[39] It was left to the *Tōhoku Mainichi* (Miyagi prefecture), however, to give unstinting praise to what had been accomplished so far, and at the same time to argue with the greatest enthusiasm the case for federation. It did so in an editorial entitled 'Why Ever Don't the Gentlemen of Tōhoku Bestir Themselves and Organize a Confederation of Progressive Parties?', the closing paragraph of which was:

We are not alone in advocating the need for a confederation of progressive parties. Most of the gentlemen of the Empire have acknowledged this need. That we have gone on even to the present day without a confederation was, as we have explained, simply due to emotion, to suspicion and to thinking about what is past and done with. At this juncture, it was the *Kyushu Kaishin-tō* which, not ready to be controlled by its emotions, not caring to be misled by its suspicions, and not prepared to cling to thoughts of the past, magnanimously broke with the fashion, and by forming a great confederation of progressive parties pitted itself against the various conservative parties of the Government. In view of this, a few of our colleagues could not help but urge the same thing on our *Tōhoku Kaishin-tō*. This was the general situation in the Empire as a whole. Now the *Kyushu Kaishin-tō* has sent delegates all the way to Tokyo in order to bring together all the Progressive parties. Therefore our *Tōhoku Kaishin-tō* must also get a move on and, by joining forces with the *Kyushu Kaishin-tō*, work for a grand national confederation of progressive parties. Now is the time! Why ever don't the gentlemen of Tōhoku bestir themselves and organize a confederation of progressive parties?[40]

The general position of the Liberals at the time of the 1890 election was clearly weakened by bad organization in the field, and a divided leadership at headquarters. As has been said, some constituencies did not have any Liberal candidates; others had too many. In addition to this, the appearance of no fewer than three different Liberal factions in the six months before polling day was little short of an insult to the gods of politics-with-elections.

Yet, despite these handicaps and omissions the Liberal groups between them had many more candidates in the field than any other political party, and they also had the advantage of wide-spread popularity among the electors. This popularity was some-thing on which the Liberals could rely from the start of the campaign to the time it was completed. To a large extent, the general climate of opinion, with its belief in progress and a considerable amount of Westernization, still favoured them;

even more beneficial was the success they had had in establishing themselves in the countryside. Nor should the wide appeal and intrinsic excellence of the Liberal manifestos be forgotten. The Whig philosophy with which they buttressed their attacks on the Government was in many ways as apposite for the times as it was formative for the future. Thus, the reduction of the land-tax or the shortening of the conscription period were matters of immediate interest to the nation at large; while the introduction of party Cabinets was the necessary next step for its political élite. Moreover, there were in the ranks of the Liberal leaders not a few men of high calibre.

Finally, it has been seen how the Liberals were not altogether incapable of taking steps to remedy their own failings. A union of the three factions had been half accomplished, and coalition with the Progressives was in the offing.

(4) THE PROGRESSIVE PARTY ('KAISHIN-TŌ')

The Progressive Party was never completely at odds with itself. Not even the shock of the resignations of its president and vice-president in 1884 had brought about its dissolution; and the party of the Centre was in 1890 far more united than either its Conservative foes to the Right or its Liberal rivals to the Left.

Very probably, the nature of the elements forming the party's nucleus had kept it united. Though its organization had penetrated the countryside, the Progressive Party, compared with the Liberals, had little influence with, and was little influenced by, the rural capitalists. It had even less in common with the forces of ultra-nationalism. The middle classes of the cities on which the Progressives mainly relied were not prone to provincialism and obscurantism. Consequently the party was relatively free from the regionalist pressures which often split both the Liberal and the Conservative groups, and also from the heady chauvinism that made some Liberals indistinguishable from Ultra-Conservatives.

In the structure of its leadership, too—a leadership consisting in the main of 'radical' bureaucrats, university-trained intelligentsia and *arriviste* businessmen—the Progressive Party was in the forefront of the modernization taking place in Japan. An élite drawn from these groups apparently found it fairly easy to act in harmony with one another. Possibly this was because the persons of whom it was composed had in common a general spirit of careful but ungrudging optimism. Tomorrow was to be well built for tomorrow's sake, not for yesterday's, and although their modernism was outwardly rather less effusive than that of the Liberals, it may well have been inwardly more thoroughgoing. Moreover, while no one could accuse the Progressives of faceless leadership, strength of character in their case did not denote an impulse to destroy rather than reform anything found objectionable, an impulse that drove extremists to fight each other as well as the Government.

Thus, the Progressive Party had a dominant bourgeois element in its following, and was controlled by men whose education or business interests had given them a good knowledge of the outside world as well as a strong belief in the essential rightness of the bureaucrats' modernization policies for their country and its economy. By virtue of both its general membership and its leadership, this party was still in 1890 the most rational in outlook and so most 'modern' in behaviour. It revealed few, if any, of the unfavourable signs of the breakdown of the feudal order—regionalism, excessive factionalism, two-sworded turbulence and recurrent attacks of xenophobia or other forms of extremism.

This is not to say that the Progressive Party did not have its handicaps. The greatest of these was the concentration of voters in the rural areas where, as has been said, the power of the party tended on the whole to be slighter than that of its adversaries. True, this disadvantage was to some extent offset by the right of any city with a population upwards of 100,000 to elect its own Member. But, in the Japan of 1890, only three provincial cities (Yokohama, Kōbe and Nagoya) other than Kyoto and Osaka did have populations of more than 100,000. All other centres of any size, such as Sendai, Niigata and Hiroshima, were linked with part of the surrounding countryside to form a joint ruro-urban constituency. This circumstance of demography gave rise to another difficulty under which the *Kaishin-tō* laboured. Its membership was probably smaller than that of the Liberal factions as a whole, even though the party outnumbered them separately, and in regions where it functioned was usually more than a match for Conservative opponents. Finally though Itagaki was able to tour the country on behalf of his following, the national leader of the Progressives, Ōkuma Shigenobu, had just left hospital after losing a leg in the bomb attack of the previous October, and was still too weak to take an active part in the election campaign. Whether the *Kaishin-tō* actually lost seats in the election because of Ōkuma's absence is a moot point, but both the party and the public must have missed some election panache through not being able to hear his oratory as well as Itagaki's.

Progressive Party candidates were generally men of distinction. Something of this can be inferred from the careers of two of the most influential men in Japanese politics. Both of them were prominent members of the party's standing committee at the time of the election; and their names have already been mentioned in connexion with formal approaches to the Liberals on the subject of federation.

Shimada Saburō was elected for Yokohama city in 1890. After studying English and working for some enterprising merchants in his youth, he made a name for himself as editor of the *Yokohama Mainichi* in the early 1870s when the paper had just been founded. As a result of his articles on politics and social reform the *Yokohama Mainichi* turned out to be an influential organ of moderate-progressive opinion. In 1875, the Government solicited his services and he was appointed Grand Chancellor of the Senate (*Genrō-in*). Later, he became Chief Secretary of the Ministry of Education, but resigned when Ōkuma fell from power in 1881.

For the next eight years Shimada worked diligently as one of the founders and policy-makers of the Progressive Party as well as publishing a number of books and taking part in the local government of Kanagawa prefecture. He was elected to the prefectural assembly, and before long was chairman of it. In 1889, he travelled widely in both Europe and North America, in order to study the political systems and actual conditions of various countries. After entering the House of Representatives in 1890, he continued to be a Member of it until his death in 1923, holding in due course the posts of deputy Speaker and Speaker of the House. He was also a minister in several party Cabinets. Keenly interested throughout his long (seventy-two years) life in social welfare and the progress of constitutional government in Japan, Shimada wrote many books and articles on these and related topics.

Shimada's career in many respects resembled that of his colleague—Ozaki Yukio.[41] Ozaki, too, had spent the earlier part of his working life as an official and had resigned in 1881 in sympathy with Ōkuma. Before going into the Treasury Department he had worked for a short while for the *Yūbin-Hōchi Shimbun*. To that paper he now returned, but soon moved to the *Chōya Shimbun*. His skill in journalism and the close relations he always enjoyed with Ōkuma naturally made him a person of importance in the Progressive Party. In 1889, he visited Europe for the first time.

Ozaki was returned for the Fifth Constituency, Mie prefecture, in the election of 1890, and thereafter sat without a break in the House of Representatives for more than fifty-five years, that is until he died a few years after the end of the Pacific War. He was as active as he was long-lived. Like Shimada, a minister of State on several occasions; the position of mayor of Tokyo was also his for three separate terms. Ozaki's chief claim to fame, however, lay in the vigour of his speeches in the Diet. These speeches advocated a Liberal interpretation of the constitution, so took the form of trenchant attacks on the transcendentalist theories of the bureaucracy. The most famous of them was to no inconsiderable extent responsible for forcing the resignation of Prince Katsura in 1913—an event that marked the beginning of the end for the *Sat-Chō* monopoly of executive power. In his old age, Ozaki continued to defend the canons of parliamentary democracy—this time, against the militarists.

With men like Shimada and Ozaki in the field, then, and they were by no means the only outstanding candidates in Progressive colours, the *Kaishin-tō* was clearly a formidably party at the time of the 1890 election. This wealth of co-operative talent must have been of great help in winning a respectable total of forty seats in the House of Representatives, but it remains likely that its chief recommendation was the more concrete merit of its policy proposals.

On what principles and objectives did the Progressives take their stand in appealing to the electors, and in what respects did their outlook differ from that of the Liberals? Generally speaking, the Progressives had from the first stood for the same things as the Liberals did; and the differences between the two parties at the time when they were originally formed in the years 1881–2 had been narrowed by the growth of conservative feeling among the Liberals since then. The two parties had also learnt during the intervening years how much they could lose by attacking each other and not the Government. Therefore when drawing attention to what did distinguish the Progressives from the Liberals in 1890, it has to be remembered that these differences of opinion or emphasis were really no more than small rocks of discord in a placid ocean of agreement.

Even in 1890, the Progressives were still more conciliatory abroad and a little more moderate at home than the Liberals. They seldom, if ever, went to prison for carrying their opposition to the Government too far. In the previous year, the majority of them had come round to supporting Ōkuma's proposals for a gradual abolition of extra-territorial rights. The Liberals, on the other hand, had joined conservative factions in a full-scale campaign for suspension of the treaty negotiations. In domestic matters, the Progressive Party fought the election on the basis of its original manifesto. In some ways, this would appear to have been a mistake, as the 1882 manifesto was already somewhat out of date by 1890 and was by no means a comprehensive statement of the party's beliefs and policies. But it is very probable that the electors knew this for themselves, and did not expect any formal revision of the 1882 manifesto so long as Ōkuma was out of action.

Comparing this 1882 Progressive statement with the three Liberal manifestos of 1890, there were two major differences, not so much of principle as of emphasis, and one serious cleavage of interest. The Progressives had neglected to give formal, black and white, adherence to two items writ large in Liberal pronouncements—institution of party Cabinets, and reduction of land-tax. Moreover, the Liberal censure of Government aid to private industry threatened the economic interests of the most important group of Progressive supporters.

The absence of a specific reference to party Cabinets in the *Kaishin-tō* manifesto was, by 1890, a notable instance of the general failure to make the official charter of the party correspond as meticulously as possible to the views it had come to hold. It should not be regarded as an indication that the Progressives were lukewarm in this respect. As much as the Liberals, the Progressives had always regarded the constitution as the bulwark of popular rights and happiness, and parliament as the means by which government was to be made conformable to public opinion. Indeed, it had been the bald demand for party rule which had made Ōkuma's 1881 memorial so repugnant to his colleagues in the Government. The most that the Progressives were prepared to concede was that there should possibly be a short transition period after 1890, during which the *Sat-Chō* bureaucrats would govern in coalition with one or other of the popular parties; and after the opening of the Diet, they joined with the Liberals in putting pressure on the Government to accept the doctrine of ministerial responsibility to parliament. Before this, the Progressive attitude of looking forward to the inauguration of party Cabinets among other things had been expressed during the election campaign in words such as these taken from an electioneering song, a fuller version of which will be given later:

Time flies like an arrow—
The First of July is at hand!
Soon our hearts' desires will be realised.

Similarly, the omission of any formal proposal to cut the land-tax in the *Kaishin-tō* manifesto to some extent belied its real intentions in 1890. By 1884, an argument had developed within the party on the feasibility of reducing the land-tax; and it was on this issue that Ōkuma and Kōno Binken had chosen to resign. Both of them had been of the opinion that the existing rate of taxation had to be maintained to keep the Empire solvent. Their departure, in effect, endorsed the views of those in the higher ranks of the party hierarchy who considered that the Government could afford to lighten the fiscal burdens it had imposed on peasants and landowners.

To some extent, of course, the whole issue of a reduction in the land-tax was more academic for the Progressives than it was for the Liberals as most of their supporters lived in the towns. Nevertheless it would have been clear to the electors of 1890 that the *Kaishin-tō* was scarcely less eager than the Liberal parties to do what it could to curtail the cost of administration in general, and achieve some alleviation of the land-tax in particular. So much could have been readily deduced from newspaper articles, political speeches, and what was known of the opinions of leading members of the party. A markedly pacific attitude on foreign relations could have been cited as additional evidence if that were needed.

Since the ideas of the Liberals and the Progressives on the role of parliament under the constitution and a reduction of taxation were identical or very similar, the only real bone of contention between them was Government subsidies to private industry. This was a relatively minor issue, however, and by no means incapable of amicable settlement.

In other points, the *Kaishin-tō* manifesto agreed well enough with those put out by the Liberals. The Progressives, too, did not want government to become completely centralized; and though they were seven years too early to make any concrete proposals for amending the Law of Election, the hope that the franchise would be gradually widened in keeping with the general progress of the people was a statement in principle of what the Liberals later asked for in practice. Finally, the *Kaishin-tō* statement did not cover such matters, but there was absolutely nothing to distinguish the attitude of the Progressives from that of the Liberals on basic popular rights—freedom of speech, assembly, and so on.

Therefore, even though the two parties represented rather different social groups and were still in a sense the separately organized following of two rival statesmen, at the time of the election the general outlook and objectives of the Progressives were very much the same as those of the Liberals. This judgement may be readily confirmed by reading the editorials published by the *Yūbin-Hōchi Shimbun* of Tokyo in the months preceding the election. This was the most influential Progressive Party newspaper; and in its political comments during this period, it usually took a line identical with that adopted by the Liberals. The following extracts from these editorials will illustrate this point, and they may be taken as good evidence of run-of-the-mill Progressive policies:

ILL-GOTTEN GAINS (2-4-90)

It is generally held that evil cannot overcome good. Nevertheless when political consciousness is still in its infancy and has not had time to develop to the full, and one is dealing with a people that is all too quick to cultivate bad habits, there may be a temporary reversal of the usual state of affairs. Upright methods will be hard pressed by dishonest stratagems, good will be overcome by evil. Of course, it is not to be supposed that the issue will be thus decided for once and for all but, regardless of whether it is for a long time or a short time, such things as the triumph of trickery over fair play should never be tolerated here in this country of righteousness.

THE PERIOD OF NON-PARTY GOVERNMENT (8-4-90)

What sort of policies will non-party Governments adopt towards the Diet?... [Government] strategists [if they try to imitate Bismarck] will be able to make a Buddha statue, but will not be able to breathe any life into it... Though we shall never believe that the schemes of these strategists will all turn out well, looking at the matter from the point of view of a Ministry that wishes to stand aloof from political parties, the best plan would surely be for such a Ministry to form an alliance with a powerful party in the Diet, and to make use of it. However the business of making a full alliance with the chosen party and winning its confidence is not just a matter of adopting the party's view. Its leaders must be prevailed upon to enter the Government; and something like a coalition Cabinet should be formed...If it should eventually fall foul of the majority in the Diet, it will simply have to resign. This will be one step towards party Cabinets.

THE CONSTITUTIONAL PROGRESSIVE PARTY (14-4-90)

Although the fortunes of the Progressive Party have inevitably been subject to fluctuations from time to time, looking back over the past ten years, one really cannot but be impressed by the overall progress made, and the degree of stability achieved. Certainly of all the political parties in our country, the Progressive Party is the most orderly and the most developed. Indeed, it is doubtful if there are any others to compare with it in these respects.

DON'T DISCOURAGE THE INDUSTRIALISTS FROM THINKING ABOUT POLITICS! (15-4-90)

There is no necessity for industrialists to mix with politicians and openly engage in political activities of their own accord. Nevertheless it is very important that they should know about politics and take an interest in them. The attitude of taking no interest in politics, on the grounds that since they are industrialists they need not concern themselves with political affairs, is an evil relic of feudal times. In those days, politics were the preserve of the samurai class and their superiors alone. The industrialists, being unable to have any say in them, were completely excluded from politics. The industrialists themselves were obliged willy-nilly to put up with this; and, losing any desire to hear about [politics] as time sanctioned the convention, they virtually gave up thinking about them. So it is hardly surprising that they should have been indifferent to politics in bygone times. But the feudal system has been abolished, and the four classes have been made equal. Moreover a Liberal system of government is gradually being put into operation, and now that we are about to be given the right to participate in the government, it is essential that industrialists should be thoroughly conversant with politics.

NOT BIASED, NON-PARTY (16-4-90)

Most of those who call themselves 'not biased and non-party' stink; and it is no accident either...If they are not completely without principles, even though they do not claim to be [members of] a political party, they will inevitably be partial to one side or another. If they are

4. THE PROGRESSIVE PARTY

not partial to one side or another, then they must be men without fixed principles. People without principles drift around like seaweed in the waves; preaching progress to-day, and favouring conservatism to-morrow. They are never constant. Is not this what is meant by 'not biased and non-party'? Well, what virtue is there in being not biased and non-party?

HESITANT REFORM AN EVIL (20-4-90)

Following the Government's decision to reform the Civil Service and get rid of superfluous officials, the bureaucracy has been in a state of jitters...From what we have seen of Government offices during the last fortnight, none of them appears to be over-worked; rather, it would seem that a certain amount of leisure has had to be sacrificed. With regard to this, all but two of the ministers of State went off to see the military and naval manoeuvres, and then stayed on to make tours of the Kyoto and Osaka regions and so forth. Therefore it is natural that there should not be any great pressure of business. All the same, the days of leisure [the bureaucrats] are enjoying now are not the same as the usual period of mid-summer relaxation from strenuous toil. Their bodies rest; but they are not easy in their minds, and are afflicted by all kinds of doubts. From the point of view of the Government, this can hardly be termed a happy state of affairs; and it is positively disagreeable for the individual officials concerned. It is clearly a matter of immediate urgency that the Government should take at once suitable steps to deal with this situation.

In order to cut down administrative expenses, and simplify the management of [government] business, unwanted officials must be dismissed.

THE PEOPLE'S STRENGTH (6-5-90)

Under an absolutist political system, decisions are made in an arbitrary fashion, and once the Government has made up its mind to do something, it can do it as and when it pleases, without having to pay any attention to public opinion. Even serious issues do not require a great deal of delicate handling and are easily settled. Under a representative system, on the other hand, the people must be consulted, and it is not possible to act without the consent of the majority of them. Consequently a considerable amount of time and trouble has to be spent on getting them to agree to anything. Politicians who have grown used to absolutism may well find these exertions beyond them, and no doubt will be full of complaints about the representative system. Nevertheless the people are on the move, and their advance cannot possibly be checked. The tyranny of a minority will have to defer to opinion of the majority. This is the inescapable outcome of the development of the strength of the people.

II. PARTIES, PRINCIPLES AND ISSUES

DANGER OF POLITICAL WORLD BECOMING ABYSMALLY DEGRADED (10-5-90)

The world of politics is always apt to be ruled by unsavoury characters; and it is frequently in danger of falling into a bottomless pit of degradation. True patriots ought to be ever conscious of the need to avoid this danger...It is natural for politicians to fight each other for the reins of power, and we have no intention of denying them this [right]. However they should be expected to conform to certain standards of conduct in their disputes.

THE ENEMIES OF LIBERTY (16-5-90)

Tyranny is the enemy of Liberty. Tyrannical actions, no matter whether they stem from governments or peoples, are all alike in being opposed to Liberty...Liberal politics are the politics of discussion. The misuse of force is nothing other than the politics of tyranny. Those who wish to violate in any way the freedoms of speech and action, no matter whether they belong to the Government or the people, must all be considered equally opposed to Liberty. The freedoms of speech and assembly, not to mention the right to life, will be secured under a Liberal system. Those who by any means whatsoever violate them in any way are all enemies of Liberty.

(Part of a speech given on 26-6-90 to the residents of the Nihonbashi ward of Tokyo by Fujita Mokichi, a local *Kaishin-tō* candidate. The *Yūbin-Hōchi Shimbun* gave a summarized version of this speech as its editorials for the three days 28–30/6/90.)

If I were to play the complete politician and tell you that the taxes levied on the country should be reduced by one half, that we will cleverly adopt policies that would enable us to meet the costs of government on only one half of the present amount brought in by taxation, my words would be highly gratifying and would no doubt gladden the hearts of the more ignorant tax-payers. Yet it is plainly impossible to do any such thing. To prate about cutting administrative expediture and reforming the methods of the bureaucracy, when one is in the position of an outsider who knows nothing about the true facts of the political situation, is just irresponsible talk.

It will be seen, then, that the Progressive Party, while remaining true to its motto of 'slow but steady', was nevertheless an organization which in 1890 could be fairly described as 'progressive' and 'popular'.

(5) SOME CONSERVATIVE PARTIES—THE 'JICHI-TŌ',
THE 'KOKUMIN-HA', AND THE 'HOSHU CHŪSEI HA'

In its editorial for 7 June 1890, the *Tokyo Nichi Nichi Shimbun* remarked that the Conservatives were as divided as the Liberals. It would have been nearer the truth if it had said that the Conservatives were even more divided than the Liberals. Not only did they resemble their opponents on the furthest Left in having a large number of splinter factions and regional associations; they made no attempt to join forces before the election. There was never any Conservative equivalent of the *Kōin Club*. The Conservative factions were closer than any other group to the feudal tradition. To an even greater extent than the Liberals, therefore, they were animated by feelings of attachment to a particular district and a particular leader. This was one of the reasons why they failed to unite. Another reason was a deep and abiding difference of outlook. There was a moderate, Westernizing, constitution-minded conservativism of the bureaucrats in power, and there was an extremist, ultra-nationalist, quasi-absolutist conservativism of a few public figures out of power.

Some of the numerous provincial Conservative parties were well established in their own districts and did well in the election—notably the National Rights Party (*Kokken-tō*) in Kumamoto prefecture, and the Miyagi Political Association (*Miyagi Seikai*) in the area round Sendai. However the influence of these groups did not extend beyond the boundaries of their respective prefectures, and the overall national strength of the Ultra-Conservatives in particular was not very great. Moreover, these regional clubs were not destined to last or develop. Consequently, unlike the *Jiyū-tō* and *Kaishin-tō*, they cannot be regarded as direct ancestors of modern political parties though, depending on their position in the conservative camp, they did keep alive a tradition of Right-wing extremism or else rallied support to the moderate conservativism of the bureaucrats.

On the national level, the Conservatives fared even worse. In fact, the only Ultra-Conservative organization with any claim to be a national rather than a provincial political party, the *Hoshu Chūsei Ha*, was just about the weakest electorally. On the other hand, the sponsor of the *Hoshu Chūsei Ha* was one of the ablest exponents of the Ultra-Conservative point of view during the Meiji period.

In these circumstances, all the main strands of Conservative thinking and practice, as revealed by the election and the characters and opinions of the principal Conservative leaders taking part in it, may be found in three of the Right-wing parties: Inoue Kaoru's *Jichi Kenkyū Kai* (Society For The Study Of Self-Government); General Tani Kanjō's *Kokumin-ha* (National Party); and General Torio Koyata's *Hoshu Chūsei Ha* (Moderate Conservative Party).

(a) Moderate Conservatism—Inoue Kaoru's 'Jichi-tō'

Inoue Kaoru was a Chōshū man, a close friend of Itō Hirobumi, and a permanent office-holder in the Meiji administration from the time of the Restoration in 1868 to the time of his formal retirement in 1898. Thereafter he continued to wield considerable influence behind the scenes as an aged and respected *genrō* (elder statesman) until his death in 1915. He founded the Society For The Study Of Self-Government in 1888, intending it to be a comprehensive political body like the *Daidō Danketsu*. Unlike the latter, however, it was to be normally pro-Government. The society had no fixed programme, and never developed one. Thus, it entered on the election without a manifesto of any sort. Originally, it had concentrated on studying different systems of self-government, with the help of foreigners who were employed in Tokyo either as official advisers to the Government or as lecturers at the Imperial University. The total membership of the Society For The Study Of Self-Government was never anything more than minute, though there were no formal restrictions on entry. It consisted of a number of Inoue's colleagues in the ranks of ministers and deputy ministers of State, together with a sprinkling of leading men of affairs outside the

Government. One of these last was Shibuzawa Eiichi, a prominent banker.

In a situation like this, it is not surprising that the *Jichi Kenkyū Kai* was regarded, by the enlightened as well as by the ignorant, as 'Inoue's party'.[42] The capital and the nation as a whole would have none of it. In a sense, this was a revived but even weaker Imperial Party. There was a desire to govern in accordance with the constitution to be sure, but in accordance with the most orthodox of bureaucratic interpretations of the constitution. Having barely survived the difficulties of its birth, the society soon broke up. Its speedy disappearance demonstrated once again that there was no room for a party that was both conservative and truly constitutional to the Right of the Progressive Party so long as most Government leaders did not intend to collaborate openly and permanently with a substantial bloc of Representatives.

Despite the virtual failure of his schemes so far as Tokyo and the greater part of the country were concerned, Inoue's efforts led to the victory of several so-called Self-Government Party (*Jichi-tō*) candidates in the election. In some areas where they were particularly successful, such as Kyoto *fu*, these *Jichi-tō* candidates do not seem to have had very close links with Inoue, and the Kyoto *Kōmin-kai* (Citizens Association) which won five seats was probably a fairly autonomous organization in its own right. On the other hand, in his home province of Chōshū (Yamaguchi prefecture), Inoue, acting in conjunction with Itō, had a large personal following. This Inoue–Itō faction was opposed by a group owing allegiance to Yamagata Aritomo, and also by an Ultra-Conservative faction headed by Torio Koyata and Viscount Miura.[43]

The *Jichi Kenkyū Kai* or *Jichi-tō*, therefore, would appear to have had three rather different existences at three separate levels: national; provincial outside Chōshū; and inside Chōshū. In Tokyo, it had been an abortive attempt to re-found a national Government party along the lines of the defunct Imperial Party; in districts like Kyoto or Wakayama prefectures, it reappeared at the time of the election as a convenient vehicle for moderate conservative opinion; in Yamaguchi, it was a well-established local party comprising the closest adherents of Inoue and Itō in the central bureaucracy as well as in the prefecture.

Although the Yamaguchi Ultra-Conservatives under Torio and Miura had made apparently fruitless approaches to the Yamagata party with the idea of forming an electoral alliance, they were bitterly opposed to the Inoue–Itō party. Thus, in Chōshū at any rate, there was no prospect of an understanding between the Ultra-Conservatives and the moderate Conservatives. This lack of sympathy is important because it delineates the frontier between conservativism and reaction. Bureaucrats like Inoue and Itō were conservative in the strict sense of the word. That is, they wished to conserve the bureaucratic connotations of the system of government first set out in the constitution. They favoured non-party Cabinets, formally subject to the Emperor alone, and regarded the people or their Representatives as privileged participants in the rites of Imperial administration. Yet, with them, there was no question of revoking the constitution once it had been granted, or of seeking to undermine in practice the popular rights on which it stood. Parliament had come to stay; so, too, had the first stages in the modernization of Japan.

(b) Ultra-Conservativism—Tani Kanjō's 'Kokumin-ha', and Torio Koyata's 'Hoshu Chūsei Ha'

The political world of Generals Tani and Torio was vastly different from this, though they usually took care to hide the discrepancies under a mask of less strident conservativism. Their real aim was total reaction. They wished to turn back from the whole constitutional and parliamentary experiment to the older collective and hierarchical order. In short, they wished to negate the ideal of Liberty—to stamp out its supposedly noxious effects in Japan, and to look forward to the destruction of its original homelands in Europe and the Americas.

Tani Kanjō was born in Tosa in 1837, the son of a samurai

of that fief. His formal education began at the age of nine, when he started going to relatives and fellow clansmen for instruction. A great deal of this childhood training seems to have been spent on acquiring proficiency in the military arts—fencing, archery and, later on, gunnery. In 1856 the Tosa fief sent him to Edo to complete his education; and it was there that he embarked on an exhaustive study of the Chinese classics, concerning which he was to become a recognized authority. The next few years saw him travelling constantly between Tosa, Edo and Osaka, becoming all the while more deeply involved in the Imperialist movement.

In 1865, Tani was recalled to Kōchi and made an assistant instructor at the fief school. Before long fief business took him to Nagasaki and this gave him an opportunity to visit Shanghai. His return to Nagasaki was followed by association with Saka-moto Ryūma and Gotō Shōjirō, two Tosa samurai who were already leaders in the Restoration plot. In 1867, he visited Osaka to have talks on behalf of his clan with Imperialist samurai from Satsuma; and later in the same year, Tani accompanied the former Daimyō of Tosa, Yamanouchi Yōdō, when he journeyed to Kyoto to take part in the deliberations held after the formal resignation of the shogun. Tani was a successful commander on the Imperialist side during the War of the Restoration. He captured the castles of Takamatsu and Marugame in Shikoku in January 1868, and later served with distinction at battles near Nikkō and Aizu.

For the next decade, Tani's career lay with the new army. By 1870, he was a major-general, and held the post of Director-General of the War Department. Shortly after this, however, a posting as Commander-in-Chief of the Kumamoto (central Kyushu) Garrison took him away from the capital. He was on the staff of the punitive expedition sent to Formosa in 1874, and had little trouble in adding to his laurels on that campaign. Two years after this, Tani returned to his former post in Kuma-moto; and, in 1877 at the time of the Satsuma rebellion, he earned deserved fame by successfully holding the castle at

Kumamoto for over a month against rebel attacks and invest-
ment. He subsequently was promoted to the rank of lieutenant-
general and became Commandant of the Military Academy,
but resigned from this post in 1881.

From this time Tani ceased to be a professional army officer,
though he kept his rank, his interests leading him into the worlds
of letters and politics. In 1884, he was made Head of the Peers
School, and created a Viscount. Chosen to be a member of the
Imperial Academy in 1885, in October of the same year he
entered the Itō Cabinet as Minister for Trade and Agriculture.
Within a few months of taking office he left for a tour of Europe,
and returned to Japan in June 1887. His trip abroad did not
lessen his nationalist sentiments in any way; and in July 1887,
he resigned from the Cabinet. Ostensibly this was because he
objected to certain changes in agricultural policies, but really
because he was profoundly dissatisfied with the Government's
attitude towards treaty revision and uncompromisingly opposed
to Westernization of the country. Viscount Tani's resignation
was the *coup de grâce* for Inoue Kaoru's schemes for treaty
revision which would have necessitated the appointment of
foreign judges to the Japanese higher courts.[44]

For the next year or two, Tani tried to follow up this success
by joining Gotō's anti-Government campaign. His was one of
the most powerful voices on the Right wing of the *Daidō
Danketsu*; and it was about this time that he founded the *Meiji
Club* to give currency to his views. From the opening of the
Imperial Diet in November 1890 to the time of his death in
1911, Tani sat in the House of Peers. There he was an eloquent
and redoubtable opponent of successive Governments, no
matter whether they had been formed by the *Sat-chō* bureaucrats or the popular parties.

As an organization, the *Kokumin-ha*, which Tani formed in
succession to the *Meiji Club*, was even more amorphous than
Inoue's *Jichi Kenkyū Kai*, and it received hardly more than a
bare mention in newspaper accounts of the election. True, there
was a report in one paper on the day of the election to the effect

that a growing number of the supporters of the rival Conservative general, Torio Koyata, were 'surrendering' to General Tani; but the report itself cast doubts on its own authenticity.[45] It would seem that the members of the *Kokumin-ha* had little to hold them together, apart from a common allegiance to 'Japanism' and to Tani himself. A formal manifesto, if issued, was not publicized, and presumably the scattered company of National Party candidates was left each to fend for himself at the election.

However, since the electors generally favoured the Liberal and Progressive parties, Tani was perhaps right to abandon tactics of publicity and direct appeal for cautiously doing what he could to get his sympathizers into parliament by the back door. For at the same time as he kept the *Kokumin-ha* at any rate in existence, he interested himself in a number of regional clubs with nationalist leanings and possibly also gave covert support to some Independent candidates. His native Kōchi prefecture was the area where he felt strongest. There the *Kokumin-ha*, calling itself by that name, challenged the Liberals in every constituency.

Unfortunately for the Nationalists, Kōchi was also the birthplace of the Liberal movement and they were defeated in all these contests. A foretaste of what was going to happen to them at the parliamentary elections had been given to the National Party by the prefectural elections in March 1890. Then, its candidates had been virtually routed by their Liberal opponents. So, even in Kōchi, Tani's election prospects were not very good, and he seems to have wisely realized that for him the election had taken on much of the character of a salvage operation. Tani was a prolific letter-writer; and a communication, dated 19 May 1890, which he sent to the Tosa *Kōyō Kai* gives some evidence of the way he went about things.

The *Kōyō Kai* was a local ultra-nationalist society with its headquarters in Kōchi city. The subject of Tani's letter to it was the collapse of the old *Daidō Danketsu* and the impending amalgamation of the three Liberal factions. The *Kōyō Kai* had apparently formed part of the *Daidō Danketsu*, and was still linked with the *Daidō Club*. By 1890, extreme Conservative groups such as it were embarrassed by their continued association with the now predominantly Left-wing *Daidō* movement. Tani, in his letter,[46] put forward two alternative plans for dealing with this problem, and asked the senior officials of the *Kōyō Kai* to consider them. The letter's contents were to be withheld from ordinary members.

The first plan was that his followers in the *Kōyō Kai* should renounce their allegiance to the *Daidō Club*, and stand as best they could on their own feet for the time being. In the opening sentences of his message, Tani recalled how the original *Daidō Danketsu* had been neither too reformist nor too obscurantist. The position had deteriorated, however, and the existing *Daidō Club* was a group of 'demagogues', whose Liberal principles stemmed from 'blatant individualism'. The disadvantage of this course of action was that the local Ultra-Conservatives would lose what little chance they had of influencing the results of the elections. Too weak to fight for themselves, their only hope lay in maintaining their co-operation with more powerful radical elements.

Tani was nothing if not realistic about this. He told his henchmen in the *Kōyō Kai* that before they finally made up their minds whether or not to secede from the *Daidō Club*, they would have to give careful consideration to whether the Ultra-Conservative organization could keep going in isolation even for a few months; to whether it could secure the election of any candidates at all; and to whether it could survive the shock of overwhelming defeat in the recent local elections. If members of the *Kōyō Kai* did decide to secede, he said, they would be forced to give up their political activities for the time being and restrict themselves to their everyday occupations in agriculture or trade, 'swallowing their shame and putting up with their misfortunes' until a more favourable opportunity arose. Speaking of himself, he wrote: 'Of course, I myself cannot participate directly in political party movements; but, indirectly, I shall help the parties which I consider to be good, and shall do my utmost for the State. Never for one moment shall I forget the principles of "Japan first!", for which I have made myself a spokesman!' Then he went on to advise them to pay attention to what they would read in the Right-wing newspaper, the *Nippon Shimbun*.

As an alternative to the above proposal, Tani also suggested that *Kōyō Kai* members might find it easier to hide their disgust with the *Daidō Club* and remain part of it, at any rate until after the election. The immediate advantage of this plan was that it would enable them to have some say in who should be elected; and he listed the names of two or three candidates whom he thought worth supporting. What he was really counting on, however, was the likelihood of a fresh split in the Liberal ranks when they came together in August to give some substance to their paper federation. Since the *Kōin Club* was merely the first step in the protracted process of Liberal reunion, Tani had some justification for calling it more than once a nominal amalgamation, and confidently predicting that the pattern of party alliances would undergo a further sweeping change later in the summer. When that happened, he argued, societies like the *Kōyō Kai* would be in a strong position to act as the nucleus of a new, Right-wing *Daidō Danketsu*. As indicated earlier, Tani was by no means alone in holding these views about the probability of the *Kōin Club* being overtaken by failure. However, in his case, they were obviously reinforced by conversations he had recently had with two of the leaders of the *Daidō Club*, Inoue Kakugorō[47] and Ōe Taku.

Naturally, as Tani pointed out, the same prospect of eventual re-affiliation with the more congenial Liberals still held good, even if the *Kōyō Kai* chose to adopt his first proposal and broke with the *Daidō Club*. Either way, it was simply a matter of beating a strategic retreat; and so the letter really boiled down to a short discussion of two alternative methods of doing just this. It is an interesting document not only because it shows how Tani played the political game, but also because of the clear indications it contains of the grave electoral weaknesses of Conservatives of Tani's stamp and the extremely fluid nature of inter-party divisions. In short, the Ultra-Conservatives were forced by their general unpopularity to be opportunistic; and their opportunism had some chance of reward by reason of the readiness of certain Liberals to treat with them.

There were many similarities between Tani Kanjō and his *Kokumin-ha* on the one hand, and Torio Koyata and his *Hoshu Chūsei Ha* on the other; but there were also some differences between them. Like Tani, Torio was a soldier turned politician. Born in 1846, he was the eldest son of a Chōshū samurai. As a child, he had been noted for his intelligence and all round ability; and in his early manhood, he joined the *kiheitai*. *Kiheitai* was the name given to a force of samurai and plebeian volunteers, which was raised in Chōshū from 1860 onwards to fight the shogunate.[48] These bellicose activities earned Torio the hostility of the greater part of his acquaintance, and eventually the extreme displeasure of his parents who formally disowned him. Undaunted, he continued to make himself known as an ardent supporter of the Imperialist cause, surviving all the perils that attended a life of political agitation in those troubled days to take part in the battle of Fushimi at the head of a little band of twenty irregulars, who were his personal followers and known as 'Torio's Twenty'. Fushimi is a place half way between Kyoto and Osaka where Imperialist forces determined the issue of the War of the Restoration by defeating the shogun's army in January 1868.

After the fighting was finished, Torio was in Kii province for a while, helping with the reform of the fief government. For a few years from 1870, he held a number of senior positions in the War Department, and in 1875 was appointed to the *Dajōkan*. In the following year, he acted as Minister for the Army for a few months before becoming Chief of the Imperial General Staff. When the Satsuma rebellion had been crushed, he was given a higher Court rank and a special award of ¥600. His next post was that of Court liaison officer to the Imperial

General Staff. He held it for only a few months until October 1879, when he was appointed Commander of the Imperial Guards. At this point, there came a break in his official career, apparently because of ill health. By February 1881, he had resigned from the Imperial Guards and also from the *Dajōkan*, and had gone to live in Osaka where he began studying Zen Buddhism. A Viscountcy was conferred on him in July 1884, in recognition of his services to the State.

In 1885, Torio re-entered public life as a member of the National Defence Council. From February 1886, he was away from Japan for a period of thirteen months most of which was spent in Europe. While overseas he was appointed to the Senate. From the relatively undistinguished rank of Senator he was raised in June 1888 to the dignity of Privy Councillor; and so he was one of those entrusted with the ratification of the constitution. In May 1890, just before the election, he resigned from the Privy Council; and later in the same year, he was successful in the election of representatives of his order to the House of Peers. In 1895, Torio reversed the step he had taken five years previously, and resigned from the House of Peers to become a Privy Councillor for the second time. He continued to serve on the Privy Council until his death in 1905.

As a publicist, Torio was perhaps not so eloquent as Tani; but he wrote well, and was, if anything, even better educated than his fellow general, as he had not only as deep a knowledge of the Chinese classics but also a virtually complete mastery of the Buddhist canon as well. He wrote several essays on political theory, which were a success in their day and are of no little interest to a student of Meiji constitutional developments. In these writings, he sought to preserve unsullied the principles of respect for the Emperor and punishment for the barbarian that had inspired his youth.

Though Torio was more successful as an essayist and a publisher of political reviews than as a leader of a political party, his *Hoshu Chūsei Ha* was, at any rate on paper, the best organized and most articulate of all the Conservative groups, moderate or otherwise. It was first launched in November 1888, when Torio circulated the prospectus of the new party among his friends. He was reprimanded by the Minister for War, Marshal Ōyama, for taking part in politics while still retaining his commission in the army. (This perhaps was a reason why Tani Kanjō felt that he could not intervene openly in politics.) The immediate upshot of this reprimand was that Torio had to issue a statement severing his connexion with the new party; and his closest aide, Fujita Ichirō, did what he could to recover the circulars that had been sent out. Then, Torio resigned from the army; and on 20 January 1889, he published the same manifesto in a magazine, the *New Conservative Review*, that he had started to bring out as a journal for his party.

This manifesto was by far the briefest of all the party platforms prepared especially for the election of 1890. What is more to the point, it was notably defensive in tone. In a few words Torio cleverly managed to steal some of the opposition's clothes, and yet at the same time made clear the fundamental conservativism of his own position. The Moderate Conservative Party's manifesto was:

Conservatism has as its aim the preservation of the existing state of affairs, and the acceptance and use of its consequences. Now, in order to elucidate this principle, I shall point to its opposite. The opposite views are those of reformism and radicalism. The advocates of reformism and radicalism abandon the fruits [of the past], and wish to make the reconstruction of the State the basis of their thinking. This idea of reconstructing the State does not recognize any limitations. (If it did, it would not be reformist, it would be conservative.) Therefore they will always be reconstructing the State and making experiments. If there is no Conservative party to check this, it will be very dangerous for the future. The differences between the two views lie in their principles and objectives. In practice, though, there is also a reforming element in the Conservative parties; and no doubt there is a conservative element in the reformist parties. [Nevertheless] since [the differences between them] stem from their principles and objectives, their intentions naturally cannot be the same. In the following, I inform my political friends of the intentions of Conservativism.

GENERAL PROSPECTUS OF THE MODERATE CONSERVATIVE PARTY

1. Our Party will stand erect among the parties that are established in our Empire of Japan—loyal and upright, steadfast and indomitable.

5. SOME CONSERVATIVE PARTIES

2. Our Party will respect the constitution granted by our Emperor of His own free will, will uphold the dignity of the Imperial Sovereignty, and will honour the rights of the people.

3. Our Party will never hesitate nor show any scruple in perfecting moral relationships and advocating righteousness.

4. Our Party, recognizing the fixed rights of the Upper and Lower Houses, [holds that] the division of power between the legislature and the executive must be made to comply with the constitution in every respect.

5. Our Party will base the national administration on frugality and simplicity. It will reduce government expenditure, foster the strength of the people, and shall be eternally resolved on a policy of sound administration.

November 1888.   Torio Koyata.[49]

On the face of it, this declaration, with its promises to respect the constitution and honour popular rights, was conservative rather than reactionary; and the last article, in particular, echoed the propaganda of the Liberal and Progressive parties. Moreover, the very choice of the name 'Moderate Conservative Party' would tend to give the same impression. However, the overtones of caution and moderation should be thought of as a smiling face put on by Torio for the purpose of doing what he could to influence an electorate which he knew to be antipathetic to his ideas. The genuinely popular parties, numerous though their mistakes and defects were, never lost the initiative. Therefore Torio chose to make it sound as if his new party was conservative but constitutional. Certainly, a comparison of the *Hoshu Chūsei Ha* prospectus with other works by Torio indicates that it was a very attenuated expression of his real opinions.

Torio deceived no one at the time with his unaccustomed air of moderation. On 28 May 1890, the *Tokyo Nichi Nichi Shimbun* reported an interview between one of its correspondents and a member of the Kumamoto Progressive Party; the subject discussed was whether groups like the *Hoshu Chūsei Ha* could be included in the Kyushu Confederation of Progressive Parties. Their conversation went as follows:

T.N.N.S. Correspondent: With regard to the new conservative party led by General Tani [*sic*], the General himself declared, when he introduced his party to the public, that he favoured a progressive outlook in politics; but what is your attitude to that party?

K.P.P. Member: Quite right! He did say he favoured progressive principles; but, here in Kumamoto, we regard him on a par with the *Shimei* faction [i.e. the Kumamoto National Rights Party, *Kokken-tō*, a locally powerful nationalist group].

T.N.N.S. Correspondent: In that case, policies such as Moderate Conservativism are at complete variance with your objectives, of course?

K.P.P. Member: Of course!

The correspondent then ended his report by noting that it would be quite impossible for Torio's organization to become part of the Kyushu Confederation of Progressives. A few days later, the *Osaka Mainichi*, itself no particular friend of the popular parties, stated that the *Hoshu Chūsei Ha* had held a business and social meeting in a hotel in the eastern part of the city where Torio was staying. The proceedings of this meeting were a strictly guarded secret, but it was known that the principal item on the agenda had been the election campaign. Not even the names and occupations of those who attended it were divulged to the press, but according to this report more than half of them were Buddhist priests.[50]

People like Tani and Torio do not appear to have objected so much to the political forms of Liberalism such as the constitution and the Imperial Diet, though these in their eyes were bad enough, as to its moral spirit. This latter, they felt, would give rise to an unhealthy sense of individualism among the Japanese, and make each of them think only of himself. The consequence of this would be that the quasi-religious ties that bound a man to his family, to his master, and to his Sovereign would snap, and human society would fall into a state of bestial anarchy. In 1890, the nation's moral culture was still preeminently Confucian, and it had but recently emerged from conditions of feudalism under which hereditary status and personal service had been immeasurably more important, in terms of prestige at least, than abstract freedoms and private wealth. Therefore the general relevance of this line of reasoning is obvious. Torio was shrewd in insisting too, as he did, that it would be impossible for everyone in a poor and populous country like Japan to secure an adequate gratification of their material desires.

Ideas of this kind were the true strength of the Ultra-Conservative reaction to the Meiji innovations; and the hints of radicalism in the objection to unfettered Liberalism's sanctioning of economic inequalities should not be missed. Thus, there emerges a paradox—the Ultra-Conservatives, though completely reactionary in their political outlook, were by no means incapable of appearing to be the poor man's friend when it came to economic or social questions. This paradox was balanced by the other already noted—the Liberal groups, and to a slightly less extent the Progressives too, as organizations of the rich, were politically emancipationist but socially conservative.

The development of Japanese parliamentary institutions was to some extent determined by these Ultra-Conservative attitudes, even though the poor electoral performance of the factions led by Tani and Torio tends to overshadow their underlying historical significance. In 1880 Torio published an essay on kingship. A remarkably able exposition of his and Tani's point of view, it appeared in translation in the *Japan Daily Mail* for 19 and 20 November 1890:[51]

Order and disorder in a nation...[are] determined by the disposition of the people. The pivot on which the public disposition turns towards order or disorder is the point where public and private motives separate...To regard our family affairs with all the interest due to our family, and our national affairs with all the interest due to our nation,—this is to fitly discharge our duty, and to be guided by public considerations. On the other hand, to regard the affairs of the nation as if they were our own family affairs,—this is to be influenced by private motives and to stray from the path of duty...

Selfishness is born in every man; to indulge it freely is to become a beast. Therefore it is that sages preach the principles of duty and propriety, justice and morality, providing restraints for private aims and encouragements for public spirit...In the Orient, from ancient times, national government has been based on benevolence, and directed to securing the welfare and happiness of the people...The inhabitants of this empire live, for the most part, by manual labour. Let them be never so industrious, they can hardly earn enough to supply their daily wants...They achieve as much as their opportunities permit...Yet there is nothing in human society that does not owe its existence to labour. Now, to satisfy the desires of one luxurious man, the toil of a thousand is needed. Surely it is monstrous that those who owe to labour the pleasures suggested by their civilization should forget what they owe to the labourer, and treat him as if he were not a fellow-being. But civilization, according to the interpretation of the Occident, serves only to satisfy men of large desires. It is of no benefit to the masses, but is simply a system under which ambitions compete to accomplish their aims...It is plain that if the mutual rights of men and their status are made to depend on degrees of wealth, the majority of the people being without wealth, must fail to establish their rights; whereas the minority who are wealthy will assert their rights, and, under society's sanction, will exact oppressive duties from the poor, neglecting the dictates of humanity and benevolence. The adoption of these principles of liberty and equality in Japan would vitiate the good and peaceful customs of our country, render the general disposition of the people harsh and unfeeling, and finally prove a source of calamity to the masses...

Though at first sight Occidental civilization presents an attractive appearance, adapted as it is to the gratification of selfish desires, yet since its basis is the hypothesis that men's wishes constitute natural laws, it must ultimately end in disappointment and demoralization... Occidental nations have become what they are after passing through conflicts and vicissitudes of the most serious kind...Just now their motive elements are in partial equilibrium, and their social condition is more or less ordered. But if this slight equilibrium happens to be disturbed, they will be thrown once more into confusion and change, until, after a period of renewed struggle and suffering, temporary stability is once more attained...Perpetual disturbance is their doom. Peaceful equality can never be attained until built up among the ruins of annihilated Western states and the ashes of extinct Western peoples.

This, then, was the voice of genuine reaction—to nineteenth-century individualism and industrialism as it affected the East. In 1890, it was little more than a voice crying in the wilderness; but fifty years later, it or something very like it had grown into the battle cry of a nation ready to fight the world if need be.

Clearly, Torio's argument was not without its fallacies of one sort or another. The physical obliteration of the Occident, a thing he yearned for, was not feasible unless Japan first industrialized herself along Western, capitalist lines—that is to say, took the course that Torio dreaded most. The principles of Liberal democracy, if carried to their logical conclusions and every indication on the Liberal side of the political struggle was that they would be, would give every subject equal voting rights, and thereby destroy the advantage of the minority over the majority so far as theoretical political power was concerned. Similarly, the author refused to consider the possibility that advances in technology and attendant ideals of general social emancipation would eventually create and distribute wealth for everybody, so providing a solution to problems of social injustice. In effect, by ignoring the whole question of a rule of law before which all men are equal, Torio was able to pretend that Liberalism's greatest safeguard against itself did not exist. These inconsistencies and omissions made his attack seem a good deal more plausible than it really was.

Nevertheless, even after we have taken into full account these and other shortcomings in Torio's essay, it is not hard to see that there was more than a particle of right in what he said. In Japan, as in other countries, parliament was first set up on the basis of a restricted and plutocratic franchise. (Much earlier than this Torio had called the *Risshi-sha* proposals for a national assembly 'upper-class democracy'.)[52] Moreover, the danger that unlimited political freedom will engender intolerable economic privations is the classic dilemma of classical Liberalism. The first Socialists and others were confronting this kind of problem in Europe during the last decade of the nineteenth century, a period which in many ways was the Indian summer of *laissez-faire*; and only a few decades had elapsed since Marx had written *Das Kapital*—in part as a protest against the animal conditions of economic life in mid-Victorian England.

These difficulties became more difficult when transplanted to the Japanese environment. In Western Europe, politics, economic conditions and general morality all sprang from the same individualistic root, and incongruities could be sorted out without threatening the structure of post-Renaissance civilization

In Japan, on the other hand, the new, imported political and economic apparatus stood at first in raw, and seemingly irreconcilable opposition to the native non-material and collectivist ethic; and a large-scale collision between the two would have destroyed the nation as a cultural entity.

Looking at the matter from a totally different point of view for a moment, the controlled fury of Torio's reaction does indicate the great influence which Liberalism had come to have on Japanese political thinking by the end of the first half of the Meiji era. Tani and Torio stood virtually alone in the small circle of governing bureaucrats, as well as in the wider world of the Meiji intelligentsia. It is not surprising therefore that the electors in 1890 should have been so unresponsive to them. The *Kokumin-ha* and the *Hoshu Chūsei Ha*, needless to say, were not helped by a situation in which the voters all belonged to classes that had most to gain from a parliamentary system. Among the newspapers, the *Nippon Shimbun* did what it could to rally support to the generals; but it had little that was original or constructive to say in the weeks immediately preceding the election, though it was full of careful analyses and devious comment after the results were known.

The general position with regard to the Conservative parties may be summarized as follows: those Conservatives who were not also reactionary scarcely existed as a recognizable party at all. Those who were reactionary came to the polls not altogether without a case to argue and leaders to argue it, but divided, demoralized, and for the time being all but impotent.

(6) INDEPENDENTS

The numerous Independent candidates by definition were non-party; and so it is not easy to pin them down as subscribers to any particular set of views. In general, however, those who succeeded in getting themselves elected to the Diet tended to side with the Government and against the popular parties. Therefore it is probably correct to think of Independent candidates who took their politics seriously as being on the whole a safe conservative group of the sort favoured by Inoue or Itō, though no doubt a few of them were willing to go to the extremes suggested by Tani and Torio. Among them were about forty serving or recently retired officials who obtained seats in the House of Representatives, after running the gauntlet of general public hostility towards anyone connected with the Government.

Suematsu Kenchō's remarks[53] on this aspect of the election were borne out by the Civil Service regulations of the time, which stated that any official who ran for a seat and lost would be compelled to resign his post. The object of this was to spare, if possible, the bureaucracy from the ignominy of even a single defeat at the hands of the 'people'.[54] At the same time, the need for such a drastic provision shows how conscious the Government was of its own weak standing with the electors. Suematsu, himself, and the more radical Okamoto Takeo mentioned above, are probably representative of the better type of Independent candidate.

Unfortunately, men like them were comparatively few and far between, when one takes a look at the bloc of Independent candidates as a whole. The great majority of them were 'self-nominated Independents'—mere nobodies at the national level, whose qualifications for giving useful service in the House of Representatives were at best only slightly less meagre than their chances of election. Considering what was involved, their numbers came near to assuming plague proportions, and they were spread more or less evenly over the country. The results for Tokyo *fu*, for instance, show that in the Second Constituency, one candidate polled 2 votes, and three others 1 vote each; in the Seventh Constituency, it was the same; in the Eleventh Constituency, seven candidates secured only 1 vote apiece; and so on. In Okayama prefecture, a certain candidate was dubbed the 'genealogy candidate'. The reason for this was that when the futility of competing against a popular favourite was pointed out to him, he replied: 'I have no expectation at all of being elected. Were I to receive only one vote in the election of Members to the House of Representatives, I should want this for my family tree.'[55]

A question arises as to why so many persons embarked on what they must have known from the first was an almost hopeless quest for a seat in the Diet. Not only hopeless but also possibly very expensive—particularly for those candidates whose appeal was no bigger than their purses. There were a number of stories of wealthy candidates having beggared themselves as a result of their enormous campaign 'expenses'.

The answer to this question is doubtless contained in the anecdote about the 'genealogy candidate'. It is clear that Japan's first parliamentary election aroused a very great degree of popular interest; and that this interest was not in any way restricted to the electorate alone, but extended to the public at large. Therefore, in the enthusiastic mood of the day, a large number of people were willing to risk both fortune and reputation to achieve what they considered to be the honour of representing their home district in the new legislature. Suematsu Kenchō said as much when he spoke of 'men of property and local repute who did not normally give a damn for political discussion' entering into the fray, and 'fighting for all they were worth'.[56] Certainly, there was enough in the newspapers of the time to vindicate his judgement.

(7) SUMMARY

Though the Buddhists were capable of a limited agitation on their own behalf, and Christianity was decidedly unpopular everywhere outside Nagasaki prefecture, religion played no direct part in the election of 1890.[57] This means that all the great national issues that occupied the minds of candidates and voters alike at that time have been considered.[58]

In conclusion, then: the election was contested by a number of distinct groups of politicians and men of affairs, including the Liberal-Progressive Parties on the Left wing, the more respectable Independents and bureaucratic candidates to the moderate conservative Right, and beyond these again the various Ultra-Conservative and reactionary factions, the members of which were reduced by the course of events to the role of little more than scheming observers. Over the whole field, like a cloud of gnats, hung the self-nominated Independents—the majority of whom were destined to be the ephemera of the hour. Put in diagrammatic form, the line of battle looked something like this:

Left		Centre		Right	
Liberals	K.C.P.P.*	Progressive	Some Inde-	Moderate Con-	Ultra-Con-
Jiyū-tō		Party	pendents	servatives	servatives
Aikoku-kōtō		(*Kaishin-tō*)		*Jichi-tō*	*Kokumin-ha*
Daidō Club				Independents	*Hoshu Chūsei Ha*
Kōin Club				Officials	

.... 'Self-Nominated' Independents ....

* K.C.P.P. = Kyushu Confederation of Progressive Parties.

Talking of the main issues raised at the election, Suematsu Kenchō made a general criticism of the party manifestos and the performances of the anti-Government candidates in these words:

Although all sorts of 'Party Principles' or 'General Principles' were adopted by each party, their wording was for the most part vague and they did not really touch public opinion. Especially in the case of the 'General Principles', they never did anything more than unthinkingly take over each other's opinions, putting them in valueless words to the effect that they would foster the national interest and promote the happiness of the people; because all the parties strove to find a basis for their arguments which would not allow other people to criticize them...The cry for curtailment of administrative expenses and a reduction of the land-tax was heard virtually everywhere...I did not hear of anyone who produced a satisfactory plan for realizing [these objectives]...Of course, plenty of proposals for equal treaties emerged; but these, too, were vaguely worded.[59]

Though there is some truth in this condemnation, it is not the whole truth. Liberal and Progressive opponents of the Government did make what was on the whole a full and intelligent use of their unprecedented opportunity to challenge its policies, thereby attempting to influence the course of events. Of all the questions they raised, that concerning the future of the Cabinet was the most crucial. Second only to this as an electoral issue of prime importance ranked the problem generated by the election campaign itself—the problem of the fairness or otherwise of electioneering tactics.

CHAPTER III

THE ELECTION CAMPAIGN:
A GENERAL SURVEY

Intended to be an outline of the 1890 election from the standpoint of relations between candidates and voters, the subject of this chapter is the campaigning part of the campaign. How did a candidate come to stand for a particular constituency? In what ways did he seek to make his mark on its voters? But first, before developing this theme, there are a few words to be said about the general body of candidates.

(1) CANDIDATES AND NOMINATIONS

It is not possible to give an exact figure for the total number of candidates who took part in the election. Newspapers gave conflicting accounts, and this information is lacking for large areas of the country. At one stage, the *Tokyo Nichi Nichi Shimbun* estimated that there was a total of 900 candidates for the 300 seats in the House of Representatives;[1] but since the same report mentions that there were from three to six hopefuls in each constituency, this figure of 900 would seem to be far too conservative. Doubtless the *Yūbin-Hōchi Shimbun* was nearer the mark when it reckoned that there were between 1,400 and 1,500 candidates for the House.[2]

This latter estimate is more in keeping with the table opposite which shows details of the ratio of candidates to seats in a handful of districts. The table has been compiled on the basis of the few reports that do give fairly specific information on this subject; nevertheless, the figures in the third column should be treated with caution, as not too inaccurate approximations rather than as statements of hard fact. There were either none or very few candidates returned unopposed.

The quality, as opposed to the number, of candidates is more readily determined. In terms of their occupations or social status,

Prefecture	No. of seats	No. of candidates	Candidates per seat
Tokyo	12	74	6
Osaka	10	51	5
Niigata	13	27	2
Aichi	11	52	5
Miyagi	5	26	5
Okayama	8	69	9
Yamaguchi	7	16	2
Wakayama	5	12	2
Total	71	327	5

they may be divided into four main categories. In all but the second of these categories, an impressive majority of the people concerned were, or had been, members of the local assemblies.

The first bloc consisted of those who may be called the professional politicians—the stalwarts of the Liberal movement and the Progressive Party. Individuals representative of this group were Kataoka Kenkichi and Ōe Taku in Kōchi prefecture, and Shimada Saburō and Nakajima Nobuyuki in Kanagawa prefecture.

Next, there was a group of 'career bureaucrat' candidates, the majority of whom had been employed in a relatively lowly capacity as sub-prefects in local administration. The most senior of them, though, was the Minister for Agriculture and Trade in the incumbent Yamagata Cabinet, Mutsu Munemitsu, who was returned for a constituency in Wakayama prefecture. In addition to Mutsu, three former Senators, eleven persons who held or had held important posts in the central government, and twenty-five prefectural or former prefectural officials were elected.[3]

The third category was made up of professional men—chiefly lawyers and journalists. One constituency had an auditor among its candidates; and a qualified doctor who had held a number of government posts was elected for the Fifth Constituency in Niigata prefecture, while physicians were also returned from Fukushima (First Constituency) and Chiba (Second Constituency). Sometimes, too, a person in private life was nominated by the residents of a constituency or else attracted attention because of his scholastic abilities. Nevertheless, professions like school or university teaching and medicine seem to have been poorly represented in the lists of candidates; and the wig and the pen between them virtually monopolized this section of the field.

The journalists, Okamoto Takeo and Seki Naohiko, and the lawyers, Tsunoda Shimpei and Oyagi Bi'ichirō, were typical of these 'professional man' candidates. Mention has already been made of Okamoto,[4] who was at the time of the election one of the most important members of the staff of the *Tokyo Nichi Nichi Shimbun*. Seki, also, was a prominent newspaperman (in 1890, he was Chairman of the *Tokyo Nichi Nichi Shimbun* Company), and enjoyed a good deal of fame as a theorist on the moderate Right wing of Meiji politics. He had been one of the leading members of the defunct Imperial Party during the period 1882–4, and was the translator of Disraeli's novel, *Coningsby*, into Japanese. Tsunoda and Oyagi were two of Tokyo's leading barristers, who fought each other for its Seventh Constituency (Kanda ward).

The fourth and largest group of candidates was composed of wealthy industrialists, merchants and farmer-landowners. Presidents of the various National Banks were quite conspicuous in this category, and most of those who listed their occupation as agriculture were in fact businessmen active in local transport and banking as well as in the more traditional rural industries such as brewing, soy sauce manufacture, sericulture and timber.[5] This mixed group of 'plutocratic' candidates was very successful in the elections; and its size and prominence is good evidence of the fairly rapid rise of the Meiji capitalist class, rural as well as urban. In general, their sympathies lay with the popular rights parties; and though in 1890 the *shizoku* still provided the leadership of the parliamentary movement, its grass-roots strength was already coming from the entrepreneurs. On 17 June, the *Tokyo Nichi Nichi Shimbun* printed the following thumb-nail sketch of one of these 'new men' of the Meiji era. Its subject is Yumoto Yoshinori, who was duly elected to the

House of Representatives where he sat as a pro-Government Member.

This gentleman, who is standing as a candidate for the House of Representatives in the Fourth Constituency (Kita Saitama, Ōsato, Hara, Hanzawa and Obusuma sub-prefectures) of Saitama prefecture, is a brewer of sake in Saitama-mura in Kita Saitama sub-prefecture and a notable man of property in that area. Rising forty this year, he played a part in politics at the time of the Restoration, and gained a great deal of popularity by this. He was a member of the prefectural assembly from the time it first opened; in 1886, he was again elected [to the assembly]. In the meantime, he became very interested in education and founded a number of schools, followed by a company for employing samurai of the former Oshi fief. He has made the manufacture of Gyōta stockings, which are a product of that area, a very prosperous [industry]. Although his influence has become so great, he is of a retiring disposition and does not boast.

These four categories of candidates all come from the upper middle class because of the rule that a citizen had to be paying not less than ¥15 a year in direct national taxes in order to be eligible for election. On the other hand, among those not thus disqualified (roughly 450,000 or 1 per cent of the total population), it was not necessarily the most wealthy who came forward as candidates or who, when they did compete, were successful. The fifteen richest inhabitants of a prefecture sent a representative to the House of Peers, and so were unlikely to be directly embroiled in the House of Representatives elections. Apart from this, persons of the local millionaire class do not seem to have been either very interested in representative institutions or over-popular with the general run of electors. A particular contest was sometimes summarized in the press as having been a tri-angular match between 'money power', 'innate abilities', and 'physical force'. In circumstances like these, the victory of the first was by no means a foregone conclusion, as the voters' sentiments often lay with the second. Moreover, too rash a use of 'money power' could easily bring down a criminal pro-secution on the heads of its manipulators.

That candidates had to be men of means but were not, generally speaking, extravagantly wealthy is borne out by some data supplied by Suematsu Kenchō on the pecuniary standing of the 300 Members of the first House of Representatives. According to it, the average amount of tax paid by Members for twenty-six of the forty-five prefectures was less than ¥ 100 per annum, and the average tax payment per Member for the House as a whole was ¥ 126 per annum. Only five individuals in the newly elected House paid more than ¥ 1,000 a year in taxes, and at least forty-eight paid less than ¥ 50.[6]

As noted earlier, officers of the army and navy were forbidden by law to take part in the election. Aristocratic younger sons, on the other hand, refrained from choice. Those descended from daimyo stock possibly had a family disdain for associating with other commoners on terms of equality, or perhaps it was simply that they had inherited their forbears' general vacuity in matters political. The less historic families of the peerage, which had been ennobled for services rendered at the time of the Restoration or after 1868, did not form a landed upper class with roots in the traditions and local hierarchies of the country-side. It can be assumed that they had neither the wish nor the opportunity to place junior members in the House of Representatives.

Broadly speaking, there were three ways in which a candidate could come to stand for a constituency. Either he simply put himself up for election; or he was adopted as its official candidate by one of the recognized national parties; or else he was nominated as a desirable Representative by a number of local residents.

The first of these methods was used by the 'self-nominated' candidates. Candidatures of this sort were usually hopeless if not downright frivolous along the lines of that of Okayama prefecture's 'genealogy candidate'.[7] An even more striking example was furnished by Wakayama prefecture, where an otherwise decorous campaign was enlivened by the activities of a person named Shiga Horissei.

This man was the second son of a sake manufacturer, and had been known for his eccentric behaviour for some time. Shortly

134

before the election campaign opened, he spent a week meeting the people of Wakayama city. The reason he had given for doing this was that he was about to depart for Europe in order to complete his studies in philosophy. When he did leave town, however, it was not for overseas. He merely climbed a not too distant mountain, Koya-san, which is one of the most historic Buddhist sites in Japan, and started living on its summit— presumably in one of the temples. Once the election campaign had begun ('perhaps under the impression that the time to save all beings had come'), he suddenly left Koya-san and, returning to Wakayama, established himself in a temple dedicated to the Amida Buddha which stood on an island in the middle of the city. From there, he introduced himself to the Wakayama citizenry as a non-party candidate for the House of Representatives. Horses were tethered and rickshaws lined up inside the temple gate, 'while he himself, attired in robes of spotless purple and a white sash, with his hair hanging down two feet at the back... gravely occupied a room, and was interviewed by admiring gentry and citizens'.[8]

Candidatures sponsored by one of the big national parties or respectable local group tended to be less colourful than this, though they enjoyed a better chance of success. In some areas like Niigata prefecture (*Daidō Club* versus *Kaishin-tō*) and Yokohama city (*Jiyū-tō* versus *Kaishin-tō*), or Kōchi prefecture (*Jiyū-tō* versus National Party) and Kumamoto prefecture (National Rights Party versus *Kaishin-tō*), the competition between candidates affiliated to rival parties dominated the electoral scene, and the campaigns became virtually two-party contests. In other places, notably Yamaguchi prefecture, there was a single established regional association which was able to field a strong team of candidates.

The system of party nominations worked tolerably well, despite the failure in a number of places to prevent competition between two or even more members of the same or allied parties.[9] There was one case of a Progressive Party member in Tochigi prefecture resigning from the party because he disapproved of its choice of candidate;[10] and at a meeting held in Nagano prefecture, 300 Liberals unanimously agreed to disown a certain candidate.[11] Ruptures of this kind were rare, however, even though the parties seemed sometimes ready to give their blessing to likely looking candidates who did not necessarily accept all their policies. These *bona fide* party nominations were frequent enough and an indication of the way in which elections were to be held on an increasingly greater scale in the future; but non-party endorsements of popularly chosen Independents were just as common and in many respects more characteristic of the political conditions of the time. Characteristic, because the history of these local nominations draws attention to two of the outstanding traits of the election campaign and, by implication, of the political world as a whole: the influence of regionalism (or localism), and the influence of personality.

Sometimes these two influences, which were present in one form or another in virtually every constituency, were seen to be opposed, as in a newspaper report on the Second Constituency in Saitama prefecture. In that one area alone, there were no fewer than two dozen candidates for two seats; and though representatives of the *Jiyū-tō* and *Kaishin-tō* were among them, the correspondent explicitly stated that:

The election in this constituency is a contest between personality-ism and regionalism, rather than strife between parties. In other words, those who put their faith in personalities hold that they should return men of the finest possible character, irrespective of whether they are inhabitants of the constituency or not; and regionalism means that at all costs one should elect a resident of the district.[12]

The exact opposite of this state of affairs could also happen, however, and in some places the strongest challenger as a personality was a local resident.

The Law of Election had stipulated that a candidate had to be paying his qualifying taxes in the prefecture from which he wished to be returned. This meant, in effect, that a person chosen for his outstanding abilities had more often than not been born in the area and continued to pay taxes on property there, but had long since left it to follow a career elsewhere. Thus Suematsu Kenchō, the Chief of the Local Government Affairs Bureau in Tokyo, returned 'home' to Fukuoka prefecture in order to stand for election. In this context, then, the 'regionalist' candidates must be thought of as having never lived outside their native districts for any length of time.

Regionalism was by no means confined to the countryside, where it generally consisted of each sub-prefecture (*gun*) in a constituency putting forward its own candidate or candidates. Exactly the same general trend was evident in the cities too; and there, perhaps 'parochialism' would be a better term. The Fifth Constituency in Tokyo exemplifies this. This constituency was made up of the two wards (*ku*) of Honjo and Fukagawa. At the beginning of the campaign, the voters in Honjo chose the former head of their ward and deputy president of the Tokyo stock exchange, Ōta Sane, as their candidate for the seat; and since he was popular in his own district at any rate, his election seemed certain. The residents of Fukagawa, however, were disappointed at not having a candidate of their own to pit against their Honjo neighbours' champion. Therefore they decided to nominate a notable man in their own midst, Shibuzawa Eiichi, and sent a deputation to ask him to agree to stand.

Shibuzawa[13] was one of those who had benefited most from the Meiji policies for social emancipation and economic progress. His family had been for generations wealthy farmers, indigo manufacturers, and money-lenders in Saitama prefecture. After the Restoration, he had held a government post until 1873, and had subsequently pursued a brilliant career in banking. Despite these successes, he was not willing to serve in the House of Representatives. Accordingly, when the delegates of the Fukagawa voters met him, and complained that: 'if there was a person in Honjo ward, there was also somebody in Fukagawa ward; and that they did not relish the idea of leaving their own shrine in the alcove in order to carry round somebody else's shrine on their backs',[14] he rejected their proposal. It transpired that he had already had several invitations to stand before this particular delegation visited him; but he was firm in his resolve not to enter parliamentary politics, even going so far as to declare that he would resign the seat if elected. For their part, the Fukagawa electors, not to be outdone, resolved to have Shibuzawa as a candidate regardless of his refusal, and sent him a jocular ultimatum announcing their intention to vote for 'the late Shibuzawa Eiichi'.

Pre-selection of candidates, both party and non-party, by a ballot of voters was quite common, but not the general rule. Like Shibuzawa, Okamoto Takeo (Second Constituency, Mie prefecture) and Seki Naohiko (Third Constituency, Wakayama prefecture) were both 'popular nominees', who were invited to stand by the voters of the area concerned without the formality of a pre-selection ballot. On the other hand, elections to choose the local candidate were definitely held in—to name but a few places—the Eighth and Ninth Constituencies in Tokyo; the Second Constituency, Fukui prefecture; the Third Constituency, Fukushima prefecture; and the Third Constituency, Shizuoka prefecture.

The situation in the capital's Eighth Constituency (Shitaya and Hongō wards) was extremely confused with several aspirants competing for some sort of public or semi-official endorsement in each ward.[15] In Hongō, the electors were asked to say in advance whom they wished to elect, but this investigation did not lead to any decisive results. Similarly, in Shitaya, there was an organized pre-selection poll, but neither of the two persons who came top was eager to stand for the constituency. Eventually, three leading local residents in Shitaya decided to hold a 'ward party' at a restaurant in Ueno, in order to try and reach some agreement on the question of who would best look after the interests of the ward in the House of Representatives. Invitations were sent to more than 250 important wardsmen, although there were only 126 voters in the ward. However, no more than thirty-eight of those invited bothered to attend the meeting. They listened to a number of people making suggestions on the subject of selecting candidates, and there were moments of angry argument. Just when matters were taking a turn for the acrimonious worst, somebody got up and made 'a half mocking, half jocular, conciliatory speech; and as a result of this, the place gradually quietened down'. The ward party ended happily enough, as a party, with a drinking session; but, as an election nomination meeting, it had done little good.

In Tokyo's Ninth Constituency (Yotsuya, Koishikawa and Ushigome wards), the position was rather better than in the Eighth Constituency since each of the three component wards was able to pin its hopes on a single individual.[16] Consequently three rival candidates emerged to contest the election itself, and all of them enjoyed the united support of their own wards. In Ushigome, the twenty-eight persons who represented the ward in the Tokyo city assembly, met together and, after a formal and secret ballot, selected Hatoyama Kazuo (a lawyer) as the official 'ward candidate'.

It is against this background of keenly felt but extremely narrow local loyalties that there developed a parliamentary and party system in Meiji Japan, though there were, of course, a number of exceptions. A few constituencies, for example Yokohama or the Second Constituency in Aichi prefecture, consisted of a single municipality or sub-prefecture; and in them, the ways in which candidates were picked and ran their campaigns naturally differed from the standard inter-ward and inter-sub-prefectural contests. In other cases, though a constituency might contain more than one sub-prefecture, a particular contestant was of such commanding influence that he enjoyed a wide measure of support throughout the constituency as a whole, and not just in one part of it. An instance of this was the Second Constituency (Yoshida and Sakai sub-prefectures) in Fukui prefecture. There, the election of one of the candidates, Sugita Teiichi, was a virtual certainty from a time long before the campaign actually opened. Sugita was immensely popular all over Fukui prefecture, and a prominent member of the national Liberal movement as well. At the time of the election, he was chairman of the prefectural assembly, and living in Sakai sub-prefecture. However, his candidature was formally approved on 7 and 8 June not only by the village headmen and voters of Sakai but also by those of Yoshida sub-prefecture.[17] Here is an instance of the 'local nomination' and 'party nomination' aspects of the campaign becoming indistinguishable.

Constituencies where there was this degree of fusion between the nascent national party movement and older district loyalties were not uncommon. The Third Constituency in Fukushima prefecture returned as its Members two leading *Daidō Club* politicians and men of affairs, Kōno Hironaka and Suzuki Man-jirō. Both of them were locally popular as well as nationally famous; and a formal nomination-of-candidates-meeting held by the *Daidō Club* in Shirakawa-machi on 19 June was carried out in the spirit of a public endorsement rally.[18] Even though there were five sub-prefectures in this constituency, Kōno alone polled more than 1,500 votes.

A notably elaborate pre-selection ballot was conducted in the Third Constituency, Shizuoka prefecture, by an organization known as the Natives Party—clearly a strictly regional body.[19] Since the constituency was largely rural, holding such a ballot took more time and trouble than it would have done in the towns. What the Natives Party did was to poll its supporters in every village in the constituency. These ballots were then sent to the town of Fujieda-machi, where on 6 June they were counted at a meeting of all those interested in securing the Natives Party nomination. Almost a thousand votes had been cast in this pre-selection ballot; the counting of them took place in a local restaurant, and lasted some twelve hours. Whether the checking of the votes was so drawn out because the candidates themselves were acting as scrutineers, or whether it was because they were working in surroundings conducive to relaxation, is anybody's guess.

These examples of pre-selection of candidates by ballots or other means give a picture of fairly vigorous local interest and community participation in the election of 1890. This picture reinforces other evidence of regionalism and communal self-government under the Tokugawa régime. Moreover, in so far as 'local nominations' were substantially the same as 'party nominations', the recently imported party movement was acquiring a basis in the traditional experience of the people. This was happening to some degree in at least one half of the total number of constituencies; and in their case, it is possible to see that Meiji politics were beginning to change the old regional and personal ties into a national and party system of eventual government.

On the other hand, what of the remaining half of the total number of constituencies, where the party movement was either not very strong or not very successful? Did the desire to elect at all costs a local 'somebody' mean that the candidate returned in such areas was usually a national 'nobody'? It was perhaps inevitable that an individual's continued residence in his native district should have sometimes outweighed different and possibly more sterling qualifications in other individuals, when it came to making a pre-selection of candidates. Yet even in those constituencies where party politics had not yet made much impact, the gulf between local and national interests was often bridged by the electors' desire, if only for reasons of parish pride, to sponsor somebody of widely recognized standing based on personal achievement. This is true, of course, only of places where there was a definite attempt by at least one responsible group of citizens to nominate a suitable candidate. In many constituencies, no such attempt was made, and they fell by default into the hands of the 'self-nominated' Independents. The practice of local nomination by a group representing the general body of voters in a district carried with it the obvious danger of splitting a constituency into several mutually antagonistic territorial parts. Nevertheless, in those areas not touched by party politics, it was better on balance to have such a practice; because the Independent candidates so chosen were usually of higher calibre than their self-nominated brethren.

All this speaks well for the political good sense of the voters and leading personalities in the areas concerned. At the same time, it should be remembered that their ability to pick the best man for the job was facilitated by the very absence of party politics in those places, by the small size of the electorates, and—last but not least—by the seeming infrequency of serious local issues of the sort that would have brought a little community into sharp conflict with the external world or divided it hopelessly against itself. At ground level, the election may be seen as a complicated tangle of regional and personal rivalries. In those places where the system of local nomination worked best, it was hardly ever regarded as an opportunity to seek redress for injuries suffered by a community (i.e. a city ward, or a rural sub-prefecture) as a whole or else to find new outlets for its internal squabbles, as once the 'official' nomination had been decided, a united front would be customarily presented to outsiders.

Generally speaking, the most desirable type of candidate for the non-party nominations was someone who had established a reputation outside the local community, and yet was prepared to look after its interests if and when he was returned to the Diet. Although Seki Naohiko owed much of his electoral strength to the support given him by relatives who had continued to live in Wakayama after he himself left it, his bid for the Third Constituency in that prefecture was undoubtedly helped by the name he had made for himself as a friend of the people a few months before the election. In 1889, Wakayama suffered extensive flood damage. Seki had set up a relief fund in Tokyo as soon as news of the disaster reached the capital; and when the Governor of Wakayama, accompanied by the chairman of the prefectural assembly and other delegates, visited Tokyo in order to enlist the aid of the Government, he did all that he could to make their mission successful.[20]

Seki's career had been one of outstanding personal achievement. His success as an individual was paralleled by that of the other locally nominated Independents mentioned: Suematsu Kenchō, Okamoto Takeo, Ōta Sane, Shibuzawa Eiichi and Hatoyama Kazuo. Electors up and down the land may well have been right in believing that national fame was an indication of strong and conscientious character. Certainly, the convergence of local affiliations and personal distinction could be expected to be irresistible when it occurred, at any rate within the restricted ambit of a ward or sub-prefecture.

For the inhabitants of Shitaya ward in Tokyo, the general election did coincide with a local issue of considerable dimensions. They had set themselves against a proposal by the Japan Railways Company to construct a line across a section of the inner city from Ueno to Akihabara.[21] The Company wished to do this in order to complete its network of lines in that area, and had made plans to lay a surface railway as this promised to be the cheapest method of construction. The people of Shitaya, whose homes and businesses lay in the path of the proposed line, objected strenuously on the grounds that it was unnecessary and would endanger their lives and be harmful to the commercial prosperity of their ward. A public petition signed by more than 3,000 was presented to the authorities in April, and the Government then made an official investigation into the matter. Since it erupted about the time of the opening of the parliamentary campaign, this purely local dispute was bound to get entangled in the general scrimmaging for popular favour that went on in the ward. At least one candidate (unsuccessful) made as much capital as he could out of his part in taking the lead in the struggle against the Japan Railways Company.

One of the most interesting contests in the election took place in the Twelfth Constituency, Tokyo *fu*—an outlying, rural region. There, the principal protagonists were Hirabayashi Kyūbei and his nephew Takagi Masatoshi. Both Hirabayashi and Takagi were self-nominated candidates, standing with a good deal of local support; and both of them were members of the prefectural assembly. Some of the villagers in the constituency were said to have given their support to Hirabayashi, because when the assembly passed a by-law against the carrying of manure during the day-time, he had been in favour of allowing this so long as the buckets used for the job were covered.[22] Though accounts of the Twelfth Constituency contest mention this detail, the play of legitimate but trivial interests like this was negligible in comparison with the force of longer standing rivalries between different villages in the area. In the event, after a campaign that involved family quarrels as well as village feuds, Hirabayashi was runner-up.

It could sometimes happen that the same locality would produce two or more publicly chosen or widely favoured candidates. For example, in the Third Constituency (Kyōbashi ward) in Tokyo, there were at least four candidates enjoying approximately the same amount of support from the electors.[23] In a few places, the local 'bosses', gangster or otherwise, were strong enough to dictate who should be chosen as candidates and to affect, if not actually to determine, the results of the voting.[24]

These instances of a number of strong candidates in one small area, or of boss control, were but extreme examples of the influence of personality. This influence, together with the more powerful promptings of localism and the lesser incentive of sectional interests, was responsible for the general pattern of constituency by constituency nominations and campaigns. These three factors were in their own way just as important as the 'national politics' of the election, such as the role of the Diet, extension of national rights, and so on. In terms of them and by means of them the parliamentary system had to work.

(2) SPEECH MEETINGS AND CANVASSING

Certain constituencies, both inside and outside the cities, suffered from a dearth of suitable candidates. The Shibuzawa contretemps, and the unwillingness of some people in the Hongō and Shitaya wards to stand for election, show this. Similarly, no candidates had been sponsored or come forward in the Fifth Constituency, Yamaguchi prefecture, as on 10 June;[25] and candidates chosen for the island of Sado (Niigata prefecture) and for an area in Hyōgo prefecture did not leave Tokyo until 26 June, because of delays in nominating them.[26]

2. SPEECH MEETINGS AND CANVASSING

Such late starts were the exception, as most of the candidates began their campaigns during May and continued them through June. Tactics employed during these campaigns varied widely, covering the whole gamut of the permissible and the not so permissible—from speech meetings, canvassing, posters, newspaper advertisements, social gatherings and other forms of entertainment, on the one hand, to bribery, slander, violence, crude intimidation and trickery on the other.

With candidates who campaigned fairly, by far the most common way of making their views known to the electors and meeting them individually was to organize a speech meeting, followed by a party. A candidate no longer resident in his native prefecture naturally found it convenient to return home for a short while, and base his efforts on a quick tour of the constituency for which he wished to be elected, making speeches and meeting as many of its inhabitants as he could—sometimes finding that he had to leave it at that, and go back to Tokyo before the date of the poll. In such a case, of course, a strong candidate relied on his supporters in the constituency to canvass for him.

Suematsu Kenchō (Independent), who was returned for the Eighth Constituency in Fukuoka prefecture, fought his electoral battle along these general lines. He left Tokyo to start nursing his constituency early in May, and apparently did not go away from it again until after the election. During this period of eight weeks or so, he gave a large number of speeches and attended many social functions. A newspaper report gives some details about three of these engagements. On 16 May, he visited the secondary school of Toyotsu, and made a speech to its students at the request of the headmaster. On 18 May, he was invited to a banquet given by a Mr Koimai, who lived in the village of Unshima in Kōge sub-prefecture. The banquet was attended by more than 400 other guests. Finally, on 21 May, Suematsu was present at a social gathering held at another village (Nishisaigawa) in Nakatsu sub-prefecture, and was asked to address the meeting.[27]

From this account of his activities, it is apparent that Suematsu's campaign exemplified the method of personal endeavour at its best and most successful. The candidate travelled widely throughout the constituency, speaking and meeting people wherever possible. His energetic approach to the problem of electioneering and the general esteem it earned him stirred the opposition faction in the constituency, the *Buzen Club*, into copying his methods. It, too, held speech meetings in Toyotsu and elsewhere, and tried hard to recruit members.

The two months Suematsu Kenchō seems to have spent in his constituency was probably rather longer than was usually the case with 'outside' candidates, and certainly longer than some of them allowed for their final campaigning. For instance, Suematsu's namesake and fellow official, Suematsu Saburō, did not arrive in the First Constituency, Yamaguchi prefecture, for which he was elected, until after 20 June. His campaign, once it did get under way, resembled Suematsu Kenchō's in that it consisted of a series of speech meetings and parties.[28] Though Saburō (a Ministry of Justice official) was so late in putting in his last appearance before the election, he had visited the constituency on a number of occasions in the previous twelve months in order to prepare the way for his candidature.

No doubt, as a newspaper editor, Okamoto Takeo found it difficult to leave Tokyo for any length of time. So far as can be judged from press reports, he was in his constituency (Second Constituency, Mie prefecture) for only four days—that is, from 26 May to 29 May.[29] On the other hand, he made full use of his four days. He started by holding a speech meeting in a theatre in one of the chief towns of the area, Yokkaichi (Mie *gun*), entertaining his audience to a party afterwards. Then he travelled to Tsu (Ano *gun*), another important local centre, to repeat the procedure. 27 May was taken up with another big speech meeting and party in the village of Isshinden (Ange *gun*); and two days later, on 29 May, he delivered his final address to an audience in Kameyama village (Suzuka *gun*), following it, too, with an entertainment. Thus, within a week, Okamoto had visited and talked to voters in each of the main divisions of his constituency. His tour, rapid though it was, was hardly perfunctory.

Speech meetings, when arranged, were popular, and the candidates do not seem to have had any cause to worry whether they could attract an audience. The custom of giving a party after the speeches may have had something to do with this, but the following audience figures are impressive, especially when the average number of voters per constituency was only 1,750:

25 May, Saitama prefecture, 'more than three hundred';
17 June, Ibaraki prefecture, 'more than fifteen hundred';
18 June, Shizuoka prefecture, 'more than three thousand';
26 June, Fukushima prefecture, 'more than one thousand'.

There was a case of an audience numbering no more than 'twenty or thirty'. This was in a village (Yoshida *mura*, Mino *gun*) in Okayama prefecture, where a speech meeting on 14 June apparently clashed with a period of exceptional activity in the rice-fields. Those villagers who did abandon their crops for politics heard the speaker talk about the need to elect industrialists (he was one himself), responsible Cabinets, the political systems of Germany and France and so forth.[30] Speech meetings were attended not only by the electors of a district but also by its other inhabitants as well; and the presence of women in the audiences was noted on a number of occasions.

What appears to have been the most spectacular speech meeting of the entire campaign was held in the main centre of Aichi prefecture, Nagoya city. It was arranged for three successive days—8, 9 and 10 June. The electoral struggle was particularly keen all over Aichi prefecture, but nowhere was it fiercer than in the First Constituency (Nagoya), where the principal candidates for the single seat were Kunishima Haku (*Kōin Club*) and Horibe Katsushirō (Nagoya Discussion Society, and chairman of the city assembly). The speech meeting was organized by the *Kōin Club*, and took place in one of the city halls. Though formal invitations were sent to only 500 voters, more than 3,000 people attended on each of the three days. Kunishima himself spoke on three main topics: the reduction of taxes and the position of ministers of State, on the first day; pruning administrative costs and the enactment of new legislation, on the second day; and problems of national defence, on the third day. Other *Kōin Club* members spoke in support of Kunishima on each occasion, and attacked the opposition groups. After the meeting, printed notes of Kunishima's speeches were distributed to electors throughout the constituency.[31]

The report of this particular speech meeting included a short description of the scene inside the hall where it was held. Such descriptions are rare.

Across the entrance to the meeting place was stretched a great curtain with the two words LIBERTY FOREVER written on it. In addition, national sun emblems and flags, inscribed with LONG LIVE THE EMPEROR, were standing crossed with each other here and there. Around the dais, there was a big banner with the words SINCERITY MOVES HEAVEN in large letters on it. Moreover, they had added brilliancy by installing electric lights.[32]

The nineteenth-century Japanese were no strangers to the idea of showmanship in the theatre, religious festivals and elsewhere. The Aichi prefecture *Kōin Club* would seem to have successfully married this tradition to the more modern requirements of Liberal polemics and national *élan*.

It was quite usual for more than one speaker to address a meeting. Generally, the candidate was introduced by a leading local supporter, and after he had made his speech, other sympathizers would speak in turn. Sometimes a single speech meeting or a series of speech meetings were conducted by local supporters of a party, without the participation of their candidate.

With the exception of Itagaki, who was ineligible because of his peerage to sit in the House of Representatives, none of the leading national politicians went on a tour to raise support for their cause in all quarters of the Empire; and most candidates confined their campaigning to their own constituencies. However, Nakajima Matagorō, who contested a seat in Fukui prefecture, spoke at a meeting held in Tokyo on 28 June; and well-known candidates sometimes spoke on behalf of political colleagues in constituencies adjoining their own. In the villages, the customary venue for a speech meeting was either a private house, a temple, or some sort of public hall; in the cities, theatres or large assembly rooms were often used. Open-air gatherings were not common. Frequently, the meetings were interrupted or brought to a tumultuous and premature close by the intervention of hecklers and semi-professional rowdies (*sōshi*).

As a variant of the orthodox, one-party type of speech meeting, a public debate between two or more rival candidates was occasionally attempted. One of the more successful of these, comparatively speaking, was organized in the Eighth Constituency, Hiroshima prefecture.[33] Persons representing eleven villages asked the three candidates for the seat if they would meet together and publicly state their views on the Imperial Diet in turn, so that the electors in their area would have a chance to determine impartially which of them was the most deserving of their support. One of the candidates, a former local official, replied that he did not yet have any special point of view on the functions of the Diet. Hearing this, the voters' delegation promptly withdrew their invitation. The remaining two candidates, Inoue Kakugorō (*Daidō Club*) and Tsugawa Migiyumi (member of the prefectural assembly), both accepted, even though the latter also stated that he did not have any definite ideas on the subject proposed for debate. As a result, a public debate in one of the village temples was arranged for 13 June.

In the Sixth Constituency of Kanagawa prefecture, some of the local people tried to arrange a similar public discussion among the three candidates.[34] This time, only one of the three agreed to the suggestion. He was Mizushima Yasutarō, a member of the prefectural assembly. Therefore, when the meeting was opened—again in a temple—at Isebara on 16 June, it took the form of a straightforward speech meeting on behalf of the Mizushima faction. The idea of holding these debates may have been a development of traditional Buddhist practice. Itinerant priests frequently visited local temples, and on occasion there were formal disputations between different groups of clerics.

The social gatherings (*konshinkai*) that normally followed speech meetings served an obvious and useful purpose in enabling the candidate to meet his supporters and the voters in a less ceremonious atmosphere. With politicians who were both honest and capable, their function was no doubt restricted to this; but if the candidate was not a very good orator, or if he was not above trying to corrupt the electors, the *konshinkai*, instead of being secondary to the speech meetings in the general priorities of campaigning, could easily take precedence over them and even replace them altogether. The border between legitimate entertainment and outright corruption was necessarily ill-defined and correspondingly easy to cross. At the very least, a party could be arranged with the tacit assumption that those invited would feel obliged to repay their host with their votes in due course.

The absence of any legal limit to campaign expenses encouraged this type of electioneering; and it was highly successful in a number of places. For example, a message from Gifu prefecture reported that in conditions of economic depression, the restaurant trade alone was flourishing 'with guests at all hours of the day and night, while singing and music issue forth'.[35] A few weeks later, a telegram from Fukui prefecture announced that: 'Among the candidates in the Third Constituency, the campaign of Mr Nakajima Matagorō's party has been specially noteworthy for its impartiality; but it seems that the banquets of the opposition party are gradually influencing public opinion.'[36] Even though a second cable modified the first[37] with the news that the 'mobile speeches' of the Nakajima faction had overcome the 'banquet opposition' of the Nagata party, it was all to no avail. Nagata won the election, without having to answer any bribery charges.

On occasion, these methods of persuasion back-fired on their users. One candidate in Tokyo was apparently very doubtful from the start of his chances of election; yet since he was a local celebrity, he felt that his prestige would suffer if he failed to stand. Consequently, he stuck up posters in his home ward announcing that he was a candidate. This brought most of the electors in the constituency to his door, wanting to hear his views on politics. Naturally, he could not give his visitors the cold shoulder, and

emptying his purse, which was not so heavy, he treated them to sake and food. For those who were important men, he bought some rather valuable objects. His household became bankrupt before the election, with his wife, children, and entire family giving loud voice to their innumerable complaints, and making his life a misery. Nevertheless, on 1 July, he riskily went out on the spree, diverting others as well as himself. But when the votes were counted on the 2nd—alas, alas—all those on whom he had been counting were turncoats. His own score— a mere three votes![38]

Graft also had its setbacks in the Twelfth Constituency of Tokyo. This constituency consisted of Ebara sub-prefecture on the mainland outside the urban limits of the city, and the Seven Islands of Izu at the entrance to Tokyo Bay. The chief contenders for it were an uncle and nephew, Hirabayashi Kyūbei and Takagi Masatoshi. The following account of some of the incidents in the strife between these two is worth re-telling in full. Not just because of its humorous qualities, but because it reveals practices and conditions which must have had their counterparts in many other regions.

A STRANGE TALE OF RIVALRY[39]

In the Twelfth Constituency of a locality which we shall not specify, there is an old man called —bayashi. For a long time he has been a member of the local assembly, and since he also served as head-fisherman, he ranked first among the distinguished men of the sub-prefecture. He had a nephew called Taka—, who, despite the fact that he was very young, had a great deal of ability. So he, too, was elected to the assembly, and the influence of the nephew was not inferior to that of the uncle. These two were on friendly terms in the local assembly, as might be expected seeing that they were uncle and nephew.

Therefore, at the time when the constitution was promulgated last year, they both had the opinion that in that sub-prefecture they were second to none. They were under the impression that running as a candidate for the Diet would in fact present no difficulties, especially if they had the assistance of their relative. Accordingly, they were unable to restrain themselves. First of all, they privately sounded out people to see how the ground lay, and having come to the conclusion that there were no other candidates and that the moment was a propitious one, they both came out [as candidates] at the same time. Whereupon, [feeling] that the person whose help they had been counting on up till then had failed them...uncle...nephew...both parted in silence.

After a while, the nephew, Taka—, fell sick; and the uncle, beside himself with joy, made full use of the chance to extend his influence. In the meantime, unfortunately [for the uncle], he [the nephew] soon recovered, and sent out celebratory [presents of] rice-cakes and dried bonito to the electors throughout the sub-prefecture. When he heard of this, —bayashi's indignation knew no bounds. 'You really are a man of gratitude! After all, those who to-day are in the assembly, and up till now have been thought of as gentlemen by the public, all enjoyed the patronage of me, your uncle...You, in particular, have long since said that you hold to the principle of honouring one's seniors; but what your lips [say] is different from what your heart [thinks], and your action in sending out rice-cakes in order to shut out your uncle is most strange and uncalled for. You'll pay for it, you...young Taka—you!'

So saying, [the uncle] summoned a family council on that very day, and declared: 'Well, I am going to seek your advice. As you will already know, I have a popularity in this sub-prefecture quite beyond my deserts, and it is my intention to run for the Diet. However a certain imprudent nephew of mine has distributed rice-cakes throughout the sub-prefecture in celebration of a recovery [from illness], so that he might cross swords with me, and seems to have had a great effect on public opinion. Since I feel that for me to be defeated by him would be the mistake of a lifetime, I have decided to spend ten thousand yen out of my own fortune on election expenses. While I do not for a moment expect you to oppose [my scheme], I am letting you know to make sure.' Since there was no reason why the listeners should object to the old man's saying that he would use his own money himself, they all said 'Very well'. Whereupon old —bayashi, with a broad smile, but without saying 'Bravo, bravo!' or anything at all [of that nature] said: 'In that case, would you at any rate please put your seals on this document to signify that you have no objections'; and they all of them covered it with their seals.

News of this quickly spread; and as this was more promising than rice-cakes, —bayashi became popular all of a sudden. —bayashi did not idle his time away; but spent money on a speech meeting in one place and a social gathering somewhere else, and entertained the electors. He also spent money on a second meeting after this. On that occasion, when the second meeting was drawing to a close, people suggested that a third meeting should be held in a local brothel. After the hero had agreed to be involved in that, they decided to make a move at once. However one old man (aged sixty) declined, saying: 'I am sixty this year, and have grandchildren. More especially, up till now I have never bought a harlot, not even once, and so I beg you to excuse me in this matter only.' Answering 'Come, come, don't say such things!', they took him by force to a certain house.

Well, the very old man had a really wonderful time. The previous night's refusal completely forgotten, he himself insisted on spending the next evening there alone. As a result, his son came to hear that he was spending his time out of doors buying harlots. After he had at last learnt the full story, the son, flaming with anger, said—'You silly old fool, —bayashi! How dare you lead my pure and spotless father into profligacy! Very well, I, too, know a trick or two.' Thereafter the son attached himself to the nephew, Taka—, and it is said that he is working very hard for Taka— and is doing his utmost to bring about the failure of —bayashi. Well, well, well.

As a postscript to this tale of misjudged endeavour, it might be added that Takagi Masatoshi after being elected for the constituency in 1890, was subsequently re-elected no fewer than fourteen times, and had a long and distinguished career in the House of Representatives.

There are no means of telling whether Hirabayashi did in fact get through the ¥10,000 he was said to have been willing to spend on his campaign. The *Yūbin-Hōchi Shimbun* stated that a candidate would have to spend at least ¥600–700 on electioneering. With the maximum figure put at several thousand yen, it calculated the mean as ¥1,000.[40] The *Tokyo Nichi Nichi Shimbun* agreed that campaign expenses for each candidate were, on the average, in the region of ¥1,000.[41] Converting these figures into pounds sterling, they represent, approximately, a minimum of £60–70, a maximum of several hundreds of pounds, and an average of £100—all estimated at values for Victorian era currency. One self-nominated Independent in Saitama prefecture was said to have sold his properties to raise more than ¥10,000 (£1,000) for his campaign funds.[42] This class of candidates was naturally expected to pay for its adventures into national politics, with perhaps a few contributions from their backers if they had any. On the other hand, candidates who had been asked to stand by a group of voters in the constituency, or else had been nominated by a party, could generally count on considerable financial assistance.[43]

Canvassing was not confined to speeches and suppers. In places where the local sub-prefect (*gunchō*) had resigned to run as a candidate, he could often rely on the village headmen and other people who were under an obligation to him to press his case. The Sixth Constituency in Osaka prefecture was an area where the former *gunchō* was elected in this way.[44] Buddhist priests, too, sometimes helped certain candidates; but, in general, the monks did not interfere very much in the electioneering. Then again, candidates would usually find their families, personal friends, admirers and, possibly, trade acquaintances ready to canvass for them. In the Third Constituency (Kyōbashi ward), Tokyo, four or five of the candidates each had his own little band of active supporters. One of these partisans was a woman who ran a hairdressing business.[45] In Asakusa ward, also Tokyo, a group of people were reported to be in favour of one candidate because they hoped to lend him money after he was elected.[46]

When a candidate was sponsored by a party or a sizeable political club, fellow members naturally often helped to solicit the voters' support by visiting their houses, distributing leaflets and so forth. Thus, a contest fought on a party basis would tend to give rise to vigorous canvassing from both sides, though this was not necessarily always the case. In Yamaguchi prefecture, the strongly entrenched *Bōchō Club* seems to have had it all its own way in three of the five constituencies.[47] On the other hand, in Chiba prefecture, a victory for the Progressive Party candidate in the Fourth Constituency appeared certain at one time; largely because there was nobody of like calibre to oppose him. The local Liberals, however, were not pleased with this state of affairs, and eventually found a suitable opponent for the Progressive champion in the managing director of a Tokyo soy sauce company, one Nishimura Jinuemon. Nishimura, accompanied by a couple of aides, canvassed the two sub-prefectures (Unakami and Sōsa) which formed the Fourth Constituency so thoroughly that he won it in the teeth of fierce counter-attacks, and despite the fact that his campaign had lasted less than a month.[48]

Yet it was probably in Aichi prefecture, where election fever was more sustained than in most other places, that organized canvassing was carried furthest. The pace was set by the *Aichi Kōin Club*, the only political body that was active in all parts of the prefecture; but rival candidates were not exactly negligent, as the following item shows.

The *Aichi Kōin Club* is publishing the pictures and personal histories of the candidates with whom it has an understanding in the columns of its paper, the *Shin Aichi*, every day. It is also holding speech meetings in every district, and is working hard to increase its influence. Moreover the other candidates, too, all have their own right hand men; and, at their own discretion, they assemble [them] together, or invite the electors to social parties, or send out canvassers and spokesmen in all directions to give explanations at every door and to seek the approval of each individual.[49]

While much of the canvassing that went on in Aichi and elsewhere was carried out by the candidates themselves and by unpaid volunteer helpers, there was also a class of professional vote-solicitors and election agents. The *Tokyo Nichi Nichi Shimbun* described on 18 June the activities of some of these professional canvassers and the candidates who employed them in an article on the election campaign in Saitama prefecture:

In the area around Kodama-machi, in the Fifth Constituency, it was a common practice last year [at the time of the election of half the members of the prefectural assembly] to distribute to the electors presents of cloth or bags for sugar, together with visiting cards on which were written the personal histories [of the candidates]...However they [the candidates] have changed their ways since the promulgation of the penal regulations on the first of this month. [Now] they make use of persons who have engaged in pettifogging activities in the past, sending them out everywhere to find the people, give presents of money, goods, or banquets, and prevail upon the electors.

These pettifoggers, whose chief stock in trade would have been a smooth tongue and a fat purse, should not be confused with another sort of 'agent' sometimes hired by candidates—the strongman (*sōshi*), with a big stick, who dealt in blows and intimidation. Nevertheless the general standards of the pettifoggers, wherever they were employed, could have hardly risen much above the level indicated.

A few candidates were fortunate enough not to have to bother much with canvassing, and so were able to do without professional agents. Seki Nachiko, for instance, was favoured by a seemingly irreversible tide of popularity. He did virtually all his campaigning from his room in the *Fujigen* hostelry, in the centre of Wakayama city.

There, he was visited, day in and day out, by a stream of relatives, friends and political supporters, who between them were sufficiently strong to ensure his election from a rural part of Wakayama prefecture. Seki, however, must have thought it prudent to set the seal on public approval of his candidature by arranging a special service in commemoration of his dead parents in one of the Buddhist temples in Wakayama. At the service, he gave hulled rice to 600 or 700 indigent citizens. 'There was not one who did not weep for joy. Each took away a bag of rice, and paid homage to the tombs of his ancestors.'[50]

Perhaps even more popular than Seki was Nakajima Nobuyuki. Originally selected as the Liberal candidate for Yokohama where he had had a redoubtable opponent in Shimada Saburō, Nakajima resigned this candidature half way through June after having accepted a request from the electors in the Fifth Constituency, Kanagawa prefecture, that he should stand there. Clearly, he cannot have had many doubts about the wisdom of this transfer. He spent the last week of the campaign on daily fishing trips out at sea off the port of Yokohama, clad in a white singlet and accompanied by a student-servant.[51] Such *sang-froid* was shown only by the handful of candidates who could be sure of success, or by the more numerous band of those who had every reason to fear the worst.

2. SPEECH MEETINGS AND CANVASSING

The effect of all this speech making and canvassing was not the same everywhere in the country. In some places—and the contest in Fukui prefecture between Nakajima Matagorō and Nagata Sadauemon was a case in point—a campaign based on lavish entertainment of the voters robbed a well-known and upstanding politician of his chance of a seat in the Diet. Nagata, though unheard of outside his prefecture, was a man of some standing and repute inside it. Such local residents, enjoying the advantages of permanent influence and connexions in the constituency, were often nuts too tough for even the most gifted of 'outside' candidates to crack.

Something similar happened in the Eighth Constituency, Hiroshima prefecture, where the seat was won by a recently resigned member of the prefectural administration, even though he had annoyed some voters by refusing to participate in a debate on the role of the Imperial Diet as an organ of national government.[52] One of his defeated opponents was Inoue Kakugorō, a national politician who spent most of his time in Tokyo. In 1890, Inoue was a leader of the *Daidō Club* and noted for his eloquence. His oratorical and open methods of campaigning had differed markedly from the victor's exercise of covert influence. On the other hand, the candidatures of Suematsu Kenchō and Nishimura Jinuemon[53]—to name but two individuals who did not normally reside in the areas for which they stood— met with complete success; and Inoue Kakugorō, himself, was subsequently elected for another constituency in Hiroshima prefecture, at a by-election held before the opening of the Diet in November 1890.

Stories of voters having been prevailed upon to give their vote to more than one candidate, or otherwise bamboozled by the tidal wave of canvassing and the less obvious pressures of village politics, were by no means uncommon. Yet the overall impact of such petty dilemmas and concealed coercions was far from disastrous to the election as a whole. The *Tokyo Nichi Nichi Shimbun* seems to have captured the ambivalence of this situation in a short humorous sketch, published on the election morning of 1 July. This indicated that although progress, in its constitutional aspects, had brought a certain amount of harassment for those citizens it had endowed with the vote, its technological improvements afforded possible means of escape—at any rate for voters living at not too great a distance from a railway station. The scene is set in the carriages of a train about to leave Tokyo for Yokohama:

While candidates are chasing round valiantly, the electors are making desperate efforts to escape. [This state of affairs may be likened to] a revolving lantern [or] scissor chess. 'Goodness, Gembei-san, you too?' 'Dear me, Hachiemon-san, you as well?' 'Ah well, I have just about had enough of ultimatums and boasting from all sides. [The election] is all very well; but if we poor merchants are silly enough to support one side, we shall lose valuable custom.' 'Neither the Diet nor the Members can take the place of trade.' 'Well I am just off to lay in stock, and at the same time to Yokohama.' 'Ha, ha, ha, me too!' The departure bell rings, the engine gives a hoot...Ah![54]

The moral that electors were able to take care of themselves was generally true for districts outside the capital as well as in it. Too much can be read into the prevalence of banquet competitions; and the unfair influence which the pressures of local interests or potentates could, and did, have over the minds of electors should not be exaggerated. Thus, there was nothing to stop an elector from being entertained by more than one candidate; and in contests where this form of electioneering was *de rigueur*, the general effect of these entertainments would have been to cancel each other out. This principle of neutralization appears to hold good not only for what occurred within a constituency, but also for comparisons between constituencies.

Even if a banquet candidate triumphed in one area, a person depending on the same tactics might well be disappointed somewhere else. A Nakajima Matagorō went down amidst the clatter of plates and drinking of glasses in Fukui prefecture; but a Nakajima Nobuyuki could be returned without having to bestir himself unduly in Kanagawa. Similarly, village and ward politics, or social considerations, did tilt the balance in favour of certain inferior candidates in several places. Yet in others, as has been shown, localism took the far less reprehensible form of an earnest desire to elect the best man available to represent the community as a whole. In keeping with this, speech meetings were well attended even when they were not followed by a party.

This sort of evidence leads to the conclusion that, despite the large number of particular instances illustrating the contrary, the general body of electors in 1890 had a mind of its own. Moreover, it was capable of expressing this mind. As a result, the first House of Representatives, in so far as it contained a clear majority of Liberal or Progressive opponents of the Government and also a substantial minority of pro-Government or Independent Members, represented, crudely maybe but none the less effectively, the settled 'public opinion' of the electorate. Dark horses of one kind or another there may well have been, even among the ranks of elected Members; but in terms of real political power, such persons were a negligible quantity.

Apart from editorial comment and reporting of important speeches, there were a number of ways in which newspapers were used or lent themselves as a means of communication between candidates and voters. The electioneering advertisements frequently displayed in the press stated that an elector or a group of electors intended to vote for a particular candidate. Such announcements appeared only rarely, if at all, in the big Tokyo papers, but were very common in the provincial journals. Assuming that they were paid for by the voters concerned rather than by the candidates, the motive behind their insertion in some instances was possibly no more than a desire on the elector's part to publicize his choice in order to be spared further approaches from opposition factions. In the great majority of cases, however, the notices appear to have been sent in to the papers by persons actively friendly to the candidate concerned. This would have been done with the idea of bringing his name to the attention of the public, and perhaps also in order to indicate to waverers which way the bandwagon was likely to move. The following example of those how-I-am-going-to-vote declarations has been taken from a Kōchi prefecture paper:[55]

III. THE ELECTION CAMPAIGN

> We hitherto belonged to the NATIONAL PARTY
> but we have seen the light and now firmly give
> our support to LIBERALISM.
>> Kōchi Sub-prefecture, Shimohayama Village, Himenono
>> Section, Ichikawa Saneyuki.
>> Ditto Sub-prefecture, Ditto Village, Shindokyo Section,
>> Takahashi Tomiji.

Advertisements like this were usually accepted by newspapers purely as a business proposition. As a result, separate notices of support for different candidates sometimes came out on the same page. There was at least one case, however, of a newspaper having refused to publish a voter's announcement,[56] and although most regional papers refrained from flagrant partiality in the electoral struggle, there were some that did not.

The latter not unnaturally made full use of their editorial columns to canvass the electorate. As the campaign grew keener, some of them devoted much of their remaining space to undiluted propaganda. This, it must be realized, was a trait of certain relatively minor provincial papers only. Though the big metropolitan dailies all sided with the Government or with one or other of the political parties, their preferences stopped short of spineless eulogy and they were never rabid in their antagonisms.

It was not always the same elsewhere. In the Ninth Constituency, Osaka *fu*, for instance, the backers of one candidate distributed free copies of the *Kansai Nippō* throughout the district because it gave him favourable publicity.[57] But once again, it is to Aichi prefecture that we must turn for some of the most striking examples of press intervention in the campaign. There, as mentioned previously, the *Aichi Kōin Club* had its own journal, a paper called the *Sin Aichi*. It, too, was sent as a gift to the home of every elector in the prefecture during the campaign. There were also other local dailies, the *Kinjō Shimbun* and the *Fusō Shimbun*, which were just as openly in favour of candidates opposing the *Kōin Club*. Consequently a veritable

160

war of pens developed in the area, with the *Shin Aichi* on the one side and the *Kinjō Shimbun*, together with the *Fusō Shimbun*, on the other side. As all these papers were published in Nagoya, the contest between Kunishima Haku (*Kōin Club*) and Horibe Katsushirō (Nagoya Discussion Society, i.e. Independent) for the seat in Nagoya city (First Constituency, Aichi prefecture) inevitably attracted most of their attention.[58]

The rancour and high feelings displayed in printer's ink in Nagoya during the last few weeks of the election campaign were considered sufficiently remarkable to be retailed in due course in the news columns of the capital too. Although first-hand documentary evidence now can be cited only from the *Kinjō Shimbun*, it is safe to assume that its standards reflected those of the *Shin Aichi* and *Fusō Shimbun* newspapers.

Let it be said at once that the standards eventually adopted by the *Kinjō Shimbun* were deplorably low. Up to about 27 June, this paper, while leaving its readers in no doubt where its sympathies lay, had reported the campaigns in Nagoya and the other constituencies in a reasonably impartial and non-sensational manner. On 27 June, all this changed; perhaps because it looked as if Kunishima was going to win the seat in Nagoya. On that day, the *Kinjō Shimbun* published a venomous attack on him. Its opening paragraph read as follows:

DISHONEST, UNPRINCIPLED KUNISHIMA HAKU

In olden days, men said that evil could sometimes look like virtue and a lie perhaps appear to be the truth. In Nagoya, there is a person called Kunishima Haku. He is evil and full of lies. He is always talking about Liberty and Equality, and though his heart is filthy and black, he wears a mask of integrity and rectitude. What is more, because his heart is filthy and black, he wants to deceive the public and make the people his dupes. But the sun and moon have not yet fallen to the ground, and the gods are still above us. No matter if there is an An Lu-shan in the world, will there not [also] be a Chang Chiu Ling[59] to prophesy rebellion? Likewise, let there be never so many Wang An-shihs, is it likely that men of the stamp of Lu Hui Ch'ing[60] to smell out their great lies will be lacking? KUNISHIMA has behaved in a DISHONEST and UNPRINCIPLED fashion before now; and by exposing this to the world we shall disillusion those whom he has ensnared by other acts of trickery and evil-doing. [Furthermore,] we shall prevail upon gentlemen who share our feelings to join us in reviling this DISHONEST AND UNPRINCIPLED KUNISHIMA. Let him be driven from the woods and forests of self-respecting citizens! Let him be banished to the furthermost regions of our country—there to become food for wolves and tigers! What follows now is a detailed record of KUNISHIMA'S DISHONESTY and LACK OF PRINCIPLE, and it is on the basis of this that we indict him. We beg the public to pay strict attention, and to take a good look at the working of this DISHONEST AND UNPRINCIPLED KUNISHIMA's heart.[61]

After this there came a further two and a half columns of newsprint. All of it simply boiled down to the accusation that Kunishima, a professional advocate, had been guilty of misleading some peasants and inciting them to public disorder for his own personal gain. He had promised to plead their case in a tenancy dispute without charging them either court costs or a lawyer's fee, and had prefaced this offer with the well-known words—'Heaven did not create any man above another, nor did it create any man below another.'[62] The next article on the same page was headed, pointedly enough:

WHO WILL HELP DISHONESTY AND BE ASSOCIATED
WITH THE UNPRINCIPLED?

and ended with the threat: 'If anybody on the first day of next month dares to vote for the DISHONEST Kunishima, the UNPRINCIPLED Kunishima, we will publish his name in the columns of our paper and make it known throughout the length and breadth of the land. Take note of this!'

This anti-Kunishima campaign was continued in successive issues of the *Kinjō Shimbun* up to and including the day of the election. The words DISHONEST and UNPRINCIPLED were splashed across any page containing articles designed to discredit him. When the Nagoya result was announced, it proved to be a victory for Horibe Katsushirō. He polled 236 votes to Kunishima's 134. Both the *Kinjō Shimbun* and the *Fusō Shimbun* were said to have proclaimed the news in special extra editions under an identical headline:

MR HORIBE BANZAI, CITIZENS OF NAGOYA BANZAI![63]

2. SPEECH MEETINGS AND CANVASSING

To this the *Shin Aichi*, making the best of a bad job, replied:

There is yet another Horibe Katsushirō in Niwa sub-prefecture at Inuyama-machi. Therefore, excluding 32 votes which are clearly marked [as having been cast for the Horibe Katsushirō living at] Funeiri-machi Nagoya city, 203 votes cannot be confirmed and must be rejected as invalid. In other words, Mr Kunishima has the greatest number of votes that are valid. Long live our party! Liberty for ever!

But after announcing a 'victory' banquet for Kunishima, and a further run of bickering, charges and counter-charges, it was at length compelled to admit defeat.

Before these final skirmishes, and before the voting took place, the public had been informed that: Kunishima had gone mad (*Kinjō Shimbun*); Kunishima had been taken into custody (*Fusō Shimbun*); Horibe had been put on trial (*Shin Aichi*); Horibe had killed himself (*Shin Aichi*).[64] Stories of this sort were not as a rule spread by the newspapers, but slandering one's opponent or circulating rumours that would act to his disadvantage was a very common ruse. Suematsu Kenchō stated that it was used most frequently by self-nominated Independents and by members of small parties which had little chance of victory, adding the comment that 'The parties with a lot of influence wanted the election to take place as quietly as possible, with no aftermath of unpleasantness'.[65] This judgement would seem to be correct as a general summing up of the situation; though in the instance recorded above, one candidate belonged to the *Kōin Club*. Campaigning by innuendo was definitely illegal under the terms of the Supplementary Penal Regulations; but it was an almost impossible task to trace a particular rumour back to its source so that a criminal action could be brought. Consequently this was a way of defying the law and harassing one's opponent that was both simple and safe.

The snakes of rumour could be made to hiss for one side or the other in a number of different ways, ingenious and not so ingenious. In Ashikita sub-prefecture, Kumamoto prefecture, where, it was said, bribery had become old fashioned, physical force was no longer interesting, and bottle and candy tactics were also out of favour, falsehood was used in a manner that incriminated the highest in the land. Supporters of the National Rights Party visited the homes of every elector in the sub-prefecture, and carefully but quite mendaciously explained that the Marquis Hosokawa (the former daimyo of the area) and the Emperor himself had both of their own free will contributed to its campaign funds. Therefore anyone who voted for the rival Progressive Party candidate would not only be guilty of disloyalty to the ex-daimyo, but would also be committing what amounted to high treason.[66] In Osaka, one candidate was everywhere maligned on account of the unpleasant friends he had;[67] and another was wrongly reported to be not eligible for election.[68]

Suematsu described a rather more elaborate trick played on him in his own constituency in Fukuoka prefecture. His anecdote is best told in his own words:

Moreover, in my own constituency, the opposition party—in order to collect an audience for a speech meeting that they were going to have—informed interested persons in the neighbourhood by letter that their candidate and I would hold a public debate. Furthermore, copying the example of the travelling advertisements for the theatre in rural areas, they went from village to village, waving flags and beating drums, to spread the news about the public debate. [By these means, they managed to] assemble a large audience. When the time came to open the meeting, they announced 'Suematsu is too frightened to come.' The slander was repeated several times, and, worst of all, they had no scruples about publishing it in the newspapers even.[69]

The same commentator, when discussing the general part played by rumour in the campaigning, mentioned that an acquaintance of his who was standing for election suddenly discovered that he was the victim of an 'arrest of candidate' story put about on the eve of the poll. In this case, all the injured person could think of doing to counteract its damaging effects was to hire a rickshaw, and drive around the constituency shouting to all and sundry 'I am So-and-so!'[70]

Suematsu felt that in his own case and by implication in other campaigns where one candidate was particularly strong, slanders of this type were of little more than nuisance value; but in places where there were two evenly matched candidates, a rumour could have swayed the issue.[71] There is not much evidence to contradict this judgement; but it is well to remember that two close rivals could be evenly matched in their propensities for making false accusations as well as in everything else. This is essentially what happened in the Horibe versus Kunishima imbroglio.

A more straightforward method of garnering votes was that whereby candidates or their agents frequently made out lists of supporters in covenant form to the effect that Messrs A, B, C, D, etc., had pledged themselves to vote for Y. The next step was to get the voters concerned to attest the accuracy of the contents of these lists by affixing their legal seals. That done, the list became a sort of covenant. These agreements had no legal validity at all; but they were found to be extremely useful, because they enabled a candidate to see exactly how he stood in terms of popular support, and because an elector was very reluctant to withdraw his vote after having once promised it in this fashion. Moreover, on the basis of such documents, two candidates would sometimes do a pre-election deal under the terms of which one of them would give up his candidature and transfer all his 'covenanted' votes to the other. The motive behind such last-minute withdrawals from the fray was in some cases personal advantage, in others party interest.

MR HORIBE BANZAI, CITIZENS OF NAGOYA BANZAI! These seven words contain the gist of the circumstances under which the great majority of candidates ran their campaigns. Public interest in the election was nowhere completely absent; and in areas where it was whetted by talented speakers or a close contest, it could rise to great heights of enthusiasm. Packed speech meetings are evidence of this. To have a good chance of winning, however, a candidate did not just have to be able to speak well. Even more important was his own standing in the district. Was he popular personally? How many influential friends did he have? Even if he was both a capable politician and had strong connexions with the people in his constituency, he was still not safe. Almost certainly there would be a number of self-nominated and scheming Independents in the field against him; and these men, too, would have their own links with the neighbourhood and maybe a virtually unlimited supply of 'money power'. Then, if he were a party man, he might have to contend with one of the other big party organizations, or at any rate a small, but embittered and active, nationalist faction. Or again, his leading opponent might be a person as well qualified to be a Representative and as locally popular as himself.

All this meant that a successful, or potentially successful, candidate had to fight hard for his victory. There was only a handful of exceptions to this rule. In the last resort, no matter whether a contestant was a permanent resident in the constituency or somebody called in from outside, no matter whether he relied on 'mobile speeches' or on 'banquet competition', his own energies and the efforts of his supporters were what usually determined the result. Given the requisite amount of local backing to start with, he had to go on from there and gain the favour of as many electors as possible—overtly or covertly, by fair means or foul. If his rivals used a particular stratagem against him, he would very probably have to retaliate in kind.

Thus, although the first House of Representatives did reflect with a fair degree of accuracy political opinion in the Empire as a whole, so far as the individual candidate was concerned, the success of his campaign depended on two factors of widespread and overriding significance—his position in the village politics of his constituency, and his own initiative. It has been shown how these same two influences gave rise to the general body of candidates, and, in particular, shaped the pattern of local nominations. Suematsu Kenchō seems to have appreciated these points when he said that in contrast to the election campaigning by more developed and centralized political parties in the West, in Japan 'candidates at present make local affinities their prime consideration, and it seems that in their campaigns, too, individual endeavour came first'.[72]

(3) BRIBES AND 'SŌSHI'

Although widespread bribing of the electors was a prominent feature of the election campaign, it is hard after the event to draw the line between innocent feasting and definitely illegal corruption. Therefore what follows is concerned only with acts of bribery that were punishable under the terms of the Law of Election and its supplementary Penal Regulations. The more common of these were conveniently enumerated and characterized in an ironic announcement appearing in the *Matsue Nippō* (a Shimane prefecture paper) for 29 May:

DIET MEMBERS AGENCY LTD.

In as much as we shall:

Firstly, for those who donate ¥ 10 or goods equivalent thereto, find one vote—a vote that is under a signed bond not to go astray.

Secondly, for those who donate ¥ 5 or goods equivalent thereto, vouch for one vote—a vote that does not have a signed bond.

Thirdly, for those who donate ¥ 3 or goods equivalent thereto, procure one vote—a vote that has been riskily half-promised.

Fourthly, to those who favour members of our company by asking them to meetings free of charge and regaling them with banquets of meat and wine, make a present of a shout to the effect that we shall let them have a vote.

Fifthly, to those who donate a box of cakes, give a whisper that there is a possibility of a vote.

We are looking forward to hearing in the near future from those of you who wish to do a deal.[73]

The above was published in a spirit of jest; but, as the *Tokyo Nichi Nichi Shimbun* remarked when it reproduced the prospectus in its own columns, some bad jokes strike at the evils of the day. There is no doubt that bribery was rife in Shimane prefecture and in most other parts of the country, especially Saitama and Aichi.[74] Concerning the latter area, one report stated that: 'There are incessant rumours here and there about bribery in connexion with membership of the House of Representatives.'[75]

Corruption was a tactic used more frequently by self-nominated Independents than any other group; but on occasion party candidates, too, had recourse to it. Thus three agents for the Progressive candidate in Wakamatsu city (Fukushima prefecture) were arrested on 26 June and charged with bribery.[76] Allegations made about Yamada Taizō, Liberal candidate in the Second Constituency, Kanagawa prefecture, seem to have remained unproven;[77] but there is little reason to doubt that the Liberals also were willing to hand out bribes in certain areas. In Aichi prefecture, where the *Kōin Club* was strong, the candidates were reported to be doing their best to reveal each other's bribes;[78] and the Liberal campaign in Yokohama became notorious for this and other misdemeanours.

The Shimane prefecture Diet Members Agency Ltd. was hardly exorbitant in its proposed scale of fees—¥ 10 for a guaranteed vote, ¥ 3 for a half-promised vote. Allowing for the Agency's commission, the actual purchase price to be paid to the voter would have been less than this. Of course, this calculation is hypothetical because the report on which it is based was a joke; but at any rate there is an indication here of the amount that might have been expected to change hands at a single transaction. Most of the bribery cases mentioned in the papers do not say exactly how much money was supposed to have been given to the voters; but the Kita Saitama affair[79] is unusually well documented. There no more than ten or twenty sen was alleged to have been given to each of the electors involved.[80] A subsequent report mentioned the sum of thirty sen, and added that in some instances the election agent had left ten sen and promised to increase it to fifty sen if his candidate was elected.[81] Ten sen would have been equivalent to about threepence. Fifty sen was only one shilling and threepence.

The electors by definition were not paupers; and it is hard to think that very many of them would have been willing to run the risk of a fine which would have been anything from five to fifty yen for such a paltry bribe. This raises the problem of the extent to which graft, admitting that it was widespread, was actually effective in securing the return of candidates. A solution, however tentative, to this problem should have as its premise two classes of bribes: small bribes indiscriminately distributed among the general body of electors; and big bribes given more sparingly to a selected few.

Small bribes would be sums of money amounting to less than three yen; also cheap goods that were useful in their way but of a definitely limited value, such as boxes of cake, boxes of dried fish, hand-towels, packets of sugar, sugar pouches and handkerchiefs. These bribes in places where they were used seem to have been handed out extensively, but in such a way that each recipient was given only one article, or at the most two articles. This method of distribution makes it feasible that they were generally regarded by the candidates and voters alike as something in the nature of a discreetly timed present designed to ingratiate the candidate with the electorate, and not as a calculated and binding attempt to suborn it. The giving of little presents has long been an established convention in business and social relationships in Japan, and although based on an ethic of strict reciprocity, has also developed into a means of advertisement that does not entail any particular obligation for those receiving them. The latter and scarcely heinous function may account for much of the petty bribery. In the Kita Saitama case, the *Tokyo Nichi Nichi Shimbun* at one time expressed surprise that a candidate was alleged to have given small gifts of this kind, because he was not only wealthy but also very popular in the area and likely to be elected anyway.[82]

If an elector was visited in succession by two agents for opposing candidates each of whom left a box of cakes or a towel, what would he do? It can only be supposed that more often than not he would simply accept and make use of both presents, and then vote for neither of the candidates, or else vote for the one whom he really preferred for quite extraneous reasons. This might have been equally well the case even if only one side was sending presents. The bogus prospectus of the Diet Members Agency Ltd. itself suggests that a box of cakes was not worth more than a whisper of the possibility of a vote; and as has already been seen, at one stage in the bitter contest fought by

Hirabayashi Kyūbei and Takagi Masatoshi in the outermost districts of Tokyo *fu*, the rice-cakes and bonito of the nephew quickly faded from the memories of the electors when they heard of the promised munificence of the uncle.

Bigger bribes—that is, anything worth from ¥3 to ¥10—presumably produced more dependable results; though even on this level of pecuniary inducement, the Shimane announcement made it clear that at least ¥10 was needed to make sure that a vote paid for would actually be given. Candidates prepared to bribe on this scale nearly all came from the group of self-nominated Independents with no chance of winning by other means. The *Tokyo Nichi Nichi Shimbun* deplored this state of affairs when reviewing the general progress of the election campaign. '[Most places] have put themselves in the hands of self-nominated candidates; and since the general body of electors is in fact being led astray by this, we find ourselves to-day in the melancholy situation that the things which are most abhorrent in elections exist in every region.'[83] Two weeks earlier than this, the *Kokumin Shimbun*, in an editorial entitled Two Hundred Thousand Yen Will Control The Assembly, had been even more explicit:

At present, unscrupulous good-for-nothings are trying to become members of the House of Representatives by the exercise of stealth. The weapons on which they rely are not [skill in] debate, and they are not personal ability. Still less can they claim to have had any experience of politics. Their one weapon is the use of bribes. Consequently ducks that have been long since dead have stretched their wings and taken flight; bottles of beer have grown feet and started walking. Electors—take care! Remember that those who send out bribes of ducks and beer will themselves naturally expect to receive bigger bribes with interest added! How can there ever be any difference between a willingness to send bribes to the electors and a readiness to take bribes from the Government once they have got into the Diet?[84]

Despite the pessimistic tone of such reports, in the case of lavish bribing, too, prevalence was well ahead of efficacy. Not very many of the self-nominated candidates of the adventurer type were in fact elected to the House of Representatives. Judicious graft might well have helped those candidates whose initially favourable prospects had deteriorated, but it would seem very doubtful whether corruption alone ever saved the day for someone whose candidature had been hopeless from the first. The cost of relying solely on bribing one's way into the Diet would have tended to be prohibitive for most.[85] This apart, self-nominated Independents having absolutely nothing to commend them and nobody to befriend them would have had to contend with regionalist loyalties and the personal appeal of rival candidates, not to mention the consciences of individual electors and restraints imposed by law.

Sakata Jōhei, respected local resident and a scholar of Chinese classics, was returned for the Fourth Constituency, Okayama prefecture. From the outset of the campaign the hopes of the electorate had been firmly fixed on him, even though he was not willing to canvass actively on his own behalf. From time to time self-nominated candidates put in an appearance and, taking advantage of Sakata's reticence, spread false rumours that he was not really willing to be elected, or else insinuated that a scholar was not the sort of person to make a suitable Representative. To these whispered allegations, Sakata replied simply that so far as the election was concerned, he would not seek it, nor would he compete, nor would he turn his back on popular approval. The self-nominated candidates failed; Sakata won.[86] Though there is no definite statement that the self-nominated candidates in this case added corruption to their methods, results for the country as a whole confirm the report's indication that a large measure of local support and strength of character were sufficient to defeat the more noxious Independents.

On the other hand, self-nominated candidates who did have a substantial measure of popular support or local influence and may have also had recourse to copious bribes were successful in a number of cases. The winner of the First Constituency, Osaka *fu*, was an old gunsmith named Awaya Shinazo. A self-nominated Independent, he was a member of both the city and the prefectural (*fu*) assemblies. His local connexions and previous experience in standing for the assemblies apparently helped him in the contest for the House of Representatives against opposition of a rather inferior calibre:

Mr Awaya Shinazo—the whale member, or doughnut candidate—is not at all liked by the public, but he is not the least concerned about such things. Already, the other day, he invited more than a thousand people—voters from the constituency, newspaper editors, acquaintances, and so on—to the *Senshin* inn in Nakanoshima and gave a big banquet, on the pretext of celebrating his sixtieth birthday. Whereupon he became extremely popular with one sort of people. More especially, electoral contests are this old man's forte. Up till now, he has always fought his way through stiff competition and been elected by a large majority, both at the election of members to the city assembly and at the re-election of members to the prefectural assembly. Though there is still no definite opinion that it is he who should sit in the Diet, from time to time he has his audiences convulsed with laughter, and at any rate he must be the one who is standing for the Diet with the highest hopes.[87]

Elsewhere in Osaka, in the Fifth Constituency, one of the candidates who came from a wealthy local family sent out presents of food to the electors. When his main opponent, a lawyer, heard of this, he summoned electors to his office and warned them of the punishments they would receive if found guilty of breaking the law.[88] The lawyer won the seat. In the Sixth Constituency, another candidate used his money to bring about the defeat of a public notary, who opposed him principally on the strength of his scholastic reputation.[89] In the end, both of these candidates were eliminated by a third, a former sub-prefect. In the Eighth Constituency on the other hand, money vanquished a candidate who was an ex-official and an eloquent speaker.

Events in Osaka were symptomatic of what was taking place generally throughout the country; and corruption, though it must have affected many campaigns, did not—in itself and by itself—decide the issue in more than a handful of them. The eve-of-poll situation in the majority of constituencies probably resembled that in the Second Constituency, Tokyo, where there had been no suggestion of unfair practices. Of the 218 voters, fifty had promised to support one candidate and forty-five his chief rival. More than a hundred were still not prepared to reveal the name of the person for whom they intended to vote.[90] If this surmise is correct, the composition of the House of Representatives must have been influenced by bribery but by no means determined by it. The relatively lowly financial status of elected Members would confirm this view.

Nevertheless, while the first House of Representatives was not unduly distorted by the grosser abuses of the campaign, it was not wholly free from the taint of corruption. This was the most lasting and reprehensible consequence of the widespread use of graft in the election of 1890. In 1892, after a period of protracted contention between the Government and the House of Representatives on the subject of budget estimates, the Government was at length enabled to pass a modified financial bill through the House after it had allegedly secured the consent of a sufficient number of its Liberal opponents by lining their pockets.[91] In this way, the forebodings of the *Kokumin Shimbun* and other organs of the press were seemingly justified and if the allegations were in fact correct, an evil precedent was set by the very first Diet to be followed with even graver consequences by later administrations and Houses of Representatives.

It is possible that Japanese electoral politics were from the start prone to corruption because of the traditional family ethic. As this was based on feelings of shame before recognized local groups and not on a sense of sin against an all-seeing and all-present God, it was less well suited to the moral problems of electioneering than the recently evolved more individualistic discipline of certain European peoples. Alternatively, Tokugawa political fragmentation and the authoritarian basis of Japanese administration have combined to produce a relative lack—not of patriotism in either its local or national forms—but of the sort of regular and unemotional civic morale that helps to safeguard the moral health of elections and Houses of Representatives. On a less exalted plane of conventional values, the timely distribution of small keepsakes to all and sundry was virtually indistinguishable from the custom of giving presents as an adjunct to introductions. Lastly and indubitably, one of the most important causes of electoral corruption in 1890 was the large number of self-nominated candidates.

The most effective measures against outright corruption were the relevant articles of the Law of Election and the Supplementary Penal Regulations. These sanctions were enforced fairly and firmly by the police whenever possible; the authorities were often aided in their efforts by information supplied by rival candidates, or by voters who had accepted bribes and then thought better of it. Newspapers representing all shades of opinion joined forces with the considerable number of honest candidates to warn voters not to allow themselves to be corrupted, and to condemn those attempting to corrupt them. In Saitama prefecture, a number of public-spirited persons founded an anti-corruption association which they called the Saitama Preservation of Righteousness Society; and there are hints of similar moves elsewhere.[92] However the village in Gumma prefecture, which put up the following notice at its approaches seems to have set a sadly isolated example:

STRICTLY NO ADMITTANCE TO ALL ALMS-COLLECTORS, BEGGARS, HAWKERS, VOTE-BUYERS, etc.[93]

Gangster (*sōshi*) activity was similar to corruption in its incidence and impact. The underworld tough, with his big stick and his blustering, bullying habits, was a figure that frequently erupted with violence into the centre of the 1890 electoral scene, and was always standing as a dark shadow in its background. Details of some of their outrages have already been given;[94] and easily the most common type of activity was physical disruption of a speech meeting:

Sixty or so influential people in the vicinity of Sōka-machi, Saitama prefecture, organized a speech meeting in that town the day before yesterday, the 25th. The audience poured in, one after the other, from 1 p.m. onwards; and when it reached a total of more than three hundred, a local enthusiast began to give a talk on science. Whereupon twenty or thirty persons looking like Liberal Party *sōshi* came in, sneered more than once [at the speaker], and disturbed the meeting place with their insults and bad language. The political discussion began after this; and while Messrs Kudama Tokutarō and Shinoda [illegible] were on the platform, [the *sōshi*] interrupted the speeches in the same way by sneering and shouting abuse. However these two gentlemen took not the least bit of notice of them, and finished their speeches.

Next Mr Noguchi Honnosuke advanced two or three steps towards the front of the platform, and was just on the point of commencing his speech when the band of *sōshi*, growing still bolder, took to shouting in unison and tried to create a general uproar. Then Mr Noguchi, raising his voice even louder, said: 'Gentlemen, you are bent on making a disturbance before I have opened my mouth even. No doubt because you feel that it would naturally be of grave disadvantage to you to let me finish my speech without hindrance. But one of my speeches is not worth it.' No sooner had he said this than one of the *sōshi* (Ebara Senzō), who had crept up alongside of the platform with a bottle in his hand, suddenly stood up, and closing in on the speaker with a flying leap, spluttered out two or three words.

As quick as a flash, all the *sōshi* got up and started a commotion in every part of the hall. The chairman of the meeting, Mr Udagawa Sonzō, rose to his feet and tried to control them, but the *sōshi* seized hold of him and assaulted him. The audience all stood up and waded in. Four or five policemen pushed their way into the middle of the scrimmage. The band of *sōshi* became increasingly destructive. The chairman was hit under the nose and blood trickled out. Bottles flew and were smashed to smithereens. Stones and pebbles were thrown through the air; flower-vases were upset. At last, the police ordered the meeting to be closed.[95]

The rest of this report, after repeating the allegation that the *sōshi* concerned were connected with the local Liberals and stating that they had travelled from Tokyo for the express purpose of attending the Sōka-machi meeting, described how the sponsors of the disrupted speech meeting immediately arranged to hold a party in a nearby restaurant. About eighty people attended the party; and after the meal had been served, the programme of speeches was resumed and completed—this time without any unseemly interruptions.

Apart from being employed to break up public meetings, the *sōshi* were also used in attempts to intimidate opposition candidates and to frighten electors. In Tokyo, a gang known as the *Dankyō Gikai* appears to have taken a fairly active part in the election. On 23 June, it sent a letter to Takagi Masatoshi in the

Twelfth Constituency advising him to yield the election to his uncle, Hirabayashi Kyūbei.[96] Similar letters were also sent to two of the candidates in Shiba ward, the capital's Second Constituency.[97] On 30 June, members of the same gang went to the house of a candidate in Shiba ward and said that they had come to investigate rumours that he had been offering bribes. The candidate apparently had heard of their intentions and was not at home. The *sōshi*, furious, conducted a fruitless search for him for the best part of seven hours.[98]

In Yokohama, the bravado of certain gangsters, who were indisputably connected with the Liberal faction, reached heights not attained elsewhere. The citizens awoke on the morning of 29 June to find that members of the Certain Death Compact Society had put up posters at every cross-roads threatening to kill, in their capacity as 'Heaven's agents', anyone who voted for the Progressive Party candidate.[99] On the afternoon of the day of election, the Progressive candidate himself, Shimada Saburō, was visited by three of the most notorious of the Yokohama *sōshi*, and after a quarrel, subjected to minor assault.[100]

Though two of the cases mentioned so far imply Liberal connivance, electioneering with the help of rowdies was by no means confined to the Liberal factions alone. Independents were, if anything, slightly more prone to adopt the practice; the Progressive candidates, if anything, rather less.

In the Third Constituency, Tochigi prefecture, the main contestants were Tanaka Shōzō (*Kaishin-tō*) and Kimura Hampei (Business Party), and the struggle was keen. Both candidates called in *sōshi*, with the result that there were incidents in the course of the campaign and some injuries inflicted.[101] On the day of the election, it was reported, they had stationed *sōshi* everywhere, but police vigilance prevented any further outbreaks of violence.[102] In Gumma prefecture, five of the six candidates in the Second Constituency were still resolutely campaigning on the eve of the election; and even though the police supervision was strict, 'fierce quarrels' were occurring in all districts.[103] In Aichi prefecture (*Kōin Club* v. Independents), gangsters were in short supply because they were liberally used by both groups of candidates.[104] In Osaka, an Independent candidate, whose campaigning methods have already been touched on,[105] took the initiative in enlisting *sōshi*, only to find his rivals quick to outdo him in this at any rate.

> The evil tide of threatening ultimatums has reached Osaka, too. A certain candidate in the First Constituency, for example—perhaps finding after all that the doctrine of doughnut and banquet entreaties was slow in having effects—whistled up a gang of gambling ruffians (What a Member!) with whom he had been acquainted on terms of friendship for some time. Having plied them with sake and greased their palms, he formed them into squads of four or five men under squad leaders, and by pushing his claims has brought influence to bear on each elector, one by one. His competitors, seeing this, decided that neither bragging nor speech meetings could match it and, adopting the same policy, took up the idea of using main force in the form of intimidation and threats. Thus, the rowdies of one side encounter and glare at the bullies of the other side in front of the gate of every elector, and the atmosphere is tense. It is to be feared that in secret, at any moment now, blood will be shed and flesh will fly. The electors for the most part find a way out by saying that they are not at home, and so down to the present have done all they could to avoid interference in electoral matters. The police, too, fearful of what may happen on the day of the election in these circumstances, have recently taken very strict precautions. Rumour has it that there will also be some unexpected arrests, and there is a general feeling of unease.[106]

As the above indicates, a *sōshi* strategy, for all its unruliness and consequent publicity, was not particularly effective. The sponsors of the Sōka-machi speech meeting had been able to continue with the programme elsewhere after rowdyism had resulted in premature closure of the meeting, though admittedly the audience had dwindled somewhat in the meantime. Likewise, Takagi Masatoshi, Shimada Saburō and one of the two threatened candidates in Shiba ward were all elected to the House of Representatives, despite open *sōshi* hostility; and there is no evidence that anyone actually voted in accordance with their dictates, or that any candidate felt it wise to give up his candidature for the same reason.

It is not too difficult to see why the hiring of gangsters should have been even less effectual than the use of bribes as a means of prevailing upon the electors to give up their right to vote for the candidate of their own choice. Since it was a relatively cheap way of exerting pressure, a candidate who employed *sōshi* would soon have his opponents following suit. As a result, one gang often found itself foiled by another, and the electors were left in comparative peace. Moreover, it was much easier for the police to prevent or, failing that, control outbreaks of public disorder than it was for them to uncover illicit transactions in money or goods. For their part, as has been shown, the police were by no means negligent in enforcing the provisions of the Law of Election, and on polling day itself succeeded in curbing the *sōshi* throughout the country.[107] Finally, although the gangs could easily disrupt speech meetings and subject a few unfortunates to acute physical discomfort, the violence displayed in the many incidents in the course of the campaign was of a not very intimidating kind. Noses might have been punched here, or kicks exchanged there; but certainly, nobody was killed. Very probably, there were no bones broken even.

Something of this can be detected in newspaper accounts of the outbreaks. Naturally, responsible opinion condemned violence as well as bribery. Yet the reports and editorials contain an under-current of amused tolerance verging on admiration for the gangs. At the very least, they gave a touch of excitement to the election, which their misbehaviour could never vitiate in the way corruption threatened to vitiate it. The following stanzas of a Progressive election song popular in Kanagawa prefecture reveal a spirit in which loathing of the *sōshi* is balanced by self-confidence in face of their menaces:

> Onwards, ever onwards!
> Though [our foes] be massed [against us]
> And the *sōshi* blindly rage,
> Advance fearing naught.
> Never retreat!
> For principles and country!
>
> Be brave, be brave, be truly brave!
> Though the *sōshi* be such,

3. BRIBES AND 'SŌSHI'

The law which shall protect us
Is stronger than iron.
Never retreat!
For principles and country!

Think, think, O think!
Though hateful people threaten,
We are resolved
Never to be threatened.
Never retreat!
For principles and country![108]

The *sōshi*, then, though fearsome enough in appearance and manner, were not so very terrible in practice. Perhaps their most useful function, from the point of view of the candidates who employed them, was the provision of a reasonably reliable personal bodyguard in case of need. Looking ahead, however, the use of gangsters by Independent and party candidates in 1890 set a bad example which was followed with far more serious results by the Government in the election of 1892, when it tried to secure a pliable House of Representatives by terrorizing the electorate. Further, the setting up of a parliamentary system in Japan did not immediately abate a thoroughly reprehensible tradition of political violence.

The *sōshi*, themselves, were members of the normal, everyday gangs of semi-professional criminals and other congenital ne'er-do-wells. They belonged to that underworld of racketeers, pimps and dishonest-penny-turners that exists in Japan or any other large country, especially in the cities. This would explain why they were so readily available to those candidates requiring them. It would also help to explain—because as members of regular gangs individual *sōshi* would be well known to the police and members of the public alike—why they did not carry their outrages too far. Also, protection rackets cease to be operable if one is too thorough about eliminating opposition racketeers. As common gangsters, the *sōshi* had as much claim to be regarded as a general and long-standing social ill as a specifically electoral evil, and from this would stem some of the relative lack of alarm at their misdeeds.

III. THE ELECTION CAMPAIGN

At a speech meeting held at Maebashi in Gumma prefecture on 22 June, some *sōshi* started a disturbance, pulled one of the speakers off the rostrum, and eventually forced the chairman to declare the meeting closed. The particular speaker interrupted in this way was not the candidate on whose behalf the meeting had been arranged, but someone who supported him and was also in favour of abolishing licensed prostitution;[109] and it may have been that in this instance the gangsters were acting in defence of their permanent and apolitical interests rather than for temporary electoral rewards. The next bit of evidence does not need to have anything read into it, and clearly shows that the *sōshi* were gangs organized on a permanent basis, and were willing to travel some distance in search of congenial employment: 'Bribery is rife among the candidates and electors at Koshigaya in Saitama prefecture. It is reported that, declaring that to leave things as they are would bring shame on their ancestor, Mr Banzuiin Chōbei, twenty metropolitan *sōshi*, each with a stick and wearing straw sandals, set off enthusiastically the morning before last to have high words in that area. Magnificent!'[110] Koshigaya is about fifteen miles from the centre of Tokyo. Banzuiin Chōbei was a famous chief of an Edo chivalrous fraternity, established at the beginning of the seventeenth century to protect the townspeople from bullying by samurai or other misfortunes.[111]

The Yokohama campaign, however, shows the *sōshi* at their most active, and so throws the greatest light on who they were, how they operated, and their role in the election. The underworld elements in that city seem to have been almost entirely in the service of the Liberals; but with the transfer of their candidate, Nakajima Nobuyuki, to the Fifth Constituency, Kanagawa prefecture, in the middle of June, the Liberal camp and its *sōshi* adherents were sadly divided among themselves.[112] In the end, a section of the Liberals joined forces with some recalcitrant Progressives, and on 27 June this coalition of former opponents nominated Hiranuma Senzō to stand against the official Progressive candidate, Shimada Saburō.

3. BRIBES AND 'SŌSHI'

Before this, however, some of the *sōshi* who had been working for the Liberals had taken the initiative and, calling themselves the Residents Club, held a party for the Yokohama electors on the 22nd.[113] At this party, it was decided to sponsor the candidature of a certain Suzuki Inenosuke. At about the same time, another *sōshi* clique, also with Liberal connexions, put forward a Totsuka Sentarō for election to the House of Representatives. Thus in the last ten days of the campaign, Shimada Saburō found himself opposed by three Liberal candidates instead of one. Furthermore, of these three Liberal candidates, two at least had been championed by rival bands of *sōshi*; and on the Liberal side, the Yokohama campaign after the sudden withdrawal of Nakajima Nobuyuki had taken on many of the characteristics of a gang vendetta.

The following account of an incident which must have taken place just before the nominations of Suzuki and Totsuka makes this clear. The 'hero' of the story, Fukui Mohei, was one of the best known of all the Yokohama *sōshi*, and was the person who assaulted Shimada Saburō on the afternoon of the day of the election.[114]

Those who are known to be leaders of the ??? in that area, Fukui, Maruyama, Umeda, Nomi, Sakurai and Takano all considered that the moment was very propitious for them to show their influence. They decided to hold a meeting as soon as possible, and as they favoured Mr Suzuki Inenosuke (a member of the Liberal Party), to nominate him as the candidate and tell the electors what they had done. For all those who had been opposed to them for a long time past —Nishimura, Ono, Kurusu, Shimada, Ishikawa and Watanabe—it was a very serious state of affairs. Saying, 'We are local people, so why should we let ourselves be trampled on by those villains without doing anything at all about it?', they hurriedly sent out a rickshaw-man as a secret messenger, and held a conference of their supporters in a certain place.

However the 'rickshaw-man'—all unbeknown to them—was actually a fully-fledged Liberal Party *sōshi*, and had taken on this disguise for reasons of ??. On hearing these [instructions], he ran of his own initiative to the camp gate of the Liberal Party, with news of what was afoot. The chief of staff there, Mr Fukui Mohei, boiled with rage, and shouted—'No matter what sort of wretches they are, it is quite

181

unpardonable of them to have given us no warning at all and to ignore others!' Then having pocketed a hand-knife, he stormed off like a demon, alone on horseback, and when he came to the meeting place of the opposition faction, prepared to burst his way in.

The latter, for its part, seems to have realized that it had no ordinary foe to deal with; and men dressed in dirty clothes and soft sashes were on guard at the gate with big sticks in their hands. Mr Fukui after taking a look, muttered 'Bah, mere greenhorns!' Holding up his knife above his head so that all could see it, he made a charge. They fell back before a countenance so terrible; but just then the nearest of the *sōshi* ran into the house, closed the door with a thud, and snapped the lock shut.

Mr Fukui, nonplussed, made a tour of inspection here and there, and while he was doing so saw Mr Kurusu Sohei standing in the lavatory to relieve himself. The fearless Mr Fukui immediately sprang on him and gave him a sudden kick. When he had overpowered him with kicks, he got on top of him and hit him with his fists, shouting in a loud voice—'You are giving aid to the *Kaishin-tō*, but now how about supporting the candidate whom we want to elect?' In the end, people inside the house ran out, and, coming in between them, quietened them down; but for a while there was a great deal of confusion.[115]

It is just possible that a gangster of Fukui Mohei's undoubted energies and strength of character was genuinely interested in Liberalism for its own sake; but it is far more likely that Fukui and all the other regular *sōshi* operating in Yokohama and elsewhere were concerned with politics only for what they could get out of them, and regarded the general election as a Heaven-sent opportunity for extending their spheres of influence. The reasons why the Liberals seem to have relied rather more heavily than the Progressives on *sōshi* support are not altogether clear. Probably, in 1890 the various Liberal factions still had an aura of populism since in the preceding decade militant members of the *Jiyū-tō* had engaged in many small skirmishes and conspiracies against the Government.

In sharp contrast to conditions in later years, few, if any, of the *sōshi* involved in the first general election were motivated by ultra-nationalism or had Right-wing affiliations.[116] This does not mean that the gangs were not on occasion capable of borrowing the propaganda or demeanour of the ultra-nationalist groups, if and when it suited them to do so; but in such circumstances their ultra-nationalism was clearly spurious. Thus at one stage, the Liberal *sōshi* of Yokohama publicly accused Shimada Saburō of treason, but this was for their own ends. Likewise, the *Kinjō Shimbun* of Nagoya threatened that a band of 200 *sōshi* would visit the homes of all those who failed to vote; because 'people who disregard the rare and wonderful right conferred on them by to-morrow's voting and do not go to the polls are guilty of extreme disloyalty to their country'.[117] Yet this particular group of *sōshi*, if it existed at all outside the columns of the *Kinjō Shimbun*, was almost certainly one of the regular Nagoya gangs and therefore apolitical.

Occasional reports of more serious outbreaks of violence, such as arson or large-scale rioting, give the impression that these were not so much electoral disturbances as manifestations of a deeper and more menacing social unrest in various parts of the Empire. The scattered but frequent peasant revolts of Tokugawa times continued well into the Meiji period; and in a debate on poor relief during the opening session of the Diet it was alleged that upwards of 4,000 paupers were dying of starvation every year.[118]

Incidents entailing damage to property were quite rare during the course of the election campaign; but on or about 25 May, a street riot broke out in Iida-machi in the Noto region of Ishikawa prefecture. (This was a district that had been specially noted for similar *émeutes* in the feudal era.) The *Chōya Shimbun*, reporting the affair stated that it had originated in the conflict between local parties, and that among the former Liberals there were 'wild and lawless fellows' who were liable to behave badly. The rioters succeeded in destroying the house of the village headman, and had also attacked the village office and the police-station. The police were compelled to draw their swords, and ten persons were arrested and many more wounded before order was restored.[119] Elsewhere, in the Third Constituency, Tottori prefecture, the town office and three adjacent houses in Yonago-machi were burnt down on the morning of 30 May. Later the following notice was put up in every quarter of the village: 'You, Endō Haruhiko, stop forgetting your place as a salaried official and running about on behalf of candidates! Your ardour for the fray will only lead in the end to the burning down of a number of offices. Four young *sōshi* proclaim this.'[120] It transpired that Endō Haruhiko, the headman of Yonago-machi, had been canvassing the area on behalf of a candidate in the parliamentary elections.

Quite apart from *sōshi* as common gangsters and *sōshi* as putative political militants of one kind or another, there were other cases of electoral fracas where the participants seem to have been indulging more in a species of larrikinism than anything else. The following (final) story will convey this. Its principals, at any rate, were both men whose everyday jobs were respectable if somewhat humdrum, and that there is no suggestion at all of political zeal.

On the evening of the 26th, the Kimura faction held a speech meeting in Umedo village, Inabe sub-prefecture, Mie prefecture. While the speakers were travelling back in a party, in rickshaws, from Umedo village to Kita Ōyashiro, six or seven *sōshi* belonging to the Amaharu faction were going along in a group. The first party, however, attempted to overtake without any word of warning. The Amaharu faction's *sōshi* criticized this rudeness, and started exchanging words with the *sōshi* guards of the various speakers. A certain Amashiro, a barber of Hachiman-Shinden and a *sōshi* of the Kimura faction, said that he would cut down the Amaharu party with an unsheathed sword that he was carrying. Whereupon the Amaharu faction retorted—'Just try it, and see if you can!' Amashiro immediately slashed Hikota, a stone-mason from Minami Ōyashiro and a *sōshi* of the Amaharu faction, from the left elbow to the wrist with the sword—at which, the irresistible Hikota gave a loud cry and fell down. The Amaharu faction, seeing his body, seized hold of Amashiro, called him a vulgar oaf and took his sword from him. Then the Kimura faction all fled on the spot, raising a great clamour. Hikota is at present undergoing medical treatment, and it is reported that his life is not in danger.[121]

CHAPTER IV

ELECTION RESULTS AND COMPOSITION OF THE FIRST HOUSE OF REPRESENTATIVES

The election itself was a success. Despite a few very minor incidents involving *sōshi* on the day of the election, the polling everywhere took place as planned and in a general atmosphere of quiet. This is not to say that the enthusiasm which had marked the campaign in most areas suddenly ebbed away in the early hours of 1 July, leaving the voters to troop apathetically to the polls. On the contrary, a mood of exuberance continued right down to the date of the election and for a short while after. In the Twelfth Constituency, Tokyo *fu*, Takagi Masatoshi kept open house for all and sundry from the time of the opening of the polling stations at 7.0 a.m. It seems that the local electors and others made full use of his proferred hospitality, for:

When word went round that the abstemious and drunkards alike could freely indulge in tea, cakes, foreign liquor, etc., in the reception rooms, there was a constant stream of people going in and out. There were ancients flicking their beads and chanting innumerable prayers, and a party of firemen in quilted coats was also seen. We understand that they had not all left by the time the polls closed; but this may be an unfounded rumour.[1]

Elsewhere in Tokyo, groups of voters made arrangements to fête successful candidates after the results of the elections had been announced;[2] and in the Fourth Constituency, Osaka *fu*, the entire population of the town of Nishihama-machi, Nishi Nari sub-prefecture, stopped work on 4 July to celebrate the victory of Nakae Tokusuke.[3]

More serious and concrete evidence of popular interest in the election is provided by the number of votes cast. Of a total of 450,365 electors, only 27,636 failed to vote. In other words, for the country as a whole, there was a 95 per cent poll, and this when there was no legal penalty for not voting. The prefectures with the highest number of non-voters were Nagasaki (11·1 per cent), Kyoto (11 per cent), Tokyo (10·9 per cent), Yamaguchi (10·9 per cent) and Yamanashi (10·9 per cent).[4] In Fukuoka, on the other hand, the abstention rate was under 1 per cent. The figures for this extraordinarily high poll must be accepted at their face value as showing that the election had given vent to a long-cherished and widespread desire to participate in national politics. The feeling which accounted in part for the large number of candidates had been even more convincingly demonstrated by the numbers of people who took the trouble to vote. Moreover, it is probable that this was no mere flash-in-the-pan interest in parliamentary politics. The sixteen-year history of the Liberty and Popular Rights Movement and crowded election meetings up and down the land would argue otherwise.

The press deserves a lot of credit for having tirelessly explained the advantages and responsibilities of constitutional government to the people. Yet even though it is pleasant to think that last-minute exhortations such as the following had some effect, by the end of this campaign they probably reflected public opinion rather than determined it:

The election of Members is almost upon us. Even though there may be some who are not interested in the election, others who are bewildered by it, others who have been perplexed by dishonest canvassing, others who have been led astray by temporary inducements, others who are unable to distinguish the good and bad points of the candidates, others who have been frightened by the threats of the orators, and so on and so forth, most of the electors are not in this position. They are all gentlemen...If unworthy Members are returned at the coming election, the electors will have to take all the blame for it. On the other hand, if good men are returned, in nine out of ten cases that will be a tribute to the gentlemanly qualities of the electorate. Apart from this, whether the gentlemen concerned [i.e. the electors] will prove enthusiastic or no, whether they will take good care or no, whether they will act with proper rectitude or no, whether the election will be ill-famed or of good repute—all must depend in the end on themselves. So theirs is indeed a great responsibility. Electors and gentlemen, each and every one of you—we beg you—live up to your responsibilities![5]

2,935 of the 422,729 votes cast were invalid.[6] This is not a large number by any standards. In this case, it is surprisingly small considering that it was the first general election ever held, that the method of voting used necessitated the writing in full of both the candidate's and the elector's names and also the address of the latter, and that not all the electors were literate. It would appear from this that the care taken to provide official scribes at the polling stations was of net advantage in that it reduced the number of spoiled votes, despite the opportunity it gave corrupt clerks to hoodwink illiterate electors.

Very little bitterness was left behind by the election. This was so, even though the competition for seats had been nearly always keen and sometimes violent. Personal and parochial rivalries, too, had come to the fore in the eight weeks preceding polling day. Yet by the end of the first week in July, when all the results had been announced, the public excitement had died down and the political scene, though it had obviously undergone a fundamental change as a result of the holding of the election, was tranquil. Doubtless only very few of the fifteen hundred or so candidates could have experienced to the full those feelings of dispassionate amity which the editor of the *Kokumin Shimbun* wished on them when he wrote on the morning of 1 July:

We rejoice that they, ever faithful to and utterly single-minded in their high ambition, have so gloriously undergone this great ordeal; and we shall pray that winners and losers will grasp each other's hand, and, putting foremost the wider interests of our country, will continue to foster the development of constitutional democracy. If the clouds and rain of discontent have no place in their hearts, above their heads will only be blue sky and a golden sun.[7]

Nevertheless 'the clouds of rain and discontent', wheresoever there were any, must have soon yielded to a 'blue sky and golden sun'; and allowing for hyperbole, the latter metaphor is not a bad one to describe the mood of hopeful and rancourless quiescence which succeeded the stress and upheaval of the election.

Moreover, the frequently expressed[8] fear that the personal animosities and regional feuds aroused in many places by the campaigns for the Diet would somehow have an adverse effect on the workings of local government proved to be unfounded. The various prefectural, city, town and village assemblies did not really function any the worse for having been involved indirectly, through their memberships, in the election for the House of Representatives. The same is true, generally speaking, of individual officials such as village headmen who had often taken a far from inactive part in the parliamentary contest. By and large, once the election was over, local affairs returned to being purely local affairs, and the new Diet was left alone to find its own place in the arena of national politics.

There were a number of different reasons for this happy state of affairs. In the first place, many of the candidates—possibly a majority of them—polled fewer than ten votes. These persons must have known from the outset that their chances of being elected were virtually non-existent, and so would have not been too disappointed by their failure. Secondly, interest in the forthcoming Diet tended to efface memories of the polls as soon as the election was over. Both the party politicians and the press had little time for recrimination; from the beginning of July, they were fully occupied in making preparations for, or having thoughts about, what would happen in the following November when the House of Representatives was due to meet for the first time. Thirdly, the Government's impartial attitude towards the election meant that there was no upsurge of popular indignation against the *Sat-Chō* bureaucrats. Thus, post-election feeling in 1890 was very different from what it was to be in 1892, when the Government's open and frequently brutal interference with the electors gave rise to a widespread and by no means transient hostility on the part of the press and the public. Fourthly, on the morrow of the voting, officials and people alike could congratulate themselves on a job well done. Unsavoury incidents and features of the campaign were not overlooked in the spate of 'over the wave' editorials and press comment. But stronger than pricks of shame was a feeling of exhilaration and not unjustifiable pride in having accomplished so much. After all, twenty-two years previously, the nation had barely heard of constitutional government. Finally, and perhaps most significant of all, the general spirit of good humour that prevailed after the first election was indicative of the fact that behind the great political issues of the day as well as behind the innumerable local rivalries, there lay a concealed but considerable and growing sense of national unity.

Of course, the political issues and local rivalries were real enough; but most of those involved were still willing, when the circumstances demanded it, to subordinate them to the interests of the Empire as a whole. It is not surprising that that extreme Right-wing newspaper, the *Nippon Shimbun*, should have filled its editorial columns for July 1890 with statements like the following:

The setting up of a House of Representatives in our country has come about as a result of collaboration between the throne and people. Never can it be compared with the conflicts between royal prerogative and popular rights in European countries. Although it is not the case that there have been no collisions between Government and people, the national condition had already become one of union of Sovereign and subjects. Therefore political evils were the fault of the governing authorities alone. Speaking from this standpoint, our country is indeed superior to any other, and is the one that produced [first] the system of making the Monarch sacred and the Prime Minister responsible, which has recently become common to all constitutional countries. Of course, many of the trends since the Restoration have accelerated this process. Yet it must be attributed, in the final analysis, to what has been made manifest in the Imperial Way and in the character of the people from the time of the foundation of the Empire.[9]

More interestingly, the Japanism of the Ultra-Conservatives had its echoes in the patriotism of the others. As already noted, the editor of the Liberal *Kokumin Shimbun* chose the morning of the election to remind candidates, and by implication the nation at large, of the need to 'put foremost the wider interests of our country'. On the same day, the *Yūbin-Hōchi Shimbun* (Progressive Party) declared that the principal business of Government, people and newly elected Members of the House of

Representatives was to make the State a solid rock at home, and a shining light abroad.[10] This common tendency to think in terms of national problems, and a fairly wide measure of agreement on the question of what constituted the most pressing national problems of the day, must not be taken to mean that there was a similar unanimity with regard to possible solutions for these problems. Nevertheless, a broad sense of national unity was one of the things which enabled the Diet to function as a genuine parliament from the first, and the nation to accept without any great misgivings the verdict of the election.

Kōin Club			Kaishin-tō			Kaishin-Jiyū-tō	
105			16			23	
Daidō Club	55					*Kyushu Dōshi-kai	19
Aikoku-kōtō	32					Gumma Kōgi-kai	3
Jiyū-tō	16					Kyoto Kōyū-kai	1
Gōdō-ha	2						
Jichi-tō			Ultra-Conservatives			Independents	Unknown
17			18			87	3
Kyoto Kōmin-kai	5		Kumamoto Kokken-tō	5			
Others	12		Hiroshima Seiyū-kai	5			
			Hoshu Chūsei-ha	2			
			Others	6			

* Same as Kyushu Confederation of Progressive Parties.

(Adapted from Hayashida Kametarō, *Nihon Seitō Shi*, vol. 1, p. 284.)

In the House of Representatives elected in 1890, the 'popular parties', i.e. the Progressive Party and the Liberal factions, had a clear but not crushing majority. The minority consisted of a mixed bag of Government supporters, Independents and a handful of Ultra-Conservatives. It is impossible to state with precision the numbers of Members belonging to each of the various parties and factions, as the newspapers reporting these details doctored them in accordance with their own political preferences. The above table, published originally by the *Tokyo Shimpō*, is reproduced here because it contains the fullest account of the state of the parties immediately after the election; but the exact numerical strength accorded to each of the groups and factions is not necessarily its true one. To begin with, the table leaves no fewer than thirty-one Members unaccounted for.

The table does at least show that all the main strands of

political opinion and major party groupings that had appeared at the time of the election campaign were represented in the new House. The *Daidō Club* had done particularly well in Niigata, Yamagata and Aomori prefectures; that is, in the area where the defenders of the *Bakufu* had made one of their last stands and where Gotō Shōjirō had had his most successful campaigns at the time of the organization of the *Daidō Danketsu*. The *Aikoku-kōtō* was strong in Hyōgo, Fukui and Kōchi prefectures; while the *Kaishin-tō* won three of the five seats in Toyama. On the other hand, the *Kaishin-tō* fared badly against the *Daidō Club* in Niigata; and the *Kōin Club* lost all but two of the eleven seats in Aichi to its pro-Government opponents. Other regions where pro-Government or Independent candidates scored major victories were Miyagi, Shiga, Gifu, Fukushima, Tottori and Shimane prefectures.

One of the most surprising results of the campaign was the comparative success of Inoue Kaoru's *Jichi-tō* (pro-Government and moderate conservative group). It had won five of the six seats in the Kyoto area and had virtually swept the board in Yamaguchi and Wakayama prefectures as well. The Ultra-Conservatives had held their own in Kumamoto and had managed to make quite a good showing in Hiroshima; but they ended with an almost total failure in Yamaguchi (Torio's home province), and did even worse in Kōchi (Tani's home province).

The Kyushu Confederation of Progressive Parties was returned for all the seats in Saga and Kagoshima prefectures. The result for Kagoshima is somewhat unusual, because Satsuma (the old name for Kagoshima) was one of the two 'home provinces' of the *Sat-Chō* Government. With the sudden deaths of both Saigō Takamori and Ōkubo Toshimichi at the end of the 1870s, the power of Satsuma in the topmost ranks of the governing hierarchy seems to have declined slowly but surely. By 1890, the chief spokesman for the Satsuma interest, Matsukata Masayoshi, was known to be quite content to follow the lead of his Chōshū colleagues. Therefore the ordinary people of Kagoshima may have felt little reason to support the existing régime on grounds of regional loyalty, and as Satsuma could no longer lord it over the Government, chose to favour the opposition. Moreover the internal politics of the former fief had been complicated in the previous year (1889) by a serious quarrel on the subject of treaty revision. The younger inhabitants of the district had wished to found a kind of Satsuma-based *Daidō Danketsu*; but the older men refused to commit themselves to the project which failed for lack of their support. This timidity on the party of the 'clan elders' weakened the local conservative parties.[11]

By the time of the opening of the Diet in November 1890, the situation in the House of Representatives had become far more coherent and stabilized. In August, the *Jiyū-tō*, the *Aikoku-kōtō*, and the *Daidō Club* dissolved themselves in order to make way for the proposed amalgamation of all the Liberal groups. This was in accordance with the agreement reached by the three factions at the time of the formation of the *Kōin Club* in May 1890. The *Jiyū-tō* and *Aikoku-kōtō* went out of existence on 4 August; the *Daidō Club* deferred its demise until 17 August. Meanwhile, the Kyushu Confederation of Progressive Parties, encouraged by news of what had happened to the *Jiyū-tō* and *Aikoku-kōtō*, dissolved itself on 7 August, and once more sent delegates hotfoot to Tokyo to preach the holy cause of a union of all true friends of the people.

Two meetings were then held, on 12 and 23 August, at which representatives of the three former Liberal factions, the former Kyushu Confederation, and the *Kaishin-tō* discussed the idea of forming one single party. Agreement was virtually reached at the second of these two meetings on a short draft proposal for an entirely new party to be founded on Liberal principles. However, the *Kaishin-tō* delegate, Shimada Saburō, asked that details of this decision should not be made public until after his party had held its general convention on 1 September; he also requested that the new organization should insert in its programme an explicit reference to the fact that it adhered to Progressive as well as Liberal principles. The others rejected his suggestions, and Shimada walked out of the meeting.[12]

The upshot of this quarrel was that the *Kaishin-tō*, when it met on 1 September, refused to disband itself, and so the prospect of a merger between the Liberal elements and the Progressives faded away overnight. The Liberals and their supporters in Kyushu went ahead with the plans for amalgamation, and on 15 September, the new *Rikken Jiyū-tō* (Constitutional Liberal Party) was brought into existence at a meeting of prominent Liberal leaders in the *Yayoi* Hall, in Shiba park. The meeting was marked by considerable disorder—heated arguments inside the building, and *sōshi* fist-fights outside it— but at length the party programme was approved. Thus by the end of September 1890, the position of the popular parties was substantially the same as it had been before the dissolution of the first *Jiyū-tō* in October 1884. There was now once more a large and somewhat precariously united Liberal Party; and the smaller, but better organized and powerful, Progressive Party continued to be a separate entity.

Both these parties found that for the convenience of conducting their business in the Diet, it was better to have an intra-mural as well as an extra-mural association. Consequently, on 2 September 1890, the Liberal Members of the House of Representatives formed themselves into a society known as the *Yayoi Club*. The name of this club was taken from the building where it was founded, the same *Yayoi* Hall in Shiba park mentioned above. The *Yayoi Club* was not really different from the *Rikken Jiyū-tō*; it was simply the parliamentary branch, so to speak, of the latter body. Likewise, on 1 September 1890, the Members of the new House of Representatives attached to the Progressive Party were authorized by the party convention to set up the *Giin Shūkaijō* (Members' Club). In the case of both the *Yayoi Club* and the *Giin Shūkaijō*, membership was available only to those adherents of the two parent parties who also had a seat in the Diet; and in both cases, all those eligible joined.

There was only one exception to this. In October, some Right-wing 'Liberals', belonging in the main to nationalist associations which had been affiliated with the former *Daidō Club*, held a meeting in Saga city, Kyushu. (There was always an active ultra-nationalist movement in the southern island.) Then in the following month, they and their sympathizers from other regions founded in Tokyo a political party of their own, which they called the *Kokumin Jiyū-tō* (National Liberal Party). Needless to say, the *Kokumin Jiyū-tō* was always nationalist and never Liberal.[13] Its sponsors hoped that it would grow into a large association which would be national as well as nationalist, and would link together all the separate Ultra-Conservative factions in the provinces; but this never happened.

The *Kokumin Jiyū-tō* had only five adherents in the House of Representatives; and in 1891, it was dissolved. However, its history though brief is not altogether without significance. For one thing, it is an indication of how many different sorts of eggs had gone into the making of the *Daidō Danketsu* and afterwards the *Daidō Club*, and—to continue the metaphor—the unscrambling of this particular omelette had been one of the problems which had held up the amalgamation of the Liberal factions earlier in the year. Then again, the formation of the *Kokumin Jiyū-tō* shows that, as always, the Ultra-Conservatives tried to make up for their lack of members by engaging in a ceaseless round of high-level activity and bombast. They were cheeky, though weak.

Meanwhile, many of the more moderate Conservatives and supporters of the Government in the new House also came to feel the need for a special intra-mural association. This they founded on 22 August, and gave it the neutral-sounding name of *Taisei-kai* (Accomplishment Society). Members of the House belonging to this group had all been elected as ostensible Independents (Non-Party and Not Biased); but in reality, almost all of them had been strongly pro-Government from the first. Naturally enough, it contained a large number of the serving and recently resigned officials who had been elected to the House. Since the Cabinet was formally committed to the doctrine of non-responsibility to the Diet, however, it was bad politics from its point of view to have an openly pro-Government party in the House of Representatives. Hence the rather cryptic title of the *Taisei-kai*. Hence, too, the fact that, unlike both the *Yayoi Club* and the *Giin Shūkaijō*, the *Taisei-kai* never had a parent body outside the House. Though it drew up its own short political credo,[14] it was never anything more than an association of those Members who had a general sympathy for the aims and methods of the Government.

Members of the House who were not enrolled in the *Yayoi Club*, the *Giin Shūkaijō*, the *Kokumin Jiyū-tō*, or the *Taisei-kai* remained as Independents. Most, but not all, of this group also supported the Government. Among the Independents were the Minister for Trade and Agriculture, Mutsu Munemitsu, and other *Jichi-tō* candidates who had been returned from Yamaguchi and Wakayama prefectures, and also most of the Members belonging to the ultra-nationalist Kumamoto National Rights Party. On the other hand, the five Kyoto *Kōmin-kai* members, also *Jichi-tō*, chose to join the *Taisei-kai*.

When the Diet was formally opened on 29 November 1890, then, the state of the parties in the House of Representatives was as follows:

Yayoi Club (Liberal)	130
Giin Shūkaijō (Progressive)	40
Kokumin Jiyū-tō (National Liberals)	5
Taisei-kai (Pro-Government)	80
Independents	45
	300

Since the *Yayoi Club* and the *Giin Shūkaijō* were able to co-operate quite successfully inside the Diet, the anti-Government popular parties had a majority of forty votes. In what seems like tacit recognition of this state of affairs, the Emperor, acting on behalf of the Government, appointed Nakajima Nobuyuki (*Yayoi Club*), who was a veteran Liberal leader but before that had been a prefectural governor, to be Speaker of the House, and the former Senator, Tsuda Mamichi (*Taisei-kai*), to be deputy Speaker.

Aspects of the first House of Representatives, other than its narrowly political allegiances and party composition, merit attention. Of the 300 Members, 109 were *shizoku* and 191 were commoners.[15] The days when the former military class had determined the politics of the Empire were over, though the ratio of *shizoku* to commoners in the House (1:2) was far higher than the corresponding ratio for the population as a whole (1:19).

The average age of Members was surprisingly low, even when one takes into account the fact that expectation of life in Japan has increased by at least fifteen or so years since the middle of the Meiji era. The following table shows that very nearly two-thirds of the total number of Members were less than forty-three years of age in 1890.[16]

Year period	No. of members born in
Bunsei, 1818–29	10
Tempō, 1830–43	59
Kōka, 1844–47	40
Kaei, 1848–53	99
Ansei, 1854–60	85
Manen, 1860	7

The oldest Member of the House was sixty-seven (Suematsu) or seventy-two (Fukuchi); the youngest just turned thirty.

The average amount paid in taxes by Members of the House of Representatives was ¥126 per annum. As mentioned earlier, most Members were assessed at a lower rate; the average figure is somewhat misleadingly high because one Member paid over ¥2,000 and three others over ¥1,000 a year in taxes. To give a clearer idea of the relative position of the Members of the House of Representatives in the plutocracy of this period, the average amount paid in taxes by the forty-five 'millionaires' representatives' specially elected to the House of Peers was ¥1,534 per annum. The highest figure in this group was ¥11,282; the lowest ¥262.[17]

Of course, only general inferences can be drawn from data of this sort; but allowing for exceptions, it is possible to begin to sketch the outstanding features of the statistically 'typical'

Member of the House of Representatives by picturing him as being (i) a commoner; (ii) a person who, though born before the fall of the *Bakufu*, was in terms of his working life of the first generation of the Restoration; and (iii) of modest to comfortable middle-class means. Already, the break with feudalism is obvious. Our imaginary Member does not so far appear to have had many links with the Tokugawa past, when the officials of the Shogunate and fief governments were all samurai; age almost invariably took precedence over youth; and those who had amassed fortunes, if they were merchants by class, often squandered them on city amusements, and could never use them to acquire political power. With the convening of the Diet in 1890, there marched for the first time to the centre of the stage of national policy-making representatives of a 'new' class, a class which had in fact been waiting in the wings with envy and increasing ferment for some considerable time. To this class we may give the generic title of Men of Enterprise.

All in all, the elections were a triumph for the middle classes, and above all for the village landlord-entrepreneurs, who in being returned to the Diet in such numbers had come into their own. The following details of the various occupations hitherto pursued by Members show this.[18]

Occupation	No. of members
Senior officials (in office or recently retired)	18
Junior officials (i.e. *Kuchō* and Gunchō in office or recently retired)	22
Agriculture	125
Trade and industry	33
Law	22
Journalism	16
Medicine	3
Others	61

Included in the 'others' are leading party politicians, such as Nakajima Nobuyuki or Hayashi Yūzō, and also members of the recognized intelligentsia, using that word in its narrower sense to mean thinkers or opinion formers. Examples of this type of Member are Seki Nachiko (*Jichi-tō*) and Ueki Emori (*Jiyū-tō*), even though the former had earned his living as a journalist and the latter can also be regarded as a politician. These are side-issues, however. The main point is that the 'typical Member' would have very probably belonged to the rural gentry class, or failing that, to the commercial and professional middle class of the rapidly expanding cities. Furthermore, the chances are that he either was or had been a member of a local government assembly. The *Nippon Shimbun*, in one of a series of articles analysing the results of the election, stated that whereas 68 of the new Members were or had been at one time in the official service, no fewer than 158 of them were or had been at one time members of prefectural assemblies.[19]

Thus, getting on for half of the Members of the House of Representatives came from the country landlord class, and more than half of them had at one stage in their career been elected to a local assembly. A good deal has already been said about these two crucial aspects of the election, and it is convenient to defer further discussion of them to the Conclusions that follow this chapter. Meanwhile, as a general comment on the result of the election of 1890, let it be said that the voters had secured a genuinely representative though not wholly effective parliament; and, by the same token, the Government had confronted itself with a not negligible, if divided and as yet untried, opposition.[20]

CONCLUSIONS

Changing, it is the same. Despite the always distending and sometimes near cataclysmic ordering of subsequent events, the politics of 1890 are of a piece with the politics of the next half century. Accordingly, it would be possible to locate the significance of Japan's first general election in the later evolution of the four great contending groups of Liberals, Progressives, Moderate Conservatives and Ultra-Conservatives against a historical background which had for its main features pre-eminent bureaucracy, revolution instigated from above, rapid modernization, industrialization, and the links between the Liberal movement and the rural entrepreneurs. While not denying the legitimacy of this approach, it would tend perhaps to be more descriptive than analytical. The hows and whys of modern Japanese constitutional history in general, and the election of 1890 in particular, are best understood in terms of continuous interaction between Government and opposition forces. Seen in this light, this history follows an inner logic of its own. It is the logic of two voices raised in argument. Now the argument is harsh and bitter with dissent; now it suddenly dies away and there is a reasonably amicable settlement of the matters under dispute; now there is fresh controversy as each side attempts to interpret the terms of the settlement to its own advantage.

The outward form of this inner logic was the process of constitutional evolution by stages; stages, that is, of rising tension, followed by partial relaxation and reconciliation, followed by renewed tension, and so on. While this process was in operation, there were constant changes in its frame of reference. Feudal institutions were disposed of; the foundations of a modern industrial State were laid. A military caste ceased to have any special status as a military caste; in the countryside, another class, the village gentry, came into its own. Rebellion broke out; individuals died, not all of them in bed. Wars occurred, and treaties were signed. Yet though these 'extraneous' events modified, they did not interrupt the essential argument in the political arena between the Government bureaucrats and the upholders of popular rights. The former wanted statism with an element of Liberalism; the latter combined an underlying commitment to the State with a Liberal programme for its organization and government. The argument persisted, and with it the process of achieving constitutionalism through interaction. In many ways, it was a mistrustful and badly geared process; but it worked, has gone on working, and has accomplished much.

It is in the terms of, and as further evidence for, this hypothesis of interaction that the following comments on the broad significance of the 1890 election are made: first, as one stage in the process; secondly, as a symbol of the process as a whole; and thirdly, as an important step in giving this fundamental process an institutional form.

Strictly speaking, of itself, the election began nothing and it decided nothing—apart from the composition of the first House of Representatives. The holding of it had been made necessary by the decision to create representative institutions, and it has been followed by other general elections at regular intervals over the past seventy years. Thus, it was not an isolated phenomenon, but one link in a chain of development. Although it took place in an atmosphere of comparative calm and goodwill, the cries from the hustings already contained the battle-notes of future challenges and conflict. The struggle for a representative assembly was over; the fight for party Cabinets was about to commence. In respect of this rather unspectacular because primarily lineal relationship to what had gone before and what was to come after in the process of constitutional development, the election occurred towards the end of a period of low tension. Further, it marked the transition of the evolutionary process from its phase of pre-constitutional contest (Bureaucrats *v.* Liberty and Popular Rights Movement, 1873–81) to its phase of post-constitutional contest (Bureaucrats *v.* Popular Parties, 1890–1918).

Yet there was more to the election than this. Did it not also to a remarkable degree contain and exemplify in itself all the various strands woven into the pattern of interaction? Each side to the great political debate was concerned with the voting in its own characteristic capacity: the bureaucrats as organizers and administrators, self-appointed guardians of public order and interests of the State; the party politicians as pace-setters and the apostles of an already considerably domesticated brand of Liberal individualism. Both sides played their part within the general framework provided by the constitution and the Law of Election; and the whole business of a parliamentary election was indisputably a Western-type innovation. In few situations were the full nature and extent of the confrontation of the two great creative forces in Meiji politics more clearly revealed. The officials were efficient and no doubt deeply interested in the results of the polling, but at the same time chary of staking the Government's future on the electors' favour since they were not yet ready to engage fully in parliamentary politics on their own account. The advocates of popular rights, for their part, had ample supplies of enthusiasm and talent but were destined, it seems, to strain for ever beyond the limits of what the general progress of society or their own party organizations would allow. The attitudes of the one side had their origin in the attitudes of the other. The very existence, perhaps, of the one side depended on the existence of the other.

This sort of dualism, when made to inhabit a house of equitable law and institutions especially designed for its expression, is the spirit and structure of representative government as it developed in Western Europe. Parliament is first a place for discussion; and there can be no doubt that once basic requirements of economic welfare and administrative technique have been met, the best of all possible political worlds is that which gives opportunities for useful debate. The election of 1890, therefore, is of interest not only as a stage in the process of interaction and not only as a symbol of that process; it is significant, too, in that it was one of the first acts by which the nation recognized the need to give itself this freedom for meaningful argument, and proceeded to do so in an official and durable way. With the constitution, the right to disagree had been embodied in the highest institutions of State, and rule by an elected majority in parliament became a feasible objective. At the election, voters availed themselves of the right in order to draw closer to the objective. Henceforward both bureaucrats and their opponents were going to have to play the interaction game in accordance (more or less!) with parliamentary rules; and 1 July 1890 was the day of the first match under the new dispensation. In other words, this force of interaction had been raised from the dust of rejection, concealment, and political battle, and was being turned into a properly constituted principle of State.

On a more cautious note—the 'three evils' of modern Japanese politics, that is, factionalism, corruption and violence were, if not exactly born at this time, strengthened as a result of the inauguration of representative institutions. Yet malpractices such as these have not of themselves destroyed Liberal democracy in Japan, despite their obviously adverse effect. Neither have they outweighed the good it has done in terms of personal emancipation and even of national progress. This is a matter of individual opinion; but it can to some extent be substantiated by what has been said of the 1890 election. Moreover, on the view that the three evils were primarily traditional elements which were liberated along with much else by the dissolution of the old society, rather than importations along with much else from abroad, the creation of parliamentary forms was probably a vital first step to effective counteraction. It was precisely by increasingly frequent reference to a modern standard of orderly and democratic government that they were to be seen as deleterious, as older criteria, based on unmitigated authoritarianism and Confucian notions of probity, became inevitably less applicable.

The internal dynamics of the bureaucrats and anti-bureaucrats are always worth investigation. What gave each of these groups its power? What drove it to seek some kind of understanding with its opposite number? Why did not the antagonism they felt for each other force them so far apart that any sort of interaction would have been impossible?

As has been said earlier, a correct understanding of the Meiji political world depends on trying to answer these questions. The dynamics of interaction grew from a common root of individual ambition and the national experience of the period immediately before and after the collapse of the *Baku-han* system as a result of collision with the West. The legacy of feudal statecraft, the pressure of day-to-day problems, concern for personal success, and the appeal of the West combined to build up in the minds of the leading bureaucrats a desire to fashion some sort of constitution and some sort of representative institutions for their reconstructed State. The agitators for liberty and popular rights acted on a similar combination of motives. Their political conduct, like that of their followers, was animated by what persisted of the Tokugawa polity and its concepts, by contemporary dissatisfactions and ambitions, and by the example of the West. What follows is an attempt to enlarge slightly on these statements by relating them to the first parliamentary election.

The influence of the West should not be thought of as having been somehow slight or superficial. On the contrary, it was this, probably more than any other single factor, which drew the reforming bureaucrats and their Liberal opponents together, and gave them a common goal in a general desire for a Western-type constitution. From 1873 to 1889, the argument was not really about the need for a constitution. When should it be promulgated? How much real power should it put in the hands of the people? These were the issues to which those who stressed State rights and those who stressed individual rights addressed themselves. Both views assumed a good deal of Westernization along with their patriotism; and, as already explained, both the moderate bureaucratic Right and the conservative Liberal Left were deeply involved in the election which they treated with due seriousness.

Moreover, the evidence of the election results, the campaigning that preceded them, and the newspapers that recorded it all, would tend to show that a modernization tantamount to Westernization had proceeded quite rapidly and penetrated quite deeply. Of course, it is not possible to claim that this process was anything like complete. Nevertheless—to take but one facet of this steady instruction in a hitherto alien culture—there existed by 1890 in all parts of the country an élite composed of men who thoroughly understood the methods, problems and opportunities of representative government. These were the men, candidates and publicists, who wrote the newspapers and toured the constituencies making speeches on Western political theory and its application to Japan. The voters and the general public responded to this initiative from above with enthusiasm for speech meetings, an almost 100 per cent poll, and a win for the anti-Government parties. The electoral weaknesses and confusions of the xenophobic Ultra-Conservative groups are another indication of this same general trend.

There emerges a picture of revolutionary change instigated from above; of change which is essentially responsive in character, taking place as it does in a mode of interaction between Japan and the West, between rulers and ruled; and of change which has for its goal a modernization in many respects identical with Westernization. This finding for the election is true for Meiji society as a whole. Moreover, it would seem to contradict the view sometimes held that during the Meiji era, Japan was—in a manner never fully explained—technologically transformed but spiritually unaffected by the West. No doubt the Meiji leadership in some ways deliberately re-affirmed the traditional value system; apart from this, democracy in Japan, even in its post-1945 phase, will always be distinctively Japanese, if only because no long-established community can be expected to lose all traces of its pre-modern character. On the other hand, ideas that change has been confined to technology, or ought to be so confined, are simply not tenable in the light of the developments of the past hundred years.[1]

However, while all this is to be kept in mind, the essential role of the Occident in Japan during the second half of the last century was that of a mentor. It gave new forms, a new impetus and something of its own spirit to forces transmitted from the native past. Quite definitely, one of the strongest of these forces was localism.

Not long after the Government had abolished the fiefs, Ōkubo wrote:

Although, in the autumn of 1871, a decree abolishing the *han* was promulgated and an order establishing the prefectural system was issued so that there would be consistency in government instructions, for almost one thousand years, the people have been accustomed to the oppressive feudal system and its unfortunate practices. Given the customs and feelings of the people, how can the country be adjusted to new institutions? Democracy, of course, cannot be established in Japan, and the old monarchy can no longer be maintained. We must develop a political system that conforms to the customs, feelings, and conditions of our nation. We must decide on a fixed statute for the State, that is, a system of constitutional monarchy.[2]

These observations show how much the senior ministers had to take into account the strength of an ordinary man's attachment to his native district when contemplating the political future of the country. Likewise, an awareness of this mountain of localist feeling must have lain behind Kido's experiment with the Conference of Prefectural Governors, and behind the *Dajō-kan's* considered policy of setting up representative assemblies in the provinces before it allowed a national assembly to be elected. Conversely, the popular rights movement drew many of its energies from this same force of localism. A sentence or two from the *Aikoku-kōtō* manifesto of 1890 adequately sums up the situation in this regard:

In the feudal era, our country went too far in the direction of regional particularism and had an administration which was seriously weakened by decentralization. The system of every little corner of territory maintaining its own independence was abolished at the time of the Imperial Restoration; but there was an unexpected tendency for the central Government to enlarge its powers and the provinces gradually grew weaker. Our party is determined to introduce a fair system of local self-government, and to bring about a proper and reasonable division of power.

Thus, both bureaucrats and Liberals were conscious of the strength of regional feeling nurtured by the old order. The former, quite rightly, felt obliged to placate it; the latter, equally rightly, used it as a shelter in times of dire trouble (Itagaki's sojourns in Tosa after 1873 and again after 1884) and as an instrument to turn public opinion against the Government. Localism and regionalism, then, taking them together, were a potent source of interaction, though by no means the only source. In connexion with this, it may be mentioned again that the local assemblies set up by the authorities after 1878 had a truly useful and vital function. In all sorts of ways, they were a veritable stepping-stone from the feudalism that was dying to the modern parliamentary State that was coming to be.

The significance of localism as a major factor in early Meiji politics is fully attested by its wide influence and thrusting power in the 1890 election. Many of the candidates of all political colours were members of the local assemblies or else had held posts in the local administrations. Many more besides these relied on parish pride or local connexions to see them home. Many of the political parties of the election were nothing more than regional associations. Even the 'national' parties were really federations of like-minded regional associations; and Liberal fragmentation after the collapse of the *Daidō Danketsu* in 1889 can be explained to some extent in terms of regional loyalties. This strong and pervasive spirit of localism was at one and the same time a strength and a weakness of the nascent parliamentary movement in Japan.

In few countries attempting representative institutions for the first time can Liberalism have come more easily and more securely to the countryside. Most nations, which though not in the direct tradition of West European Liberal culture have experimented with its type of government, have found that this could make some headway among the intelligentsia of the cities but failed in the rural areas. In Japan, this was not so. The village gentry who after 1868 could be projected by localism into national politics, were at least the compeers of, and in some respects ahead of, the city dwellers in their radical leanings. The ready acceptance up and down the land of the new ideas by this important class of persons—who, it must be stressed, were not the younger sons of established landlord and village industrialist families, but were the heads of these families in their own generation—must have done much to foster their rapid growth and practical application from, say, 1873 to 1924. Long enough, that is, for the parliamentary system to become customary for the nation as a whole, and to that extent an established and native institution.

On the other hand, the economic flesh of the rural proprietors and capitalists was destined to become the enemy of their political spirit; and, in the twentieth century, men of this class weakened representative government by using it to consolidate their financial hold over the less fortunate group of tenant farmers and village poor. This divergence, between the economic interests of the rural capitalists and their Liberalism, did not have any serious effects until after the end of the Meiji period. Before then, it is the cohesiveness of their economic power and political behaviour which is important, and not any potential conflict between these two aspects of their activities. However the *laissez-faire* attitudes of the Liberal manifestos in 1890, to say nothing of the anti-plutocratic outlook of the radical Right, contain more than a hint of future developments.

Apart from this, it is obvious that, if localism is carried too far, it will disrupt the essential business of the central government, distort the operations of a national parliament, and fragment any movement based on an appeal to the people. In the Japan of the Meiji era, there was always a danger that this would happen. This was probably one of the reasons why the bureaucrats, intent above all on firm national government to handle a national reconstruction, were so reluctant to hand over executive power in 1890. It was certainly one of the reasons why their opponents were not more united.

From whatever angle we look at it, the exuberant and many-sided localism of the first general election was, like its factionalism, a manifestation of a society in transition. It was the mark of the old trying to fashion itself for the new; alternatively, it was the mark of the new trying to adapt itself to the old. Furthermore, there can be no doubt that the localism of 1890 was nothing other than a continuation in different forms of the *han* and village autonomy of Tokugawa times.

Though the connexions between the village capitalists and localism are important, their role as supporters of individualism is just as significant. Generally speaking, people in this group were not so distinguished as individuals as the top rank of national leaders; but they were the element that gave the Liberty and Popular Rights Movement its popular backing, and provided the new parliamentary system with that backbone of continuous public interest without which it could not have functioned. They were the soldiers whom the generals led to the war. Without them, there might very well have been no war, or else it would have ended rather differently. They were the community which was so well represented in the first House of Representatives.

What motivated them? Basically, their objection to arbitrary taxation, coupled with their dislike of centralization and the *Sat-Chō* monopoly of power. What made them sufficiently confident in themselves to join Itagaki's crusade? Basically, the economic power they had acquired under the old order. As a rule, the village gentry who participated in the election were not *shizoku*. Therefore under the Tokugawa Shogunate, men of their station could not have had anything more than an off-stage voice in national or fief politics. Yet the vigour and non-conformity with which they interested themselves in political questions after the Restoration show that this class must have been a reservoir of latent Liberal-type individualism by the end of the Tokugawa era. This potential for political action the gentry had gained from the freedom they had had before 1868 to make good in the economic sphere. Of many a candidate or elected Member it was reported that his family had been influential farmers (i.e. rich peasants who were also money-

lenders, traders and small manufacturers) for several generations. This capital, this substance, which underlay the influence
enjoyed by a particular family over the others in its neighbourhood, must itself have been obtained by the exercise of a fair
degree of individualism—astute and self-interested and mer-
cenary. Accordingly, given the opportunities that came with the
Restoration, it was a comparatively easy matter for the gentry
to extend to the political field attitudes and methods they had
inherited in the economic one.[3]

Just as localism was present in the great cities as well as in
the villages, so was individualism a power among other groups
in the population besides the rural entrepreneurs. Indeed this
individualism, sometimes called 'personality-ism', was one of
the dominant themes in national life at the time of the election
and during the Meiji era. Inevitably, the way in which it made
itself felt differed from group to group.

On the whole, what was true of the rural capitalist was also
true of his urban counterpart, but to a noticeably less marked
degree. For reasons already adumbrated, although the city
merchants, too, espoused Liberal individualism, their opposition
to the bureaucrats was not so vehement.[4]

On a rather different level of emotion and experience, many
of the more able members of Meiji society, irrespective of
whether they were *shizoku* or not, seem to have welcomed the
chance it gave them to cultivate their own personalities. Feudalism had naturally tended to prevent an individual from developing his own nature outside certain fixed and rather narrow
patterns of behaviour; seemingly, the higher the social rank, the
greater the constraint. Feudal elements apart, familistic notions
also held people in thrall. While duty to the smaller (family,
village, district) or larger (State) collectives continued to be the
accepted norm, however, it manifestly ceased to be the only
acceptable norm. A great deal of the dynamism of the new era
must have come from this gradual breaking down of restrictions
and inhibitions in the field of individual action for individual
ends. For the first time for several hundreds of years, people

could begin to feel that the world really was their oyster; and society benefited more than it suffered from this discovery. The career of Ōkuma Shigenobu was especially notable in this respect. He was a man who derived all that he could from the opportunities presented by his age; he was also a vigorous personality who did much for his countrymen in that and later periods.

Ōkuma was not alone in this. Electoral politics, as might be expected, was a sphere where this change soon showed itself, and already in 1890 candidates competed, obviously and openly, for reasons not least of which were a concern with purely personal gratification and prestige. So much so that the newspapers sometimes made fun of 'genealogy candidates', i.e. those who justified their candidatures in more conventional terms of family honour. It is impossible not to believe that the great majority of candidates liked standing for the House of Representatives just as much as they enjoyed travelling abroad when they could, and found similar satisfaction in their careers as lawyers and journalists, in belonging to the prefectural assemblies, or in sitting on the local school, public health and conscription boards. So here, in a very real sense, was a frontier zestfully crossed.

Not only were the traditionally encouraged individualism of heroes and the traditionally tolerated individualism of the pleasure quarters now free to run in wider and unprecedented courses. To them was joined a totally new and still unofficial concept of an individualism of rights. It is true, of course, that things did not turn out so well as they promised in this respect: conflict between the nascent claims for the individual and a far older and more thoroughgoing sense of obligation to the group has been endemic. However, against a background of this sort, the rise of the individual, sustained by a more slowly developing idea of individual rights, has been an important adjunct of Japanese modernization.[5]

The breeze of individualism, then, had entered Meiji politics partly as an extension of, and partly as a reaction to, the spirit and institutions of the Tokugawa State. It blew on bureaucrats and Liberals alike. Ōkubo, Kido, Itō and the other senior *Sat-Chō* ministers were not just patriotic statesmen; they were also professional administrators anxious to stay in office. Itagaki, Gotō and Ōkuma were not just public-spirited denouncers of evil; they were also seekers of power. While all this made for a certain amount of opportunism, it also helped to produce that empiricism which was such an important element of interaction. Moreover, with this individualism there went a prevailing mood of iconoclasm towards the past, enjoyment of the present, and optimism for the future; and nearly all the influential men of affairs in the Meiji era shared to some degree in this mood. This was another factor that made it relatively easy for them to come to terms with one another when they so desired. After all, if there is a general though tacit agreement that there is nothing fundamentally wrong and the national future looks promising, why carry disputes to the point of seriously endangering this state of affairs?

This is almost to write of the politics of consensus. The term has been avoided so far because its passive, if not flabby, connotations hardly suit the purposeful activism of the period under review. Interaction is a better description of this axiom of Japanese political behaviour as it operated between 1867 and 1890, in a grand rallying and metamorphosis of forces at home to counteract and exploit pressures from abroad. Interaction, though, was incapsulated in, and fortified by, habits of consensus. Thus, before the Restoration, ideas that action could rightly proceed only from a formal unanimity of opinion, and that group conflicts could be harmonized away, had been staunchly upheld by the Confucian orthodoxy. Afterwards, they were to find an ultimate source of authority in the far more nebulous tenets of the Emperor system. Their role in recent Japanese history would have been deeply significant even if the country had been socially and politically a completely unified nation state since 1600. It is all the more striking in that such a condition did not begin to come about until after 1868.

Everything that has been said about the feudal past and the way it shaped and coloured the 1890 election would indicate that the Tokugawa polity, though all but static in its hierarchy and techniques of political control and virtually closed in its relations with the outside world, was neither monolithic nor absolutist. Rather, it was a honeycomb equilibrium of diverse elements: a compound of law and power; of a formal dictatorship working through the machinery of discussion and based on a doctrine of moral obligation; of *Bakufu* rights and *han* rights; of daimyo rights and village rights; of samurai interests and capitalist interests; of emphasis on personal initiative, ostensibly at least, for the public good; of the empire of Chinese learning as opposed to the principalities of the National and Dutch Learnings; of agrarianist bias together with class and regional divisions as a setting for private commercial enterprise, group autonomy, and a slowly growing national consciousness. This was its considered, institutional nature. At the same time, it was also six or seven generations of ordinary human life— life large enough to include all its customers. The world of restaurants and big city gangsters had preceded the Meiji Restoration.

It was this richly variegated and pluralist society, which also had some fifteen centuries of history as a national and cultural entity, that broke under the impact of the West and its own reaction to that impact. But it was the fixed and outward political–social order, with its underlying idea of permanence, that disappeared; not the diverse elements and their inter-relation in a single, albeit pluralistic, whole. These elements, of course, underwent great modifications and changes of form after 1868— the *Bakufu* became the new bureaucracy; the *han* became the prefectures; the samurai became the new *shizoku* élite; the rural entrepreneurs became the backbone of the new Liberal movement, and so on. Nevertheless, despite these transformations, the inner natures and separate existences of these elements did not alter so much. They survived to determine the pattern of the Meiji history of constitutional conflict culminating in parliamentary institutions. Therefore—given always the force, timing and quality of the contacts with the West—the events leading up to the election and the election itself were 'foretold', so to speak, in the pluralist structure of the Tokugawa State and its political ethic of quasi-constitutional rule by a mixture of written regulation, custom and consensus. Meiji interaction was rooted in a Tokugawa tradition of multiple traditions.

Mid-Meiji society, as observed through a study of the election, resembled while going beyond that of the preceding period in its vigour and diversity. The Tokugawa savants had often indulged in polemics, but their discussions were for a long time strictly academic and usually carried on in discreet seclusion. The mid-Meiji publicists, on the other hand, embraced controversy in the most fervent and open manner imaginable. Their newspapers, memorials and speeches were full of it. Not even the throne was entirely outside the arena of public debate. The mass of the people ruled by the shoguns and the various daimyo doubtless maintained a fairly cheerful view of life and their individual fortunes through each successive generation. The subjects of Meiji inherited this optimism from their forefathers; but they applied it not only to their personal destinies, but also to the common destiny of their nation and society as a whole. This was a big difference. In its two and a half centuries of existence, the Tokugawa polity had experienced some concealed but far-reaching alterations in its economic and social apparatus. These alterations were frequently not fully recognized by the ruling classes; or when they were, not welcomed by it. In a nearly complete contrast to this, mid-Meiji society was vibrant with change, the knowledge that it was changing, and the will to change even faster. There was some uncertainty about the ultimate destination; but the twin concepts of Westernization and national greatness loomed large in most minds and hearts.

This was the society for which the election and the newspapers that reported it acted as a mirror; from the prudent and hard working integrity of Yamagata and Suematsu Kenchō, through the reasoned eloquence and high-minded fulminations of Itagaki and the other Liberal or Progressive leaders, to the spurious sixtieth birthday party and even more nefarious activities of an Osaka gunsmith with political ambitions. But the election did not merely reflect. Themselves both a manifestation and a vehicle of consensus between governors and governed, and having roots in domestic as well as foreign tradition, the first and subsequent general elections have helped preserve Japanese society through a future by no means so assured as that prognosticated for it in 1890.

APPENDICES

I. IMPERIAL RESCRIPT OF 14 APRIL 1875

After ascending the Imperial Throne, we called together the entire Court and swore the Charter Oath to the gods, establishing the policies of the Empire and seeking the welfare of all our subjects. Happily, as a result of the efforts of the Spirits of Our Ancestors and as a result of the efforts of the whole body of Our Court, We have to-day achieved a semblance of peace. Yet the Restoration is not long since past, and there still remain not a few changes and reforms to be undertaken in the internal administration.

We, now, in fulfilment of the principles of Our Oath, hereby set up a Senate to broaden the source of legislation, and a Supreme Court to strengthen the powers of justice. Moreover, by summoning the officials from the provinces, We shall be informed of the conditions of the people, and shall take counsel for the public good.

It is Our desire to introduce by degrees a system of constitutional government for the nation and to join with you, Our subjects, in looking forward to that auspicious event. You must not adhere too rigidly to the customs of former times; neither should you let your zeal for progress lead you into rash actions.

Mark well these Our words, and give Us your support.

(Miyakoshi, *N.K.K.S.* p. 186)

II. IMPERIAL RESCRIPT OF 12 OCTOBER 1881

We, sitting on the Throne which has been occupied by Our dynasty for over 2,500 years, and now exercising in Our name and right all authority and power transmitted to Us by our Ancestors, have long had in view gradually to establish a constitutional form of government, to the end that Our Successors on the Throne may be provided with a rule for Their guidance.

It was with this object in view that in the 8th year of Meiji, We established the Senate, and in the 11th year of Meiji, authorized the formation of Local Assemblies, thus laying the foundation for the gradual reforms which We contemplated. These Our acts must convince you, Our subjects, of Our determination in this respect from the beginning.

Systems of government differ in different countries, but sudden and unusual changes cannot be made without great inconvenience.

Our Ancestors in Heaven watch Our acts, and We recognize Our responsibility to Them for the faithful discharge of Our duties, in accordance with the principles, and the perpetual increase of the glory, They have bequeathed to Us.

We therefore hereby declare that We shall, in the 23rd year of Meiji, establish a Parliament, in order to carry into full effect the determination We have announced, and We charge Our faithful subjects bearing Our commissions to make, in the mean time, all necessary preparations to that end. .

With regard to the limitations upon the Imperial prerogative, and the constitution of the Parliament, We shall decide hereafter and make proclamation in due time.

We perceive that the tendency of Our people is to advance too rapidly, and without that thought and consideration which alone can make progress enduring, and We warn Our subjects, high and low, to be mindful of Our will, and that those who may advocate sudden and violent changes, thus disturbing the peace of Our realm, will fall under Our displeasure.

We expressly proclaim this to Our subjects.

(McLaren, *Jap. Govt. Docs.* p. 86)

III. 'JIYŪ-TŌ' MANIFESTO, OCTOBER 1881

1 We shall endeavour to extend the liberties of the people, preserve their rights, promote their happiness, and improve their social condition.

2 We desire to establish a constitutional form of government of the best type.

3 We shall strive to realize our objects by uniting with those of our compatriots who approve of our party and its principles.

(Miyakoshi, *N.K.K.S.* p. 385)

IV. 'RIKKEN KAISHIN-TŌ' MANIFESTO, MARCH 1882

The Emperor has graciously given us a constitution. The people of our Empire have been favoured with an unprecedented stroke of good fortune. At this juncture, what plan can we devise, what duty perform, in order that the people of the Empire will not disgrace themselves? There is nothing for it but to join all together in a political party and so make manifest our strength. Come brethren, let us organize a party and do our duty as subjects!

Happiness is something we expect of humanity. However we are not interested in the privileged happiness of a small minority. In the final analysis, this sort of happiness is self-interest, and is contrary to that glory of the Imperial House and prosperity of the people for which we stand. The glory of the Imperial House and the prosperity of the people are what we greatly desire. However we do not want the glory and prosperity of a brief moment. That sort of glory and prosperity are of limited duration, and are contrary to the boundless glory and eternal prosperity for which we stand. Therefore, should there be one or two who make our Empire their plaything, who despise the glory of the Imperial House and the prosperity of the people, and who, basking in the transient ease of the present time, have no thought for permanent injuries, we shall regard them as public enemies. We shall try to form this party from those who hope for a glory that will enable the Imperial House to be maintained for ever, and for a prosperity that the people will enjoy for ever. Come brethren, join our party and make manifest these hopes!

Political reform and progress shall be our unceasing aspirations. If there is neither reform nor progress in politics, it is futile to look for a boundless glory, and a waste of time to plan for an everlasting prosperity. In the end, it would be impossible to perfect the body politic. Though we hope for political reform and progress, we do not favour violent change. To think in terms of imprudent and sudden transformation is simply to disorganize society and hamper political progress. For the same reason, we reject and cannot share our aspirations with those who, lost in the darkness of their own narrow minds, cling vainly to the past and, emulating the violence of the extremists, like to get excited. We desire to reform politics by truly proper and orderly methods, and to achieve progress through a policy of steadiness and honesty. The following are the two articles of our covenant:

A Our Party shall be called the Constitutional Progressive Party.
B Our Party shall unite those subjects of the Empire who desire the following:
   i The preservation of the glory of the Imperial House, and the perfecting of the prosperity of the people.
   ii Improvements in the internal administration before any extension of national rights.
   iii The elimination of interference by the central authorities, and the setting up of the basic structure of local self-government.
   iv The widening of the franchise to be in keeping with the general progress of society.
   v The reduction to an absolute minimum of diplomatic bargaining and the strenuous promotion of trade relations, in our dealings with foreign countries.
   vi The maintaining of the principle of 'hard money' in the coinage system.

(Miyakoshi, N.K.K.S. p. 403)

v. 'RIKKEN TEISEI-TŌ' MANIFESTO, MARCH 1882

Our Constitutional Imperial Party humbly bases itself on the Imperial Rescript of 12 October 1881. At home, we shall preserve the national polity unbroken for ages eternal and shall strengthen the rights and happiness of the people; abroad, we shall extend national rights and look forward to the upholding of the honour of the Empire in every land. We shall follow a path of gradual advance. We shall not adhere too stubbornly to the past; neither shall we commit ourselves to frenzied change. All we desire is that order and progress should go together. In this way, we shall preserve the peace of the country. Accordingly, we consider it to be of the utmost importance that there should be a plan for progress, and have determined the programme of our Party as follows:

i His Majesty has made it clear that a Parliament will be opened in 1890. Our Party respectfully accepts this, and will not countenance discussion of the terms or timing of the Imperial Rescript.

ii His Majesty has declared that the constitution will be a matter for His own august decision. Our Party will respectfully abide by this, and will not fail to observe the provisions of a constitution sponsored by His Majesty.

iii It is beyond dispute that the sovereignty over the Empire rests in the Emperor alone, but its practical application will be regulated by a system of constitutional government.

iv The Diet should consist of two Chambers.

v In the election of Representatives, there should be a restricted franchise.

vi The Diet should be empowered to frame laws for the internal affairs of the Empire.

vii The Emperor should have the prerogative of approving or rejecting the legislation of the Diet.

viii Military and naval officers should not be allowed to intervene in politics.

ix The officials in charge of the administration of justice should be made independent as soon as the legal system has been put in order.

x Assembly and speech, so long as they are not prejudicial to national safety and order, are public freedoms. Speeches, newspapers and publications should be free within the limits laid down by law.

xi With regard to finance, the existing paper currency should be gradually replaced by convertible bank notes.

(Miyakoshi, *N.K.K.S.* p. 456)

VI. SUPPLEMENTARY PENAL REGULATIONS
FOR THE LAW OF ELECTION of the MEMBERS OF THE
HOUSE OF REPRESENTATIVES (Summary)

1 Forbids corruption of electors by supplying them with refreshment, transport or lodging in connexion with their attendance at polling stations or declaration of poll meetings.
2 Forbids interference with electors' right to vote by means of intimidation, abduction or deceit.
3 Forbids innuendo.
4 Forbids unruly demonstrations.

(*Kampō* No. 2,073. 30 May 1890)

VII. 'JIYŪ-TŌ' MANIFESTO, 23 FEBRUARY 1890

Principles

Our Party is based on Liberalism.

Main Objectives

Our Party will seek only to enhance the perpetual union of Emperor and people by extending liberty, by protecting rights, by esteeming virtue, and by fostering the commonweal.

Party Platform

1 We shall bring in party Cabinets.
2 If the officials of the Court of Administrative Litigation, either deliberately or else by accident, harm the rights of the people, we shall see to it that [the latter] are indemnified.
3 We shall make equal treaties with foreign countries.
4 We shall introduce the jury system.
5 We shall improve the education system and encourage the spread of learning.
6 We shall improve the military system and shorten the period of reserve service.
7 We shall abolish the system for retiring public officials.
8 We shall cut the costs of administration and reduce the number of officials.
9 In general, when fixing the rates for taxes, we shall pay attention to profits.
10 We shall reduce the land-tax.
11 We shall increase the number of income-tax grades.
12 We shall overhaul the arrangements for the upkeep of government property, and shall pay great attention to the management of this.
13 We shall abolish the tax qualification for election candidates.
14 We shall give the vote to those who pay ¥5 or more in direct national taxes.

15 We shall make the age qualification for election candidates 25 years, and that for electors 20 years.
16 We shall make the election constituencies bigger.
17 We shall do away with special protection for home industries.
18 We shall strengthen the organs of local self-government, and we shall reform the prefectural system.
19 We shall reform the Registration Law.
20 We shall use the property belonging to the government as the basis for local self-government.
21 We shall enlarge the freedoms of publication and assembly.
22 We shall abolish the Peace Preservation Ordinance.
23 We shall reform the time limit for paying taxes on fields.

(Hayashida, Nihon Seitō Shi, 1, 264)

VIII. 'DAIDŌ CLUB' MANIFESTO, 4 MAY 1890

Party Platform

1 We shall uphold independent sovereignty.
  i We pledge ourselves to consult the Imperial Diet in advance on matters of diplomacy or treaty making that affect the liabilities of the nation.
  ii It is necessary to carry out treaty revision by signing completely equal treaties.
  iii We pledge ourselves to improve the organization of the Army and Navy, and to enlarge them gradually as the nation grows stronger.
  iv We pledge ourselves to curtail the period of military conscription, and to increase the number of soldiers available in times of war.
2 We shall introduce responsible Cabinets.
  i We pledge ourselves to make the Ministers of State fully responsible to the Imperial Diet as well as to His Majesty the Emperor.
  ii We pledge ourselves to make clear the distinction between policy-making officials and executive officials, and not to cause them needlessly to rotate at every change of Cabinet.
  iii We pledge ourselves to use the Privy Council purely as an advisory body.
  iv We pledge ourselves to establish the system of administrative litigation on a perfect and enduring basis.
  v It is necessary to amend the regulations governing appointments to the Civil Service, and to devise ways of appointing men of talent.
3 We intend to put the financial administration in order, and to foster the strength of the people.
  i We pledge ourselves to simplify the structure of government by

reforming the Civil Service, by re-arranging the government departments, and by reducing the number of public officials.

ii We pledge ourselves to make differences of salary correspond to the type of work done, to enact a definitive Civil Service Pensions Scheme, and to abolish the existing retirement regulations.

iii We pledge ourselves to present a statement of the previous year's accounts to the Diet at the same time as we shall submit the annual Budget estimates.

iv We pledge ourselves to maintain the independence of the Board of Audit.

v We pledge ourselves to rescind as far as possible policies that obstruct the enterprise of the people.

vi We pledge ourselves to reform the tax laws, and to simplify their procedure.

4 We shall make perfect the system of local self-government.

i We pledge ourselves to reduce to the minimum the interference of the central Government with the local officials and assemblies.

ii We pledge ourselves to entrust, as far as possible, the management of police affairs, public works, hygiene, education, and other matters to the organs of local self-government.

iii We pledge ourselves to make local custom the foundation of the Municipal and the Town and Village Codes.

5 We shall make complete the freedoms of speech, assembly and association.

i We pledge ourselves to reform the Speech, Assembly and Publications Regulations, and to abolish the Peace Preservation Ordinance.

Addenda.

i We pledge ourselves to have election constituencies consisting of one prefecture.

ii We pledge ourselves to lower the tax qualifications for candidates and voters.

iii We pledge ourselves to make the age qualification for candidates 25 years and to let the tax qualification for them be valid irrespective of locality.

iv We pledge ourselves to alter the date of election.

v We pledge ourselves to allow Hokkaidō, Okinawa *ken*, and other places to elect Representatives in proportion to their population.

vi We pledge ourselves to refrain from allowing the courts and police to make discriminations in their handling of affairs on the basis of social position, Court rank, or official rank.

vii We pledge ourselves to reform the Registration Law.

(Hayashida, *Nihon Seitō Shi*, 1, 267)

IX. 'AIKOKU-KŌTŌ' MANIFESTO, 5 MAY 1890

On this fifth day of May 1890, having met in Tokyo and formally established the *Aikoku-kōtō*, we make the following declaration:

Our party made its first appearance in 1873. At that time, we solemnly swore that we would protect the rights which Heaven has given to all men, and would make the nation free and absolutely independent. Our party was the first to speak the name of Liberty to the Empire, and the idea of making this a principle of national policy was born in those days. Even though many changes have taken place since then and circumstances are different, we have always remained true to our belief in Liberty. So we have now given this party the old name. Its principles continue to be the same.

Liberalism is a fundamental principle of government. There is nothing under Heaven that does not have a fundamental principle. How can it be that government alone lacks a fundamental principle? We desire to inaugurate the best possible type of rule by seeking for fundamental principles and making clear our primary allegiances. Government must be suited to the times, and it is not possible to put all one's fundamental principles into operation at once. Nevertheless, we consider that a political party which, neglecting fundamental principles and subverting its primary allegiances, wants only to govern in accordance with the exigencies of the existing situation, will usually be mistaken in its policies. This is why a political party has need of principles.

A country is made up of its people. As each is dear to himself, it must be that everyone loves our country; and to love that is to have a wide and generous love of humanity. Ah, if all the gentlemen in our party understand that to sacrifice themselves eagerly for their country, with the principles of Liberalism on their lips, is more important than any one individual in the country, then, by extending self-love to the entire country, we shall secure the happiness of the people as a whole. This is what Liberalism really is.

Liberty is bestowed upon us all by Heaven. Our party will never suppress this truth, and will never follow the precedent of governing by half-measures. The security of the State really lies in making the people free. To pretend that Liberty is dangerous and to deprive the people of their rights is to transgress the universal law of Heaven. Our party's assiduous demand for party Cabinets means that we wish to invest the Prime Minister with the responsibility for the general policies of State, and that we wish to raise the Imperial Household to the lofty peaks of tranquility, as a result of not allowing this [responsibility] to devolve upon the monarch. Looking carefully at the state of affairs in the outside world, what really happens to monarchs who have both absolutist parties and Liberal parties? Liberalism is the true support of reigning dynasties. Not only will it enhance the dignity of the Imperial Household above, and improve the welfare of the people below; but also, look where you will, you shall not find outside the Liberal principles of our party the means of protecting the independence of our country and of securing the public peace.

Our party, on this the occasion of its founding, is anxious to attain to these objectives by relying on these its principles. Generally speaking, what a political party needs to do is: firstly, to establish fixed principles; secondly, to work for the general welfare of the country; and thirdly, to accept the restraints of public opinion. If it fails in any of these respects, it is thereby crippled as a political party. A political party takes its stand on the principles of Liberalism and wishes to join forces with others and so grow into a very large organization. The reason why England has so much success with party Cabinets is that her parties are very large. The reason why Germany still does not have party Cabinets is her great number of small parties. If a Cabinet does not have the support of a large party behind it, it cannot take up a firm position and it cannot carry out its own policies.

As our party is one of established principle, it has to have fixed policies based on those principles. Nevertheless, the actual execution of these policies will be based upon consideration of the circumstances, and our plan provides for this throughout. Moreover, we have no wish to settle with a stroke of the pen weighty matters, the consequences of which will affect the State for a hundred years. Nor do we wish to issue documents of no real worth. However, looking back over a good many years of experience both in speech and in action, we have found it possible to summarize the fruits of this experience in the form of a public statement consisting of a number of separate clauses and articles. This is:

1 We shall reduce government intervention to the minimum.

   The business of government is to further the people's rights and to compel them to discharge their obligations. Moreover, for the good of the general public, the Government must also play some part in the management of education, communications, agriculture, trade and so on. Nevertheless, desiring as we do to govern in accordance with the principles of Liberalism, our party will reduce intervention to the minimum.

2 In internal affairs, we shall avoid the centralization of power and shall emphasize the separate rights of the provinces.

   The institutions of the various countries differ in accordance with their general conditions. In the feudal era, our country went too far in the direction of regional particularism and had an administration which was seriously weakened by decentralization. The system of every little corner of territory maintaining its own independence was abolished at the time of the Imperial Restoration; but there was an unexpected tendency for the central Government to enlarge its powers and the provinces gradually grew weaker. Our party is determined to introduce a fair system of local self-government, and to bring about a proper and reasonable division of power.

3 In external affairs, we shall maintain relations of equality with every country.

Diplomacy should concern itself with nothing else but the freedom and independence of our country. Our party will never take it upon itself to flatter the powerful nations while despising the weak, to be of service to the great while oppressing the small, to incur the dislike of one country in the hope of currying favour with another, to break faith, to show partiality, and to indulge in actions that do not of themselves provide their own clear justification. In such matters as those of the treaties and trade, so long as the other parties involved fully and fairly discharge their obligations towards us, we for our part will acknowledge their rights. In this way, we shall mutually protect each other's equal rights. This, indeed, is a basic objective of our party.

4 In military preparations, we shall lay stress on defence.

Since our main purpose in undertaking military preparations will be the defence of our independence against foreign Powers, we must make sure that we shall meet this commitment in full. Yet our party has no intention of defraying enormous sums regardless of the resources of the State, or of adopting a policy of aggression to the detriment of the State. If our country is put to shame and there is no help for it, we shall have to try and avenge this so far as our military strength will allow. But our basic objective shall be the legitimate defence of our national rights.

5 In financial administration, we shall make retrenchment our objective and shall make expenditure correspond to the resources of the people.

Administration of the finances is the thing which most closely touches the life and welfare of the people, or so we think, and it is necessary when managing this to reform all sorts of tax laws, to make the people's burden as light as possible, and to treat all tax-payers with strict impartiality. Moreover, though we shall, of course, meet all essential expenditures of the State, our party will not needlessly expand the structure of government without regard for the resources of the people. Our party intends to make large reductions in expenditure, and to nourish the strength of the nation.

Our party is anxious to legislate on the basis of the above principles and to bring about a reform of government. The reforms for which our party will surely strive are so numerous that it is scarcely possible to list them all at this stage. But the officials and people of our country are still unaccustomed to parliamentary government; and besides this, the people have not yet completed their exploration of the actual workings of government. In dealing with matters of vital importance to the State, then, the utmost care and accuracy is required both in framing a single parliamentary bill and in subjecting it to several months of painstaking examination. If we try to reform everything at once, there is a danger that our labours will miscarry. Even though we hope to carry out all sorts of reforms, it is not possible to rush our investigations. Consequently, if we are to make thorough investigations, a long time will have elapsed before they are completed and we can table legislation. Only in the case of the most urgent matters shall we table bills; and what is more, as soon as the elections to the Diet are over, we shall announce the results of our investigations, and shall submit them for consideration and debate. Though there will doubtless be additions or eliminations made to [this list], the items for discussion that our party wishes to have adopted first are, in general, as follows:

1 Reduction in the land-tax.
2 Reduction in government expenditure.
3 Reform of the tax laws.
4 Amendment of the Newspaper, Assembly and Publications Regulations.
5 Abolition of the Peace Preservation Ordinance.
6 Improvement of the police system.
7 Improvement of the prison system.
8 Discontinuation of special protection for private industry.

In the above legislative programme, the reform of the tax laws and related matters are the most urgent pieces of business. Speaking of the existing system, though it is not hard to see what is wrong with it, as we still have not completed all our investigations, we shall decide about this at a later date. The prison regulations are drawn up in the form of an Imperial ordinance; but we shall try to make them matters of law and so be in a position of being able to amend them. The three sets of Regulations [i.e. Newspaper, Assembly and Publications] we consider to be the greatest obstructions to putting representative institutions into practice and elevating public opinion. Again, the excessive secrecy of the police system has its abuses, and we shall reform it. By making easiness and simplicity our standards, it should be possible to reduce administrative costs.

Furthermore, reduction of the land-tax is an objective long entertained by our party, and is nothing more than what was discussed by its members in every region, when the Petition On Three Serious Matters was published some time ago. Although we do not claim that there are no other taxes which can be reduced, the land-tax amounts to almost one half of the total revenues of the Government. The land-tax for the most part is a tax on agriculture, and the taxes on agriculture are disproportionately heavy when compared with those levied on other activities. As for the great dependence on agricultural taxes, in feudal days, it was easy to use them as the basis of finance and so this sort of unfairness came to be perpetrated. Now, it is not the same as it was in days gone by; similarly, it is impossible to hold that tax laws which place unequal burdens on the citizens of a constitutional State are just. Though a cut in the land-tax will reduce the amount of money coming into the national treasury, one way of making up for this is to curtail administrative expenditures. As for curtailing administrative expenditures, we shall secure a severe retrenchment either by reducing the number of officials or else by re-organizing the government departments.

Moreover, there are other ways of making up for the deficit. Things like giving special protection to private trade and industry account for a great deal of the public expenditures; moreover, they are wrong in principle. In the case of such things as sea traffic or railways which concern the public interest, the grant of subsidies by the Government is wholly for the public good. The giving of special subsidies to private trade and industry is nothing more nor less than a misuse of public funds. As a result of this, industry is turned into the exclusive monopoly of a few, with whom it is impossible for the majority of industrialists to compete. Thus, the development of independent business is gravely hampered.

The things which our party, basing itself on the doctrines of Liberalism, would seek to reform when in power are by no means limited to these. The above are really the most urgent of urgent matters. We have decided to table bills on them in this year's House, and hope that they will win a wide measure of support.

Nevertheless, when one looks carefully at these [items], [one can see that] our party, with a truly heroic restraint and after checking the aspirations of many years, has taken up only these urgent problems. Though we wish for reforms in these matters, we fully realize how very difficult it will be. Why? It is a question of interpreting the constitution. Now, in all constitutional countries, parliament has the right to discuss financial policies. If a parliament does not have this right, it is without any real authority. Moreover, the right of discussing financial policies belongs first and foremost to the popular Chamber. Accordingly, by the terms of our country's constitution, the budget has to be introduced first into the Lower House. Further, it is laid down that the revenues and expenditures of the State must receive every year the approval of the Imperial Diet in the form of a budget. Our party, as a matter of constitutional government and as a matter of interpretation of the constitution, believes that the House of Representatives possesses the right to discuss financial policies. However, if some explanations of the words 'previously fixed expenditures' etc. are to prevail, the Diet will scarcely have any right to deliberate on financial policies.

On the eve of standing for the Diet, we desire to affirm that we shall strive to attain to these objectives by fair and lawful means. The principles, objectives and programme of our party are of this nature. Our party will defend itself by means of these. It shall move forward by means of these. Expecting those hardships, it hopes to carry out these things. Our party has firm faith in itself. The day when we achieve these objectives shall be the day when the people are truly secured in their Heaven-given universal rights, and the day when they will be made free and completely independent. We assert the rights of the people and their Representatives; we stand for party Cabinets. To use the common phrase—we shall enhance the glory of the Imperial Household on high, and shall foster the prosperity of the nation below. We shall uphold the majesty of our Sovereign, and we shall establish the happiness of our country. If we succeed in putting into general effect the Liberal principles of our party, we shall for the first time stand inviolable on the same lofty peaks as the Western countries and shall be on terms of complete equality with them.

The great spirit of Liberty is a harmonious and auspicious one. Blowing like the soft winds of a vernal day, it shall make the officials and people as one, and, changing the absolutism of former times into a new rule of the constitution, it shall build a great and independent nation in the Orient. Ah, our land of the dragon-fly is an orphan isle! If we are ardent in our devotion to true Liberty, shall we not make our country's glory shine through the five continents?

Our party is steadfastly resolved on this, and will not fail to observe this declaration.

(Hayashida, *Nihon Seitō Shi*, I, p. 270)

X. 'KOKUMIN JIYŪ-TŌ' MANIFESTO, NOVEMBER 1890

How can we preserve the independence of Japan and extend her influence in this present age of intense rivalry among the different Powers? Of all political questions, there is none more important than this. Needless to say, we stand for progress. Needless to say, we esteem liberty. Yet, we believe in true progress and true liberty.

When establishing a nation in this world, one must foster its own special qualities abroad and perfect its unity at home. Progress which preserves special qualities is true progress. Liberty which goes with unity is true liberty. Not a day passes but we wish to accomplish this sort of liberty and plan for that progress. Men call the copying of foreign things progress, and the advocacy of personal rights liberty. This will destroy the special qualities of our nation, injure its unity, disrupt and endanger the true spirit of the people, and will eventually bring us to enslavement by other countries. How can that be progress and liberty?

Those who try to protect their political power by making selfish use of military force are public enemies of liberty. Those who want to capture political power by encouraging parties and factions are public enemies of liberty. We shall regard it as our duty under a constitutional system to check these public enemies. The union of Throne and people, and the thing that makes development possible, is what we call the nation. Political power should always be fully and firmly in the hands of the nation as a whole.

Anyone agreeing with these principles is one of us. We believe that all upright gentlemen in the Empire must agree with these principles. The competition of the Powers is indeed a danger to the Orient. Is not a danger to the Orient a danger to the Japanese nation? Those who do not really care for their country vainly bustle round inside its boundaries, boasting of its small reputation; they dare to make a plaything of the constitutional system even. We, for the sake of the future of the Japanese people, wish to pledge ourselves to the duty of stopping this. Our intentions are as herein stated.

(Ōtsu Jun'ichirō, *Dai Nihon Kensei Shi*, III, 456)

XI. 'TAISEI-KAI' DECLARATION, 22 AUGUST 1890

Briefly, our objectives are the prosperity of the State and the happiness of its people; and we hope to attain to these objectives by upholding righteousness and paying attention to public morality. We are not a Government party; neither are we an opposition party. Though we welcome progress, we shall not push forward too quickly. Though we value law and order, we shall not be blindly conservative. Thinking only of the good of the country and the welfare of the people, we shall confine ourselves to adopting policies that are both sound and honest and shall tread the great road of fairness and impartiality. At the present time, the reduction of the fiscal burden borne by the people is an important task; yet from the point of view of enlarging national rights, we cannot be parsimonious about national expenditures. We look forward to making the legal system as complete and as perfect as possible; but we have to take into account the condition of the country and the state of the people. Naturally, the introduction of responsible Cabinets is an urgent matter; but we must see to it that the transfer of governmental power does not lead to bad feeling because of personal greed and ambition. The need for treaty revision is indisputable; yet it must be achieved in a manner creditable to ourselves, and we are against damaging the national interest through rash actions.

In short, statements of general principles are dependent on reality. What is that reality but practical problems? Therefore we have dispensed with a statement of general principles, and hope to bring about parliamentary government by making up our minds about practical problems one by one. This is why we have held this meeting.

(Hayashida, Nihon Seitō Shi, I, 298)

NOTES

INTRODUCTION

1 For a translation of the text of the constitution, see Itō, *Commentaries;* or McLaren, *Jap. Govt. Docs.* pp. 136–44.

2 The Emperor had the power to nominate distinguished citizens to the Upper House, and the fifteen most wealthy tax-payers in each of the three *fu* (metropolitan prefectures) and forty-two *ken* (prefectures) had the right to elect one of themselves to it.

3 The *Dajōkan* was an ancient Court institution which had been revived in 1868 as the supreme governing body of the Empire. It continued in this role, acting also as a Regency Council, until it was replaced by a modern Cabinet system in 1885.

4 For an account of this dispute, see Ike, 'Triumph of the Peace Party in Japan 1873', *Far Eastern Quarterly*, II.

5 Cf. A. Burks, 'Administrative Transition from Han to Ken: The Example of Okayama', *Far Eastern Quarterly*, XV

6 For the text of this document see Hayashida Kametarō, *Dai Nihon Seitō Shi*, I, 19–24.

7 The fruits of the Osaka Conference were made public in the Imperial rescript of 14 April 1875, setting up a Senate (*Genrō-in*) and a Supreme Court (*Daishin-in*). Power of appointment to both these bodies was in the hands of the Emperor. This rescript also announced that a constitutional system would be introduced gradually. See Appendix I.

8 Lay, 'Rise of Political Parties in Japan', *Transactions of the Asiatic Society of Japan*, XXX (1902), pt. III, 384.

9 See Appendix II.

10 See Appendix III.

11 Cf. J. C. Lebra, 'Ōkuma Shigenobu and the 1881 Political Crisis', *Journal of Asian Studies*, XVIII. Also A. Fraser, 'The Expulsion of Ōkuma in 1881', *JAS*, XXVI.

12 See note 9 above.

13 Miyakoshi, *Nihon Kensei Kisō Shiryō*, p. 311. Translated as Appendix VI to G. Beckmann, *The Making of the Meiji Constitution*.

14 For its original manifesto, see Appendix IV.

15 R. Tsunoda (ed.), *Sources of Japanese Tradition*, p. 694.

16 McLaren, *Jap. Govt. Docs.* p. 428.

17 I am indebted to Dr Sheldon for pointing this out.

18 Beckmann, *Making*, p. 63.

19 Appendix V.

20 C. Yanaga, *Japan Since Perry*, p. 160. Scalapino offers a rather different explanation, see his *Democracy and the Party Movement in Pre-War Japan*, p. 111.

21 McLaren, *Jap. Govt. Docs.* p. 573. For the original, see Miyakoshi, *N.K.K.S.* p. 101.

22 For a trans. of Ōkubo's memorandum, see Appendix II to Beckmann, *Making*. For the original, see Miyakoshi, *N.K.K.S.* pp. 106–22.

23 Ōkuma (ed.), *Fifty Years of New Japan*, I, 126.

24 Cf. Herschel Webb's chapter in M. Jansen (ed.), *Changing Japanese Attitudes Toward Modernization*.

25 McLaren, *Jap. Govt. Docs.* pp. 7–15. See also Wilson, 'The Seitaisho', *Far Eastern Quarterly*, XI.

26 For the full text of the Oath, see Miyakoshi, *N.K.K.S.* p. 33. For a rather different assessment of its historical significance, see Uyehara, *Political Development*, pp. 63–70.

27 McLaren, *Jap. Govt. Docs.* p. 506.

28 Cf. Steiner, *Local Government in Japan*, p. 31. For translations of the new local government codes, see McLaren, *Jap. Govt. Docs.* pp. 331–404.

29 Beckmann, *Making*, p. 129. For the original, see Miyakoshi, *N.K.K.S.* p. 274.

30 Beckmann, *Making*, p. 132. For the original, see Miyakoshi, *N.K.K.S.* p. 296.

31 *Fukuzawa Yukichi Zenshū*, X, 238–40.

32 *Aikoku-kōtō* memorial of 17 January 1874. See note 6 above and McLaren, *Jap. Govt. Docs.* pp. 426–33.

33 Cf. T. Smith, *Political Change and Industrial Development in Japan*.

34 Cf. J. Hirschmeier, *The Origins of Entrepreneurship in Meiji Japan*, pp. 69 ff.

35 Ōkuma (ed.), *Fifty Years*, I, 128.

CHAPTER I: *Organisation and administration*

1 McLaren, *Jap. Govt. Docs.* pp. 170–211.

2 See Record of Senate Deliberations (*Genrō-in Kaigi Hikki*) for 2 March 1889.

3 Hayashida Kametarō, *Meiji-Taishō Seikai Sokumen Shi*, I, 172–7.

4 These areas were excluded from the election because the system of local and municipal self-government had not yet been extended to them.

5 For information on the way in which the seats were distributed see the following:

    1 Kaneko Kentarō's memoirs in Hayashida Kametarō, *Meiji-Taishō Seikai Sokumen Shi*, I, 172–4.

2 Suematsu Kenchō's account of the election in *Meiji Bunka Zenshu*, III, 200–21, especially pp. 200–1.

3 Hayashida Kametarō, 'Shūgi-in Giin Senkyō Hō Kaisei Iken', *Kokumin-no Tomo*, XIII (August 1893), no. 198, 170–1.

6 Suematsu Kenchō, 'Nijūsan'nen-no Sō Senkyō', *Meiji Bunka Zenshū* (hereafter cited as *MBZ*), III, 205–6.

7 Hayashida Kametarō, *Meiji-Taishō Seikai Sokumen Shi*, I, 174.

8 Suematsu, *MBZ*, III, 203–4.

9 Hayashida Kametarō, *Meiji-Taishō Seikai Sokumen Shi*, p. 175.

10 Hayashida Kametarō, 'Shūgi-in Giin Senkyō Hō Kaisei Iken', *Kokumin-no Tomo*, XIII (September 1893), no. 201, 366. The statistics given by Hayashida relate to 1892, but there could not have been much change between 1890 and then.

11 Hayashida Kametarō, 'Shūgi-in Giin Senkyō Hō Kaisei Iken', *Kokumin-no Tomo*, XIII (August 1893), no. 198, 171.

12 Suematsu, *MBZ*, III, 216. Also report on the Osaka *fu* campaigns in *TNNS* (*Tokyo Nichi Nichi Shimbun*) for 20 June 1890.

13 *TNNS*, 1 July 1890.

14 *Ibid.* 3 July 1890.

15 *Ibid.* 1 July 1890. See also *Kokumin Shimbun*, 3 June 1890.

16 *Ibid.* 18 June 1890.

17 *Ibid.* 19 June 1890.

18 *Ibid.* 25 June 1890. Cf. M. B. Jansen, 'Ōi Kentarō: Radicalism and Chauvinism', *Far Eastern Quarterly*, XI.

19 Suematsu, *MBZ*, III, 217.

20 *TNNS*, 22 June 1890.

21 When a sub-prefecture and a city were united in one constituency for which the sub-prefect was returning officer, the mayor prepared a list of voters in the city for despatch to him. If the mayor, himself, was returning officer for such a ruro-urban constituency, he still had to make the list for the municipal part of it.

22 *TNNS*, 24 June 1890. Apparently, revaluations of property for taxation purposes had deprived a number of influential people of their electoral rights in the previous year, and had caused quite a furore on the occasion of the re-election of half the members of every prefectural assembly in March 1890. See also *Yūbin-Hōchi*, 5 April 1890.

23 *TNNS*, 2 July 1890.

24 *Ibid.* 15 and 28 June 1890.

25 Suematsu, *MBZ*, III, 203 and 216.

26 *Ibid.* p. 217.

27 *TNNS*, 14 June 1890.

28 *Ibid.* 20 June 1890.

29 *Ibid.* 18 and 21 June 1890.

30 *Ibid.* 25 June 1890.

31 *Ibid.* 26 June 1890.

32 Exactly how many of the electors were unable to read or write is

not easy to say. Illiteracy must have still been common in Japan in 1890, as universal and compulsory primary education had started only a few years previously. However the total number of spoiled votes was just under 3,000 and it is highly unlikely that many who paid ¥15 or more a year in national taxes were wanting in this respect (cf. Dore, 'Education in Japan's Growth', *Pacific Affairs*, XXXVII, no. 1, and the editorial in the *Sanyō Shimbun*, 12 June 1890).

33 Art. 39.
34 Suematsu, *MBZ*, III, 217.
35 McLaren, *Jap. Govt. Docs.* pp. 243–7.
36 *TNNS*, 27 June 1890. Numbered 'arrival cards', issued in exchange for entrance tickets, were used in polling stations which had to handle relatively large numbers of electors. The elector in these cases could not vote until his number was called.
37 *TNNS*, 19 June 1890.   38 *Ibid.* 1 July 1890.
39 Suematsu, *MBZ*, III, 217.   40 *TNNS*, 19 June 1890.
41 Cf. Suematsu, *MBZ*, III, 214.
42 *TNNS*, 1 July 1890.
43 Cf. the account of the Election Meeting for the First Constituency, Kanagawa prefecture (Yokohama), published in *TNNS*, 3 July 1890.
44 *Yūbin-Hōchi*, 6 July 1890.
45 Art. 78.
46 For example, the election manifestos issued by two of the Liberal factions contained proposals for widening the franchise, lowering the qualifications for candidates, reforming the system of seat distribution, etc. (cf. Appendices VII and VIII). Kaneko Kentarō declared that 'the choice between big or small constituencies had been the most difficult problem confronting the drafters of the Law of Election (see Hayashida Kametarō, *Meiji-Taishō Seikai Sokumen Shi*, I, 172).
47 Uyehara, *Political Development*, p. 171.
48 Cf. Hayashida Kametarō, 'Shūgi-in Giin Senkyō Hō Kaisei Iken', *Kokumin-no Tomo*, XIII, no. 198, 170 ff.
49 *TNNS*, 3 July 1890.
50 Hayashida Kametarō, 'Shūgi-in Giin Senkyō Hō Kaisei Iken', *Kokumin-no Tomo*, XIII, no. 201, 365.
51 Hayashida Kametarō, *Meiji-Taishō Seikai Sokumen Shi*, I, 172.
52 *Yūbin-Hōchi*, 3 and 4 July 1890.
53 Suematsu, *MBZ*, III, 217.   54 *TNNS*, 29 June 1890.
55 See Appendix VI below.   56 *TNNS*, 4 June 1890.
57 *Yūbin-Hōchi*, 31 May 1890.
58 *Kokumin Shimbun*, 31 May 1890.

59 *TNNS*, 14 June 1890.
60 *TNNS*, 18 June 1890.
61 *Ibid.* 4 June 1890.
62 *Ibid.* 2 July 1890.
63 *Ibid.* 12 June 1890.
64 *Ibid.* 21 and 27 June 1890.
65 *Ibid.* 26 June 1890.
66 Cf. *ibid.* 4 June 1890.
67 *Ibid.* 29 June 1890.
68 *Ibid.* 2 July 1890.
69 *Ibid.*
70 *Ibid.* 3 July 1890.

CHAPTER II: *Parties, principles and issues*

1 Hayashida Kametarō, *Nihon Seitō Shi*, I, 241–4.
2 *Ibid.* pp. 246–7.
3 *Ibid.* pp. 247–8.
4 *Ibid.* pp. 248–52.
5 Cf. Ōmachi Keigetsu, *Hakushaku Gotō Shōjirō*, p. 647. A slightly fuller version of the same story is on p. 528 of Zōga Hakuai's *Ōe Tenya Denki*. For an interesting (and not so amiable) impression of some of Gotō's business activities, see J. McMaster, 'The Takashima Mine', *Business History Review*, XXXVII (1963).
6 Hayashida Kametarō, *Nihon Seitō Shi*, I, 258.
7 Cody, *Itagaki Taisuke*, pp. 216 ff.; also Ōmachi Keigetsu, *Hakushaku Gotō Shōjirō*, pp. 640 ff.
8 Hayashida Kametarō, *Nihon Seitō Shi*, I, 258–61.
9 See Appendix VII.
10 See Appendix VIII.
11 See Appendix IX.
12 Suematsu, *MBZ*, III, 216.
13 *Ibid.* pp. 202–3.
14 Cf. Mason, 'Poor Relief in the First Meiji Diet', *Journal of the Oriental Society of Australia*, III (1965), no. 1, 14 ff. Itagaki himself, however, showed an increasing concern with social problems after 1880 (see Cody, *Itagaki Taisuke*).
15 *TNNS*, 24 June 1890.
16 He was to use more or less the same words at the beginning of his Mito speech.
17 *TNNS*, 20 June 1890.
18 Cf. Sansom, *The Western World and Japan*, pp. 388 ff.
19 *TNNS*, 4, 5 and 6 June 1890.
20 *Ibid.* 28 June 1890.
21 *Ibid.* 3 June 1890.
22 Cf. Ōkubo Kagao, *Shūgi-in Giin Kōhosha Retsuden*, pp. 220–52.
23 *TNNS*, 4 June 1890.
24 *Ibid.* 20 June 1890.
25 *Kokumin Shimbun*, 2 June 1890.
26 *TNNS*, 16 May 1890. Also Hayashida Kametarō, *Nihon Seitō Shi*, I, 279–81.

27 *TNNS*, 3 June 1890.
28 *Ibid.* 4 June 1890.
29 *Ibid.* 22 and 24 June 1890.
30 *Ibid.* 18 June 1890.
31 *Ibid.* 25 June 1890.
32 *Ibid.* 12 and 13 June 1890.
33 *Ibid.* 3 June 1890.
34 *Ibid.* 6 June 1890 and *Yūbin-Hōchi* 6 June 1890.
35 *TNNS*, 6 June 1890.
36 *Ibid.* 7 June 1890.
37 *Ibid.* 7 June 1890.
38 *Yūbin-Hōchi Shimbun*, 27 May 1890.
39 *Sanyō Shimbun*, 10 June 1890.
40 *Tōhoku Mainichi*, 6 June 1890.
41 Cf. D. Mendel, 'Ozaki Yukio', *Far Eastern Quarterly*, xv.
42 Hayashida Kametarō, *Nihon Seitō Shi*, I, 262.
43 *Chōya Shimbun*, 25 May 1890.
44 Cf. F. C. Jones, *Extraterritoriality in Japan*, pp. 109 ff.
45 *TNNS*, 1 July 1890.
46 *Tani Kanjō Ikō*, II, 556–9.
47 H. Conroy, *The Japanese Seizure of Korea*, especially pp. 135 ff.
48 Cf. Craig, *Chōshū in the Meiji Restoration*, especially pp. 270 ff.
49 Hayashida Kametarō, *Nihon Seitō Shi*, I, 262–3.
50 *Osaka Mainichi*, 2 June 1890.
51 See also Lafcadio Hearn, *Glimpses of Unfamiliar Japan*, II, 676–81.
52 Ike, *Beginnings*, p. 59.
53 Cf. note 12 above.
54 *TNNS*, 4 July 1890.
55 *Ibid.* 15 June 1890.
56 Suematsu, *MBZ*, III, 202.
57 *Ibid.* p. 216.
58 Local issues will be discussed in the next chapter.
59 Suematsu, *MBZ*, III, 215.

CHAPTER III: *The Election Campaign: A General Survey*

1 *TNNS*, 26 June 1890.
2 *Yūbin-Hōchi Shimbun*, 5 June 1890.
3 *Kokumin Shimbun*, 6 July 1890.
4 Cf. pp. 83–5 above.
5 Cf. Fukuchi Shigetaka, 'Kensei Shoki-no Daigishi-no Seikaku', *Nihon Rekishi*, no. 79 (December 1954).
6 Suematsu, *MBZ*, III, 204–5, 209–10. Suematsu warns that he had great trouble in compiling this particular table (cf. Fukuchi Shigetaka, 'Kensei Shoki-no Daigishi-no Seikaku', *Nihon Rekishi*, no. 79, p. 29).
7 Cf. p. 127 above.
8 *TNNS*, 17 June 1890.
9 *Ibid.* 29 June 1890.
10 *Ibid.* 21 June 1890.

11 *TNNS*, 18 June 1890.   12 *Ibid.* 29 June 1890.
13 Cf. Obata Kyūgorō, *Life of Viscount Shibusawa.*
14 *TNNS*, 2 July 1890.   15 *Ibid.* 6 and 10 June 1890.
16 *Ibid.* 27 June 1890.   17 *Ibid.* 11 June 1890.
18 *Ibid.* 21 June 1890. For further information about Kōno Hiron-
    aka see Ward and Rustow (ed.), *Political Modernization in Japan
    and Turkey*, pp. 395–7.
19 *TNNS*, 11 June 1890.   20 *Ibid.* 17 June 1890.
21 *Yūbin-Hōchi Shimbun*, 25 April 1890.
22 *TNNS*, 2 July 1890.   23 *Ibid.*
24 *Ibid.* 24 June 1890.   25 *Ibid.* 10 June 1890.
26 *Ibid.* 29 June 1890.   27 *Ibid.* 1 June 1890.
28 *Ibid.* 26 June 1890.   29 *Ibid.* 3 June 1890.
30 *Sanyō Shimbun*, 17 June 1890.
31 *TNNS*, 11 and 13 June 1890.
32 *Ibid.* 13 June 1890.   33 *Ibid.*
34 *Ibid.* 21 June 1890.   35 *Ibid.* 6 June 1890.
36 *Ibid.* 28 June 1890.   37 *Ibid.* 29 June 1890.
38 *Ibid.* 4 July 1890.   39 *Ibid.* 11 June 1890.
40 *Yūbin-Hōchi Shimbun*, 7 June 1890.
41 *TNNS*, 26 June 1890.   42 *Ibid.* 18 June 1890.
43 *Ibid.* 4 June 1890.   44 *Ibid.* 21 June 1890.
45 *Ibid.* 2 July 1890.   46 *Ibid.*
47 *Ibid.* 15 June 1890.   48 *Ibid.*
49 *Ibid.* 12 June 1890.   50 *Ibid.* 17 June 1890.
51 *Ibid.* 29 June 1890.   52 Cf. p. 149 above.
53 Cf. pp. 145 and 155 above. 54 *TNNS*, 1 July 1890.
55 *Kōchi Shimbun*, 30 June 1890.
56 *TNNS*, 15 June 1890.   57 *Ibid.* 21 June 1890.
58 *Ibid.* 13 and 17 June 1890.
59 Chinese minister in the reign of the T'ang Emperor, Hsüan Tsung.
60 Chinese minister in the reign of the Sung Emperor, Shen-Tsung.
61 *Kinjō Shimbun*, 27 June 1890.
62 Fukuzawa Yukichi, *Gakumon-no Susume*, p. 1.
63 *Nippon Shimbun*, 5 July 1890.
64 *TNNS*, 5 July 1890, also *Kinjō Shimbun*, 30 June 1890.
65 Suematsu, *MBZ*, III, 217–18.
66 *TNNS*, 14 June 1890.   67 *Ibid.*
68 *Ibid.* 21 June 1890.   69 Suematsu, *MBZ*, III, 218.
70 *Ibid.* p. 218.   71 *Ibid.*
72 *Ibid.* p. 215.   73 *TNNS*, 5 June 1890.
74 *Ibid.* 18 June 1890.   75 *Ibid.* 26 June 1890.
76 *Ibid.* 28 June 1890.   77 *Ibid.* 26 June 1890.
78 *Ibid.* 29 June 1890.   79 See p. 54 above.

80 *TNNS*, 14 June 1890, and *Kokumin Shimbun*, 14 June 1890.
81 *TNNS*, 18 June 1890. 82 *Ibid.* 17 June 1890.
83 *Ibid.* 18 June 1890.
84 *Kokumin Shimbun*, 4 June 1890.
85 Assuming that ¥5 would have been enough to secure a guaranteed vote, then the average ¥1,000 expenses would have bought only 200 voters; and the average number of voters per constituency was approximately 1,700.
86 *TNNS*, 15 June 1890, and *Kokumin Shimbun*, 15 June 1890.
87 *TNNS*, 19 June 1890.
88 *Ibid.* 20 June 1890.
89 *Ibid.* 21 June 1890.
90 *Ibid.* 1 July 1890.
91 Cf. Akita, 'The Meiji Constitution In Practice', *Journal of Asian Studies* XXII, 36.
92 *TNNS*, 18 and 21 June 1890.
93 *Ibid.* 14 June 1890.
94 Cf. pp. 55–7 above.
95 *Yūbin-Hōchi Shimbun*, 27 May 1890.
96 *TNNS*, 24 June 1890. 97 *Ibid.* 26 June 1890.
98 *Ibid.* 1 July 1890. 99 *Ibid.*
100 *Ibid.* 2 July 1890. 101 *Ibid.* 1 July 1890.
102 *Ibid.* 2 July 1890. 103 *Ibid.* 1 July 1890.
104 *Ibid.* 29 June 1890. 105 Cf. above pp. 171–2.
106 *TNNS*, 29 June 1890. 107 Cf. pp. 57–8 above.
108 *TNNS*, 26 June 1890; cf. p. 103 above.
109 *Ibid.* 24 June 1890. 110 *Ibid.* 25 June 1890.
111 Cf. 'A Story Of The Otokodate Of Yedo', in A. Mitford, *Tales of Old Japan*.
112 *TNNS*, 29 June 1890.
113 *Ibid.* 22 June 1890.
114 Cf. p. 176 above.
115 *TNNS*, 21 June 1890.
116 The disturbances caused by the National Rights Party in Kumamoto prefecture and the *Sanyō Gikai* in Hyōgo prefecture may have been exceptions to this rule (cf. pp. 55–6 above).
117 *Kinjō Shimbun*, 30 June 1890.
118 Cf. Mason, 'Poor Relief in the First Meiji Diet', *Journal of the Oriental Society of Australia*, III, no. 1, p. 13.
119 *Chōya Shimbun*, 26 and 27 May 1890.
120 *Kokumin Shimbun*, 21 June 1890.
121 *TNNS*, 1 July 1890.

CHAPTER IV: *Election Results*

1 *TNNS*, 2 July 1890.
2 *Ibid.* 28 June and 3 July 1890.
3 *Osaka Mainichi*, 5 July 1890.   4 Suematsu, *MBZ*, III, 206–7.
5 *Sanyō Shimbun*, 29 June 1890.
6 Suematsu, *MBZ*, III, 214.
7 *Kokumin Shimbun*, 1 July 1890.
8 *TNNS*, 3 July 1890; *Nippon Shimbun*, 8 July 1890; and *Sanyō Shimbun*, 8 July 1890.
9 *Nippon Shimbun*, 12 July 1890.
10 *Yūbin-Hōchi Shimbun*, 1 July 1890.
11 *Kokumin Shimbun*, 9 May 1890.
12 Hayashida Kametarō, *Nihon Seitō Shi*, I, 285–7.
13 See Appendix X for a translation of its manifesto.
14 See Appendix XI.
15 Suematsu, *MBZ*, III, 205. Fukuchi Shigetaka argues that *shizoku* Members were almost half the total (cf. his 'Kensei Shoki-no Daigishi-no Seikaku', *Nihon Rekishi*, no. 79, December 1954, p. 31).
16 Suematsu, *MBZ*, III, 214.
17 See table in *MBZ*, III, 188–9.
18 *Kokumin-no Tomo*, no. 88 (July 1890), p. 93 ff., and other sources.
19 *Nippon Shimbun*, 15 July 1890.
20 For a list of Members returned at the election, see Ōtsu Jun'-ichirō, *Dai Nihon Kensei Shi*, III, 338 ff.

Conclusions

1 These are of course *ex parte* statements in the argument over the nature of Japanese political and ideological modernization. For able exposition of a different point of view, see Scalapino (*Democracy And the Party Movement in Prewar Japan*) and Bendix (*Cultural-Educational Mobility: Japan And The Protestant Ethic*). The present writer's opinion derives mainly from research for this book; and an attempt is made in this section to conceptualize some of the underlying reasons for holding it in terms of inter-action, pluralism and widened scope for individualism. More generally, it is also based on premises or ideas noted in the Preface. For some general support of the position taken here, see Soviak, ('The Case of Baba Tatsui', *Monumenta Nipponica*, XVIII); Akita ('The Meiji Constitution In Practice', *Journal of Asian Studies*, XXII); and Pittau ('Inoue Kowashi, 1843–1895', *Monumenta Nipponica*, XX). The last two authors mentioned have recently published book-length studies of Meiji-period political developments. Unfortunately, these have still not been available

for consultation at the time of writing, but they are listed in the Bibliography.

2 Trans. Beckmann, *Making*, p. 112. For the original, see Miyakoshi, *N.K.K.S.* p. 108.

3 Within the villages, emergent families were already presenting a political challenge to privileged groups before 1868 (cf. Smith, *Agrarian Origins*, pp. 183 ff.).

4 See pp. 102–4 above.

5 Cf. Dore, *City Life in Japan*, pp. 91 ff.; also Tsuchiya Takao, 'The Modernization of the Economy', *Japan Quarterly*, XIII.

SOURCES AND BIBLIOGRAPHY

NEWSPAPERS

Kampō, Kinjō Shimbun, Kōchi Shimbun, Kokumin Shimbun, Niigata Shimbun, Nippon Shimbun, Osaka Mainichi, Sanyō Shimbun, Tōhoku Mainichi, Tokyo Nichi Nichi Shimbun, Toyō Shimbun, Yūbin-Hōchi Shimbun.

OTHER SOURCES CITED

Akita, G. 'The Meiji Constitution in Practice: The First Diet', *Journal of Asian Studies*, XXII (1962).

Beckmann, G. *The Making of the Meiji Constitution*. Lawrence, 1957.

Bendix, R. 'A Case Study in Cultural and Educational Mobility: Japan And The Protestant Ethic', reprinted by the University of California Institutes of Industrial Relations and International Studies (Reprint No. 291, 1966) from N. J. Smelser and S. M. Lipset (ed.), *Social Structure And Mobility In Economic Development*. Chicago, 1966.

Burks, A. 'Administrative Transition from *Hab* to *Ken*: The Example of Okayama', *Far Eastern Quarterly*, XV (1956).

Cody, C. *A Study of the Career of Itagaki Taisuke (1837–1919): A Leader of the Democratic Movement in Meiji Japan*. University Microfilms, Ann Arbor, 1965.

Conroy, H. *The Japanese Seizure of Korea 1868–1910*. Philadelphia, 1960.

Craig, A. *Chōshū in the Meiji Restoration*. Cambridge (Mass.), 1961.

Dore, R. *City Life in Japan*. London, 1958.

'Education in Japan's Growth', *Pacific Affairs*, XXXVII (1964).

Fraser, A. 'The Expulsion of Ōkuma from the Government in 1881', *Journal of Asian Studies*, XXVI (1967).

Fukuchi Shigetaka. 'Kensei Shoki-no Daigishi-no Seikaku', *Nihon Rekishi*, no. 79 (December 1954).

Fukuzawa Yukichi. *Fukuzawa Zenshū*. 10 vols. Tokyo, 1925.

Genrō-in Kaigi Hikki. The Senate Record for the period after 1885 is available in an edition contained in the Imperial Household Library and printed for official use only. For earlier years see Meiji Hōsei Keizai Kenkyūjō, *Genrō-in Kaigi Hikki*. Tokyo, 1943.

Hayashida Kametarō. *Meiji-Taishō Seikai Sokumen Shi*. Tokyo, 1926. *Nihon Seitō Shi*. 2 vols. Tokyo, 1927.

'Shūgi-in Giin Senkyō Hō Kaisei Iken', *Kokumin-no Tomo*, XIII (1893).

Hearn, L. *Glimpses of Unfamiliar Japan*. 2 vols. London, 1894.

Hirschmeier, J. *The Origins of Entrepreneurship in Meiji Japan*. Cambridge (Mass.), 1964.

SOURCES AND BIBLIOGRAPHY

Ike Nobutaka. *The Beginnings of Political Democracy in Japan.* Baltimore, 1950.

'Triumph of the Peace Party in Japan in 1873', *Far Eastern Quarterly,* II (1942).

'Political Leadership and Political Parties. A. Japan', in Ward, R. and Rustow, D. (ed.), *Political Modernization in Japan and Turkey.* Princeton, 1964.

Itō Hirobumi. *Commentaries on the Constitution of the Empire of Japan.* Tokyo, 1906.

Jansen, M. 'Ōi Kentarō: Radicalism and Chauvinism', *Far Eastern Quarterly,* XI (1952).

(ed.), *Changing Japanese Attitudes Toward Modernization.* Princeton, 1965.

Jones, F. *Extraterritoriality In Japan and the Diplomatic Relations Resulting In Its Abolition, 1853–89.* New Haven, 1931.

Lay, A. 'History of the Rise of Political Parties in Japan', *Transactions of the Asiatic Society of Japan,* XXX (1902).

Lebra, J. 'Ōkuma Shigenobu and the 1881 Political Crisis', *Journal of Asian Studies,* XVIII (1959).

Mason, R. 'The Debate on Poor Relief In The First Meiji Diet', *Journal of the Oriental Society of Australia,* III (1965).

McLaren, W. *Japanese Government Documents, Transactions of the Asiatic Society of Japan,* XLII (1914).

McMaster, J. 'The Takashima Mine: British Capital and Japanese Industrialization', *Business History Review,* XXXVII (1963).

Mendel, D. 'Ozaki Yukio: Political Conscience of Modern Japan', *Far Eastern Quarterly,* XV (1956).

Mitford, A. (Lord Redesdale). *Tales of Old Japan.* London, 1910.

Miyakoshi Shin'ichirō. *Nihon Kensei Kiso Shiryō.* Tokyo, 1939.

Obata Kyūgorō. *An Interpretation Of The Life Of Viscount Shibusawa.* Tokyo, 1937.

Ōkubo Kagao. *Shūgi-in Giin Kōhosha Retsuden.* Tokyo, 1890.

Ōkuma, S. (ed.). *Fifty Years Of New Japan.* 2 vols. London, 1909.

Ōmachi Keigetsu, *Hakushaku Gotō Shōjirō.* Tokyo, 1914.

Ōtsu Jun'ichiro. *Dai Nihon Kensei Shi.* 10 vols. Tokyo, 1927.

Pittau, J. 'Inoue Kowashi, 1843–1895 And The Formation Of Modern Japan', *Monumenta Nipponica,* XX (1965).

Sansom, G. *The Western World And Japan.* London, 1950.

Scalapino, R. *Democracy and the Party Movement in Prewar Japan: The Failure of the First Attempt.* Berkeley, 1953.

Smith, T. *The Agrarian Origins of Modern Japan.* Stanford, 1959.

Political Change and Industrial Development in Japan: Government Enterprise, 1868–1900. Stanford, 1955.

Soviak, E. 'The Case of Baba Tatsui: Western Enlightenment, Social

SOURCES AND BIBLIOGRAPHY

Change and the Early Meiji Intellectual', *Monumenta Nipponica*, XVIII (1963).
Steiner, K. *Local Government In Japan*. Stanford, 1965.
Suematsu Kenchō. 'Nijūsan'nen-no Sō Senkyō', *Meiji Bunka Zenshū*, III.
Tani Kanjō. *Tani Kanjō Ikō*. 2 vols. Tokyo, 1912.
Tsuchiya Takao. 'The Modernization Of The Economy', *Japan Quarterly*, XIII (1966).
Tsunoda Ryūsaku. *Sources of the Japanese Tradition*. New York, 1958.
Uyehara, G. *The Political Development of Japan 1867–1909*. London, 1910.
Ward, R. and Rustow, D. (eds.). *Political Modernization in Japan and Turkey*. Princeton, 1964.
Webb, H. 'The Development of an Orthodox Attitude Toward the Imperial Institution in the Nineteenth Century' in Jansen, M. (ed.), *Changing Japanese Attitudes Toward Modernization*. Princeton, 1965.
Wilson, R. 'The Seitaisho: A Constitutional Experiment', *Far Eastern Quarterly*, XI (1952).
Yanaga Chitoshi. *Japan Since Perry*. New York, 1949.
Zōga Hakuai. *Ōe Tenya Denki*. Tokyo, 1926.

OTHER WORKS

Akita, G. *Foundations of Constitutional Government in Modern Japan, 1868–1900*. Cambridge (Mass.), 1967.
Allen, G. *A Short Economic History of Modern Japan*. London, 1962.
Araki Moriaki. 'Dai-ichi Gikai-ni okeru Jinushi Giin-no Dōkō', *Shakai Kagaku Kenkyū*, XVI (1965).
Beasley, W. *The Modern History of Japan*. London, 1963.
Bellah, R. *Tokugawa Religion: The Values of Pre-Industrial Japan*. Glencoe, 1957.
Benedict, R. *The Chrysanthemum and the Sword*. Tokyo, 1954.
Blacker, C. *The Japanese Enlightenment: A Study of the Writings of Fukuzawa Yukichi*. Cambridge, 1964.
Brown, S. 'Kido Takayoshi: Japan's Cautious Revolutionary', *Pacific Historical Review*, XXV (1956).
Chambliss, W. *Chiaraijima Village: Land Tenure, Taxation, and Local Trade 1818–1884*. Tucson, 1965.
Crawcour, E. 'The Japanese Economy On The Eve Of Modernization', *Journal of the Oriental Society of Australia*, II (1963).
Dai Nihon Teikoku Gikai Shi Hankōkai. *Dai Nihon Teikoku Gikai Shi*, I. Tokyo, 1926.
Denda Isao. *Kindai Nihon Keizai Shisō-no Kenkyū*. Tokyo, 1962.
Dore, R. *Land Reform in Japan*. London, 1959.
'The Meiji Landlord: Good or Bad?', *Journal of Asian Studies*, XVIII (1959).

Earl, D. *Emperor and Nation in Japan: Political Thinkers of the Toku-gawa Period*. Seattle, 1964.

Embree, J. *A Japanese Village: Suye Mura*. London, 1946.

Fairbank, J., Reischauer, E. and Craig, A. *East Asia: The Modern Transformation*. London, 1965.

Gubbins, J. *The Making of Modern Japan*. London, 1922.

Hackett, R. 'Nishi Amane: A Tokugawa-Meiji Bureaucrat', *Journal of Asian Studies*, XVIII (1959).

Hall, J. *Tanuma Okitsugu*. Cambridge (Mass.), 1955.

'The Castle Town and Japan's Modern Urbanization', *Far Eastern Quarterly*, XV (1955).

'Materials for the Study of Local History in Japan: Pre-Meiji Records', *Center For Japanese Studies*, Occasional Papers No. 3. Ann Arbor, 1952.

Hamada Kengi. *Prince Ito*. Tokyo, 1936.

Iddittie Junesay. *The Life of Marquis Shigenobu Ōkuma: A Biographical Study in the Rise of Democratic Japan*. Tokyo, 1940.

Ike Nobutaka. *Japanese Politics*. New York, 1957.

Inada Masatsugu. *Meiji Kempō Seiritsu Shi*. 2 vols. Tokyo, 1960.

Itō Takashi. 'Meiji Jūshichi-Nijūsan Nen-no Rikken Kaishintō', *Tokyo Daigaku Shakai Kagaku Kenkyujō Sōritsu Jūgo Shūnen Kinen Rombun*. Tokyo, 1963.

'Meiji Jūnendai Zempan-ni okeru Fukenkai to Rikken Kaishintō', *Shigaku Zasshi*, LXXIII (June 1964).

Iwata Masakazu. *Ōkubo Toshimichi: The Bismarck of Japan*. Berkeley, 1964.

Jansen, M. *Sakamoto Ryōma and the Meiji Restoration*. Princeton, 1961.

'Tokugawa and Modern Japan', *Japan Quarterly*, XII (1965).

Kawamura Matasuke. 'Meiji Jida-ni okeru Senkyōhō-no Riron oyobi Seido-no Hattatsu', *Kokka Gakkai Zasshi*, LVI, nos. 11, 12 and LVII, no. 2 (1942–3).

Kudō Takeshige. *Teikoku Gikai Shi*. 3 vols. Tokyo, 1901.

Lebra, J. 'Yano Fumio: Meiji Intellectual, Party Leader, and Bureaucrat', *Monumenta Nipponica*, XX (1965).

Lockwood, W. *The Economic Development of Japan: Growth and Structural Change, 1868–1938*. Princeton, 1954.

(ed.). *The State and Economic Enterprise in Japan*. Princeton, 1965.

Miller, F. *Minobe Tatsukichi: Interpreter of Constitutionalism In Japan*. Berkeley, 1965.

Moore, H. 'The First General Election In Japan', *The New Review*, III (1890).

Mounsey, A. *The Satsuma Rebellion*. London, 1879.

Nakayama Yasumasa (comp.). *Shimbun Shūsei Meiji Hennenshi*. 15 vols. Tokyo, 1936.

16-2

Nishida Taketoshi. *Meiji Jidai-no Shimbun to Zasshi*. Tokyo, 1961.

Nivison, D. and Wright, A. (eds.). *Confucianism In Action*. Stanford, 1959.

Norman, E. *Japan's Emergence as a Modern State*. New York, 1940.

Oka Yoshitake. *Kindai Nihon-no Keisei*. Tokyo, 1947.

Passin, H. *Society and Education in Japan*. New York, 1966.

Pittau, J. *Political Thought in Early Meiji Japan*. Cambridge (Mass.), 1967.

Sakai, R. 'Feudal Society and Modern Leadership in Satsumahan', *Journal of Asian Studies*, XVI (1957).

Sakata, Y. and Hall, J. 'The Motivation of Political Leadership in the Meiji Restoration', *Journal of Asian Studies*, XVI (1956).

Scalapino, R. 'Japan: Between Traditionalism and Democracy', in Neumann, S. (ed.), *Political Parties: Approaches to Comparative Politics*. Chicago, 1956.

Sheldon, C. *The Rise Of The Merchant Class In Tokugawa Japan*. New York, 1958.

Shūgi-in Jimu Kyoku. *Dai-Ikkai Gikai naishi Dai-Yonjūhachikai Gikai Shūgi-in Giin Tōsekiroku*. Tokyo, 1924.

Shūgi-in and Sangi-in. *Gikai Seido Shichijūnen Shi*. 12 vols. Tokyo, 1960.

Simmons, D. and Wigmore, J. 'Notes on Land Tenure and Local Institutions in Old Japan', *Transactions of the Asiatic Society of Japan*, XIX (1891).

Smith, W. *Confucianism in Modern Japan*. Tokyo, 1959.

Storry, R. *A History of Modern Japan*. London, 1960.

Takeda Kiyoko. 'Yoshino Sakuzō', *Japan Quarterly*, XII (1965).

Takeuchi Tatsuji. *War and Diplomacy in the Japanese Empire*. Chicago, 1935.

Toriumi Yasushi. 'Shoki Gikai-ni okeru Jiyūtō-no Kōzō to Kinō', *Rekishigaku Kenkyū*, no. 255 (1961).

'Teikoku Gikai Kaisetsu-ni itaru "Mintō"-no Keisei', *Rekishigaku Kenkyū Hōkoku*, no. 10: '*Rekishi to Bunka*' (March 1963).

Van Straelen, H. *Yoshida Shōin: Forerunner of the Meiji Restoration*. Leiden, 1952.

Various. *Economic Development and Cultural Change*, IX, no. 1, pt. 2 (1960).

Wigmore, J. 'Starting a Parliament in Japan', *Scribner's Magazine*, X (1891).

Yoshida Tōgo. *Dai Nihon Chimei Jisho*. 7 vols. Tokyo, 1940.

INDEX

245

INDEX

Nakajima Matagorō, 52, 148, 150, 157, 158
Nakajima Nobuyuki, 9, 90, 93, 131, 156, 158, 180, 195, 197
Nakakanbara *gun*, 57
Nakanoshima, 172
Nakatsu *gun*, 145
National Banks, 132
National Defence Council, 119
National Learning, 212
National Liberal Party, see *Kokumin Jiyū-tō*
National Party, see *Kokumin-ha*
National Rights Party (*Kokken-tō*), 109, 135, 164, 195
Nationalism, 23–4, 98–9, 166, 193–5; in Kōchi prefecture, 115–18; in Kumamoto prefecture, 55; and *sōshi*, 182–3; see also *Kōyō-kai*, National Party, National Rights Party, *Sanyō Gikai*, Ultra-Conservativism
Natives Party, 140
Navy, 34, 69, 70, 134; *see also* Electoral rights
New Conservative Review, 120
Newspaper Regulations, 72
Newspapers, *see* Press
Nihonbashi ward, 31, 108
Niigata, 99
Niigata prefecture, 34, 55, 57, 131, 135, 144, 191
Nikkō, 113
Nippon Shimbun, 117, 126, 189, 198
Nishi Nari *gun*, 185
Nishihama-machi, 185
Nishimura Jinuemon, 155, 157
Nishisaigawa village, 145
Nobility, *see* Peerage
Noguchi Honnosuke, 175
Noto, 183

Ōe Taku, 63, 117, 131
Ogasawara (Bonin) Islands, 27
Ōi Kentarō, 35, 63, 65
Ōita prefecture, 48
Okamoto Takeo, 83–7, 127, 132, 138, 142, 146–7
Okayama prefecture, 45, 96, 127, 134, 147, 171
Oki Islands, 28, 32
Okinawa, 27

Ōkubo Toshimichi, 3, 10, 18–19, 21, 24, 191, 205, 211
Ōkuma Shigenobu, 3, 20, 22, 59, 100–5, 210–11; rejoins government 1888, 61–2; resigns from government and founds *Kaishin-tō*, 10–11; resigns from *Kaishin-tō*, 16; and treaty revision, 61–3; wounding of, 63
Ono Azusa, 11
Osaka, 7–8, 11, 25, 41, 46, 61, 64–5, 93, 99, 107, 113, 118, 154, 160, 164, 185, 214; campaigning in, 171–2; *sōshi* activities in, 177
Osaka city assembly, 171–2
Osaka Conference, 7–8, 20, 21
Osaka Court of Petty Offences, 35
Osaka Mainichi, 122,
Osaka prefectural assembly, 171–2
Ōshima Islands, 32
Ōta Sane, 137, 142
Ōta-machi, 80, 82
Oyagi Bi'ichirō, 132
Ōyama Iwao, 120
Ozaki Yukio, 11, 95, 101–2

Parties, convivial (*konshinkai*), 145–7, 150–3, 159, 175, 181
Parties, political, 23, 114, 200–1, 206; and candidates, 86; and corruption, 167–8; and Diet, 76; dissolution of, 16; and election campaigning, 148–9, 154–5; and election expenses, 154; and election results, 190–2; formation of, 8–15; and House of Representatives, 195; and Independents, 76; Itagaki's views on, 78–80; and nomination of candidates, 135–6; proliferation of, 15, 88–9, 109; re-formation of, 16–17, 59–68; and slander, 163; and *sōshi*, 176–7; weaknesses of, 65–8; *see also* Liberty and Popular Rights Movement
Patriotic Party, see *Aikoku-kōtō*
Patriotic Society, see *Aikoku-sha*
Peace Preservation Ordinance, 60–1, 69, 72, 74, 82
Peerage, 34, 134
Peers School, 114
Perry, Matthew, 4

251